P9-CDU-555

Pests & Diseases

The TIME LIFE
Complete ◑ Gardener

Pests & Diseases

By the Editors of Time-Life Books
ALEXANDRIA, VIRGINIA

The Consultants

Scott Aker is the Integrated Pest Management (IPM) Specialist at the U.S. National Arboretum in Washington, D.C. In 1992, he established the arboretum's IPM Program, which was cited by President Clinton for achieving a 70 percent reduction in pesticide use. Aker also pioneered an IPM curriculum sponsored by the arboretum aimed at educating people on all horticultural levels—from backyard gardeners to professional nursery growers to landscape designers. He studied horticulture at the University of Minnesota and the University of Maryland, and served with the Maryland Cooperative Extension Service.

Ethel Dutky is a plant pathologist with the Department of Plant Biology at the University of Maryland in College Park and the director of the Plant Diagnostic Laboratory for the Maryland Cooperative Extension Service. With more than 15 years' experience diagnosing diseases in all types of plants and crops, she has written many fact sheets, bulletins, and articles on plant diseases. She is a regular contributor to professional journals and an active member of the American Phytopathological Society. Dutky also works with greenhouse and nursery growers to improve their disease-management programs.

Library of Congress Cataloging in Publication Data
Pests and diseases / by the editors of Time-Life Books.
p. cm.—(The Time-Life complete gardener)
Includes bibliographical references (p.) and index.
ISBN 0-7835-4103-1
1. Garden pests. 2. Plant diseases. 3. Garden pests—Control. I. Time-Life Books.
II. Series
SB603.5P46   1995   635'.049—dc20 95-6155   CIP

© 1995 Time Life Inc. All rights reserved.
No part of this book may be reproduced in any form or by any electronic or mechanical means, including information storage and retrieval devices or systems, without prior written permission from the publisher, except that brief passages may be quoted for reviews.
First printing. Printed in U.S.A.
Published simultaneously in Canada.
School and library distribution by Time-Life Education, P.O. Box 85026, Richmond, Virginia 23285-5026.

TIME-LIFE is a trademark of Time Warner Inc. U.S.A.

This volume is one of a series of comprehensive gardening books that cover garden design, choosing plants for the garden, planting and propagating, and planting diagrams.

Time-Life Books is a division of **TIME LIFE INC.**

PRESIDENT and CEO: John M. Fahey Jr.
EDITOR-IN-CHIEF: John L. Papanek

TIME-LIFE BOOKS

Managing Editor: Roberta Conlan

Director of Design: Michael Hentges
Director of Editorial Operations: Ellen Robling
Director of Photography and Research:
John Conrad Weiser
Senior Editors: Russell B. Adams Jr., Dale M. Brown, Janet Cave, Lee Hassig, Robert Somerville, Henry Woodhead
Special Projects Editor: Rita Thievon Mullin
Director of Technology: Eileen Bradley
Library: Louise D. Forstall

PRESIDENT: John D. Hall

Vice President, Director of Marketing:
Nancy K. Jones
Vice President, Director of New Product Development:
Neil Kagan
Vice President, Book Production: Marjann Caldwell
Production Manager: Marlene Zack
Quality Assurance Manager: Miriam Newton

THE TIME-LIFE COMPLETE GARDENER

Editorial Staff for *Pests & Diseases*

SERIES EDITOR: Janet Cave
Deputy Editors: Sarah Brash, Jane Jordan
Administrative Editor: Roxie France-Nuriddin
Art Directors: Cindy Morgan-Jaffe(principal), Kathleen Mallow
Picture Editor: Jane A. Martin
Text Editors: Sarah Brash (principal), Darcie Conner Johnston
Associate Editors/Research-Writing: Katya Sharpe, Robert Speziale
Technical Art Assistant: Sue Pratt
Senior Copyeditor: Anne Farr
Picture Coordinator: David A. Herod
Editorial Assistant: Donna Fountain
Special Contributors: Jennifer Clark (research); Vilasini Balakrishnan, Linda B. Bellamy, Susan S. Blair, Jocelyn C. Lindsay, Rosanne C. Scott (research-writing); Rita Pelczar (writing); Marge duMond (editing); John Drummond (art); Lina B. Burton (index).

Correspondents: Christine Hinze (London), Christina Lieberman (New York). Valuable assistance was also provided by Liz Brown (New York), Judy Aspinall (London).

Cover: A plump larval-stage Colorado potato beetle feeds on a leaf alongside newly laid eggs. Within a week the eggs will hatch and the larvae and adult beetles (back cover) will decimate the plant's foliage. End papers: Setaria verticillata, an annual weed known as foxtail, grows wild in a Kentucky field. Title page: A twining patch of dodder, a parasitic weed, slowly smothers a stand of purple loosestrife, also a weed, in a garden near College Park, Maryland.

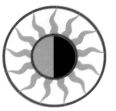

CHAPTER ONE

Pests in Your Garden

Insects are everywhere, in astonishing variety and equally astonishing numbers—worldwide, there are some 2 million species. Although only a tiny fraction of these species inhabit a typical American garden, a diligent census taker would find millions upon millions of individuals within its boundaries. On the face of it, these are numbers to fill the heart of a gardener with dismay. In reality, though, only about 1,000 of the world's 2 million insect species qualify as pests. Moreover, on the scale of a particular garden in a particular place, fewer than a dozen species are likely to feed destructively on the plants growing there. For the knowledgeable gardener, controlling that handful of pests is a manageable business rather than an unending battle.

This chapter describes an effective, environmentally sound program of pest control that relies on common sense and is easy for the gardener to put into practice. It involves basic good-gardening practices and smart plant selection, which will minimize pest problems. Learning to recognize undesirable insect species is also essential, as is the ability to identify beneficial creatures that prey on pests, and those garden denizens that are quite harmless. Once you know the enemy, you can choose among an array of control methods, from techniques as simple as handpicking caterpillars off plants to spraying with pesticides. If you decide a problem warrants such chemicals, follow the recommendations in the final section of this chapter to ensure your personal safety and the health of your garden.

NATURAL PEST CONTROL
On a spring day, a cardinal feeds her offspring a tomato hornworm, one of the garden's most voracious caterpillars. Birds and other predators help keep the pest population within bounds and reduce the need for chemical controls.

Creating a Pest-Resistant Garden

No matter what you do in or to your garden, insects will always be among the creatures sustained by its elements—soil, mulch, water, turf, the compost pile, the flowering annuals and perennials, the shrubs and trees. How you approach the ones that can eat their way through your thoughtfully chosen plants is an important matter. Whatever steps you take against the destructive few will also affect the garden's benign creatures, from invisible soil microbes to pest-eating ladybird beetles to the songbirds that enliven the scene.

Tolerance in the Garden

The most sensible course is to accept insects, including the pests, as a fact of garden life. Trying to rout them altogether with a chemi-cal assault is a losing battle, and, more important, it is environmentally unsound.

A corollary of tolerating a varied population of insects is learning to live with imperfection. Tolerating a certain amount of pest damage is fundamental to the environmentally friendly philosophy of pest control known as Integrated Pest Management, or IPM. It calls for using a variety of cultural, physical, biological, and chemical methods that work together to keep the damage done by pests at an acceptable level while preserving the overall health of the garden environment.

When you practice the cultural measures described on the following pages, you do not compromise the attractiveness of your garden. On the contrary, the basics of good gardening are also the basics of sensible pest control. Providing good growing conditions has two capital advantages: Your plants will be far more likely to reach their full potential in beauty, and they will be healthy. By keeping your plants strong and vigorous, you will maximize their natural ability to withstand pests.

Doing the Essential Groundwork

The single best guarantee that your plants will be healthy is soil of the highest quality. For the most complete picture of your garden's soil, have it professionally tested. When the soil is reasonably dry, dig up samples to about 4 inches deep from several spots around the garden. Combine them and send about one pint of the mixture to your local Cooperative Extension Service or any private soil-testing lab. The results will reveal your soil's pH level, available nutrients, the presence of organic matter, and the soil's texture, determined by the proportions of sand, silt, and clay particles it contains. The ideal soil type is loam—a crumbly, loose combination of sand, silt, and clay that drains well and contains sufficient organic matter, nutrients, air, and water.

You may be lucky enough to have loamy soil. More likely, however, you'll need to amend your soil to bring it closer to the ideal.

How to Buy a Healthy Plant

Follow these guidelines when you purchase new plants to avoid importing problems into your garden:
- Shop at a garden center or nursery known for the quality of its plants, the expertise of its salespeople, and a fair return policy in case a plant proves unsatisfactory.
- Check a plant for the presence of pests and for pest damage such as webs or egg masses on stems or leaves, or holes chewed in the leaves. Be sure to examine the undersides of the foliage.
- Look for foliage with good color and form. Reject plants that show wilting, curling, spotting, or yellowing.
- Carefully lift a container plant out of its pot to check that roots are white and moist, not brown or soggy. They should fill the soil ball but not encircle it.
- Look for plants that have good branch structure, with no broken stems or bark wounds.
- Choose plants with full, healthy buds or, if the growing season has begun, new foliage and stems.

Drawing on Nature's Diversity

A garden abounding with plants of different kinds—exotics, natives, perennials, annuals, broadleaf evergreens, conifers, flowering shrubs and trees—is far less vulnerable to devastating infestations of pests than a garden designed with a more restricted plant palette. Selecting a garden's principal furnishings from only a handful of plant families—roses, boxwood, iris, and dogwood, for instance—is a risky business, since an equally small handful of pest species has the potential to devastate your entire garden.

In short, the closer a garden comes to monoculture, the more it is deprived of the protective mechanisms that exist in natural plant communities, which are characteristically rich in species. A garden like the one shown here is attractive to pest predators such as birds, beneficial insects, lizards, and toads. It supplies many different food sources such as nectar, pollen, fruit, and seeds over a long season. And its range of trees, shrubs, and herbaceous plants of varying sizes and densities create habitats for a variety of species. With good planning, the elements that make the garden beautiful will also discourage pests, and at no environmental cost.

A heavy clay soil must be amended to let air, water, and nutrients penetrate it easily and reach plant roots. To lighten clay, mix it half-and-half with coarse sand or organic matter such as peat moss or compost. These materials can also be used to improve the structure of dense, silty soil, which, like clay, is prone to waterlogging. In light, porous, sandy soils, water drains away quickly and takes plant nutrients with it. The solution in this case is to dig in clayey topsoil or an organic material such as composted manure to improve the soil's capacity to hold moisture.

It is also important to keep your soil's pH within a healthful range. Most plants will grow well in soil that is slightly acid, with a pH between 6 and 7. When the pH is too high or too low, plants aren't able to draw essential nutrients from the soil, and as a result they grow poorly. You can correct a soil that is too acidic by digging in dolomitic limestone, which is alkaline. When a soil is too alkaline, on the other hand, use iron sulfate to increase its acidity. Test your soil's pH every year or two to be sure that it remains within a desirable range.

The Myth of Companion Planting

Many gardeners wouldn't think of planting a vegetable garden without a liberal larding of the aromatic plants reputed to keep insect pests away from their crops. Nevertheless, research suggests that this so-called companion planting doesn't deserve the faith that gardeners place in it. It is true that certain plants hinder the proliferation of undesirable organisms. For instance, it has been shown that marigolds can control pest nematodes, tiny worms that live in soil and infest plants. The problem is that the marigolds suppress the nematodes only when the plants are spaced so densely that there is virtually no room left in the garden for a food crop. The pest-repelling abilities of other favorite companion plants have been tested under controlled conditions and have been just as disappointing.

Supplying Nutrients

A soil test will also reveal whether your soil provides enough of the three nutrients essential for healthy plant growth—nitrogen, phosphorus, and potassium. Garden fertilizers are labeled to show what percentage they contain of each of these elements, and the numbers are always arranged in the same order. Thus a fertilizer designated "12-4-4" is by weight 12 percent nitrogen, 4 percent phosphorus, and 4 percent potassium; the remaining 80 percent is made up of inert fillers.

You have a choice of using either a chemical fertilizer, which is manufactured or mined, or an organic fertilizer, which is derived from plant or animal material. The two types are equally nourishing to plants and equally convenient to use. However, the organic fertilizers have an important advantage—the nutrients they contain are released gradually over a period of time. Chemical nutrients, by contrast, are often immediately available to the plants, increasing the risk of burning plant roots if you happen to overfertilize.

Not all plants thrive on the same regimen of nutrients. The nitrogen-rich diet that turf grasses demand, for instance, would stimulate rapid, floppy growth if it were applied to herbaceous perennials, making them targets for aphids. A general-purpose fertilizer will suffice for most plants, but be sure to accommodate those plants that have special needs. The encyclopedia that begins on page 125 will help you recognize the symptoms of several deficiency diseases that can be corrected with the right fertilizer.

Plants to Suit the Site

Choosing the plants that will fulfill your vision for your garden is an intensely personal, aesthetic exercise—and an eminently practical one as well. Even as you're making decisions on such matters as flower season and color, the height of a shade tree, or the combination of foliage textures for a mixed hedge, you will want to compare each plant's cultural requirements with the general conditions your garden offers. You'll also want to identify any microclimates on the site, such as a sunny corner sheltered from winter winds.

In creating a profile of your garden conditions, you'll need to consider several things:

- The hardiness zone of your area, based on the average minimum temperature.
- Temperature and humidity in summer. Are nights cool or hot? Plants adapted to cool nights often do poorly where summers are muggy.
- The average amount of rainfall and its distribution over the course of the year. If your area has dry spells lasting 2 weeks or so, as much of the United States does during summer, drought-tolerant plants would be likely candidates.
- The hours of sun and shade that different parts of the garden receive in different seasons of the year, and the quality of that shade—dappled or dense?

• Soil composition, acidity, and drainage in various parts of the garden.

Once you have collected this information, you can see whether there is a good match between a plant's cultural requirements and your garden's environment. What you learn from your analysis may also explain why certain plants in your garden, or in nearby gardens similar to yours, have flourished while others have grown poorly or died.

Pest-Resistant Plants

In addition to a plant's visual appeal and its ability to thrive in your garden, you will want to consider how vulnerable it is to pests. Some species are naturally resistant to pest damage, and in some cases horticulturists have developed new hybrids and cultivars offering such resistance. Some popular pest-

Pest-Resistant Shrubs and Trees

**DECIDUOUS
FLOWERING SHRUBS**

***Abeliophyllum
distichum***
(white forsythia)
***Acanthopanax
sieboldianus***
(five-leaf aralia)
Berberis thunbergii
(Japanese barberry)
Buddleia davidii
(butterfly bush)
Calycanthus floridus
(Carolina allspice)
Caragana arborescens
(Siberian pea shrub)
***Chionanthus
virginicus***
(fringe tree)

Clethra alnifolia
(sweet pepperbush)
Cytisus scoparius
(Scotch broom)
Deutzia gracilis
(slender deutzia)
Deutzia* x *rosea
(deutzia)
***Enkianthus
campanulatus***
(red-veined enkianthus)
Euonymus alata
(winged euonymus)
Forsythia* x *intermedia
(border forsythia)
Fothergilla major
(large fothergilla)
***Hippophae
rhamnoides***
(sallow thorn)

Hypericum prolificum
(shrubby St.-John's-wort)
Jasminum nudiflorum
(winter jasmine)
***Philadelphus* spp.**
(mock orange)
Potentilla fruticosa
(bush cinquefoil)
***Spiraea* spp.**
(bridal wreath)
Stewartia ovata
(mountain camellia)
***Symphoricarpos* spp.**
(coralberry, snowberry)
Viburnum sieboldii
(Siebold viburnum)
Weigela florida
(old-fashioned weigela)

Note: The abbreviation "spp." stands for the plural of "species"; where used in lists it means that many, but not all, of the species in a genus meet the criterion of the list.

**ORNAMENTAL TREES
LESS THAN 30 FEET
HIGH**

Carpinus caroliniana
(American hornbeam)
Cornus mas
(cornelian cherry)
***Elaeagnus
angustifolia***
(Russian wild olive)
Franklinia alatamaha
(franklinia)
***Koelreuteria
paniculata***
(golden rain tree)
Lagerstroemia
'Natchez', 'Biloxi',
'Muskogee'
(crape myrtle)
Magnolia stellata
(star magnolia)
Myrica pensylvanica
(bayberry)
Parrotia persica
(Persian parrotia)
Pistacia chinensis
(Chinese pistachio)
***Stewartia
pseudocamellia***
(Japanese stewartia)
Styrax japonicus
(Japanese snowbell)

*Parrotia persica
(Persian parrotia)*

Deutzia x rosea (deutzia)

resistant deciduous shrubs and small trees are listed on page 11.

Plants actively counter pests with a variety of mechanical and physiological measures. Two examples of mechanical, or physical, defenses are tough outer membranes that prevent insect pests from feeding on leaves or pods, and needlelike thorns that discourage browsing animals, such as deer (see pages 40-41 for a list of deer-resistant plants). A covering of hairs on stems and leaves, which on some plants can be sticky, traps pests that land on them and prevents the insects from feeding. Physiological defensive tricks include releasing toxic or repellent compounds to deter pests. Oak trees, for example, contain bitter-tasting compounds called tannins that thwart bark beetles and boring insects, and geraniums contain a chemical that paralyzes Japanese beetles.

Plants are classified according to the degree of resistance they possess. "Immune" means that a plant cannot be harmed by a particular pest; "resistant" identifies plants that are rarely infested by specific pests and suffer only minor damage if they are attacked; "tolerant" describes a plant that is subject to infestation but does not suffer any permanent damage. Finally, the word "susceptible" is a red flag for gardeners because it indicates that a plant is highly vulnerable to one or more pests. There are also species and varieties that are innately resistant to disease *(list, pages 48-49)*.

Native Plants, Native Pests

Plants that grow naturally in your geographical area can usually be counted on to perform reliably in the garden, since they are adapted to the prevailing climate and soil. Many of these native species are also resistant to native pests. Over eons of coexistence, plants that evolved effective defenses against the indigenous pests were more likely to succeed than their susceptible cousins.

Not all natives are trouble free, however. In the eastern United States, for example, native cherries are often beset by ugly masses of tent caterpillars, while some of the exotic species imported from Asia are less attractive to these pests. And, of course, every part of the country has its share of imported pests, against which native plants have no defense.

For information on ornamentals native to your area, contact your local Cooperative Extension Service. Numerous mail-order nurseries also specialize in native plants, and more and more retail nurseries are stocking natives. See the box on page 8 for buying guidelines.

Maintenance Practices That Foil Pests

Proper techniques of watering, fertilizing, and sanitation keep a garden growing well and also help fend off pests and diseases. How often you need to water depends on the amount of precipitation your garden receives and on soil type—sandy soils dry out quickly, clayey soils more slowly. To determine whether it's time to water, check the soil's moisture level by digging down 3 or 4 inches with a trowel or soil auger. If the top 1½ to 2 inches are dry, the garden is due for a watering.

In the absence of sufficient rainfall, a rule of thumb is to provide at least 1 inch of water per week, dispersed slowly and evenly during one long soaking. When plants are watered deeply at longer intervals instead of more frequently and lightly, they develop tougher outer layers that protect them from moisture loss and discourage pests from feeding. In addition, root systems are encouraged to grow downward to soil levels that retain moisture. As a result, the plants develop a greater tolerance for drought. For additional information on good watering practices, see page 50.

A 2- to 4-inch layer of organic mulch such as shredded bark or compost will help conserve soil moisture, suppress weeds and, especially when compost is used, provide a slow-release source of plant nutrients. Mulch also helps keep the soil rich in the microorganisms that break down fallen leaves, dead animals, and other organic matter into humus—the single most vital ingredient of high-quality soil.

Weeds compete with ornamentals and vegetable crops for space, light, water, and nutrients. And since weedy areas frequently harbor crickets, grasshoppers, slugs, snails, stink bugs, and other pests, eliminating weeds eliminates a source of trouble.

Clear garden beds of spent flowers, fallen leaves and fruit, weeds, or other debris that could harbor pests, and add them to the compost pile. In the case of diseased plant materials or weeds that have gone to seed, dispose of them in the trash or incorporate them into a compost pile that gets hot enough to render them harmless—at least 140° F.

Identifying Insect Pests

Sometimes even a culturally pest-resistant garden comes under attack by insects. If they inflict damage on your plants that is beyond your threshold for tolerance, you will want to deal with them quickly and effectively. To do this, you must first identify the insects, then choose an appropriate method of control. Since every pest-control method has its attendant costs in time, effort, money, and environmental risk, it's important to have a good understanding of the several types available—physical, biological, and chemical *(pages 19-35)*—before you make your choice.

This may seem a straightforward approach, but it all hinges on a somewhat complex task—correct identification of a pest and its stage in the life cycle. Identification is easier with a basic understanding of insect anatomy *(right).* Since the aim is not to eliminate every creeping creature in your garden, learning about anatomy and life cycles will also help you distinguish between the pest insects and the beneficials *(pages 11 and 24-29).* Most beneficial insects feed on pests or use them as hosts for their young. In this way, they are a naturally assertive biological control, keeping pest populations in check.

One key to avoiding major pest problems is to monitor your garden regularly. This entails weekly checking of your plants for signs of pests and pest damage. At the height of the growing season, you may want to check as often as once a day.

Keep a garden diary. When you see pest damage, record the date, the approximate number of leaves or plants infested, and the location of the damage on the plant. If you can see the pest, note the type of insect, if you know it, and how many there are—this will help you detect changes in the population from week to week or from day to day. Also make note of any unusual environmental conditions such as unseasonable temperatures, drought, or extra rain-

fall; these can affect pest populations as well as the plants themselves.

Remember, too, that not all plant damage can be blamed on pests. Nutritional deficiencies, diseases, or environmental stresses such as pollution can weaken a plant. But if your once-thriving plants are failing and you can rule out stress, soil problems, and weather-related hardships, chances are that pests are to blame.

With any pest problem, 90 percent of the solution lies in identifying the culprit. The clearest evidence you can get is to observe the insect feeding on your plant. If you can't see the pest, however, you will have to base your diagnosis on the damage it has done *(page 14).*

Whatever region, climate, or zone you live in, you face a fairly limited number of insect pests. Learn to recog-

Head

Thorax

Abdomen

AN INSECT'S COMMON ANATOMY
Like this chinch bug, all insects have four distinct features: three body sections—head, thorax, and abdomen—and six legs. Many also have antennae, which help them find food, and wings. Variations in the colors or sizes of these features will help you identify the particular insects in your garden.

Common Plant Pests

Identifying the damage pests inflict on your garden is often a confusing task. However, there are some telltale indications that will quickly enable you to zero in on your plants' attackers. The havoc wreaked by several of the more commonly found insect pests and insect relatives is illustrated below.

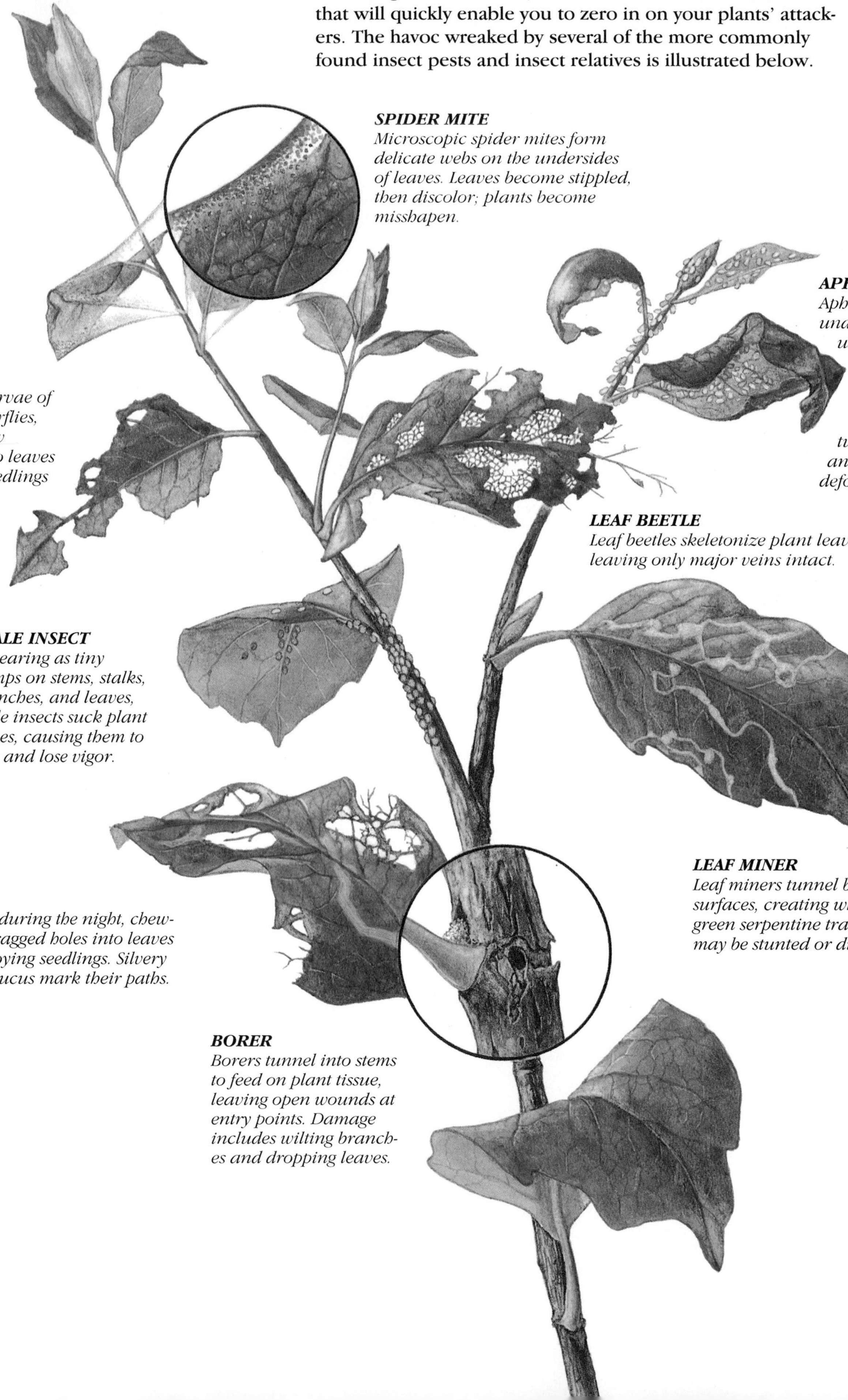

SPIDER MITE
Microscopic spider mites form delicate webs on the undersides of leaves. Leaves become stippled, then discolor; plants become misshapen.

APHID
Aphids cluster on the undersides of leaves, usually attacking new growth first. Leaves curl under at the edges and turn brown. Buds and flowers are deformed.

CATERPILLAR
The wormlike larvae of moths and butterflies, caterpillars chew ragged holes into leaves and often eat seedlings off at soil level.

LEAF BEETLE
Leaf beetles skeletonize plant leaves, leaving only major veins intact.

SCALE INSECT
Appearing as tiny bumps on stems, stalks, branches, and leaves, scale insects suck plant juices, causing them to wilt and lose vigor.

LEAF MINER
Leaf miners tunnel beneath leaf surfaces, creating white or light green serpentine trails. Seedlings may be stunted or die.

SLUG
Slugs feed during the night, chewing large ragged holes into leaves and destroying seedlings. Silvery trails of mucus mark their paths.

BORER
Borers tunnel into stems to feed on plant tissue, leaving open wounds at entry points. Damage includes wilting branches and dropping leaves.

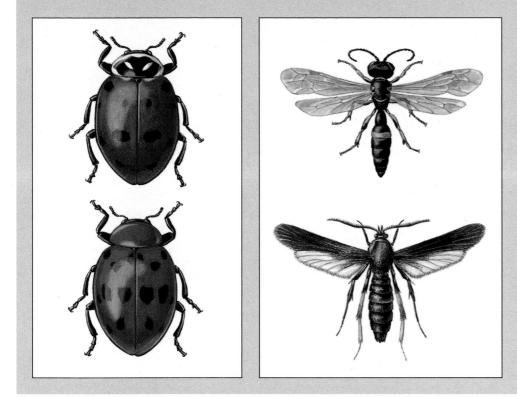

Many insect pests have markings and body shapes similar to those of beneficial insects, and even the most knowledgeable gardener will have to take a closer look to tell plant friend from foe. It is especially easy to confuse the destructive Mexican bean beetle *(far left, bottom)* with the helpful ladybird beetle *(far left, top)*. The trick is to count spots: The number will vary from one ladybird beetle to another, but all Mexican bean beetles have exactly 16 spots. In the case of the destructive peach tree borer moth *(bottom left)* and the digger wasp *(top left)*, a beneficial that preys on caterpillars and other pests, the difference lies in body contour: The troublesome moth has a thick middle, while the wasp has a narrow waist.

nize the usual suspects by anatomy, habit, and damage pattern. To find out which pests you are likely to see, use the *Range* and *Host* information given at the top of each entry in the insect encyclopedia at the back of this book. When examining insects, it's useful to look at them through a hand-held 10x magnifying lens, the kind available for around 15 dollars through well-stocked garden centers or mail-order catalogs. Once you've become familiar with the local troublemakers, any newcomer will be obvious to your trained eye.

Many people lump all garden creatures that creep, crawl, and fly into a single category, called bugs. True bugs, however, are only one of the 28 orders in the class Insecta, and account for just a tiny fraction of the more than 2 million insect species. All insects, bugs included, share a unique anatomy: They have three body sections—head, thorax, and abdomen—and all have six legs, arranged in three pairs *(page 13)*. An insect body is exoskeletal—that is, the skeleton is on the outside, much like a suit of armor—and most are less than three-quarters of an inch long. Some insects have antennae, which they use for smelling or tasting. Most insects have one pair of compound eyes, one on either side of the head; many have additional, simple eyes, on the upper part of the face. They have no lungs but breathe through tiny holes along the sides of the body, taking in oxygen directly to various internal organs. Much of an insect's internal equipment is geared toward reproduction.

Most insects also have wings. Their ability to fly lets them travel great distances, especially if drawn by an attractive host plant. This, coupled with their prodigious reproductive powers, explains how pest populations can explode overnight. Insect life cycles are short, allowing some species to produce 25 generations in a season; many lay eggs by the hundreds. This is another reason to deal quickly with any pest infestation.

Feeding Habits as Evidence

Insects live to eat, and they do so in a variety of ways. Some chew, some suck, and some bore through leaves, roots, stems, and even through thick tree bark. As you become better acquainted with different pests and their habits, you'll quickly recognize the damage they create and be able to match it to the offending pest.

Sucking insects such as aphids, cicadas, leafhoppers, lace bugs, psyllids, and whiteflies feed on a plant by inserting a feeding tube into a leaf and sucking the juice out. This causes the leaves to discolor and eventually fall off. Chewing insects eat holes into the leaves, stems, and flowers of plants, marring their appearance. The chewers include beetles, caterpillars, crickets, grasshoppers, and weevils.

Borers, the other large group of insect pests, eat away at the insides of plants through feeding tunnels. Borers are hard to detect because you can't see them until the damage is done, when plants yellow and wilt or, in more advanced cases, branches and stems die back.

This group includes bark beetles, tree borers, stalk borers, and wood wasps.

When you see the insects themselves in your garden, their numbers are another clue to their identity. Most pest insects tend to act in groups when they attack a plant. By contrast, most of the beneficial insects are predators that feed on the pests, so they usually appear in smaller numbers in your garden.

Knowing When an Insect Becomes a Pest

Other clues to identifying insect pests lie in knowing which plants they attack and at what stage of their life cycle they act as pests. For example, the sod webworm and the tomato

Metamorphosis: Simple or Complete

On their way to adulthood, insects not only grow, they also undergo a transformation called metamorphosis. This transformation can be either simple or complete. In simple metamorphosis *(right)*, insects such as aphids, crickets, and plant bugs alter very little as they grow from eggs to adulthood. This contrasts with complete metamorphosis *(far right)*, in which insects such as beetles, butterflies, and wasps experience drastic physical changes before emerging as adults.

Unlike animals that nurture their eggs until they hatch, insects commonly lay their eggs and leave them to gestate on their own. Insect eggs come in many shapes and sizes, and because they are independent, they are often covered with a protective layer of tiny hairs or a shellaclike coating. The eggs are normally laid on or near the plants or host insects that will provide food for the nymphs or larvae. Some insects lay eggs singly; most deposit them in batches ranging from 50 to hundreds of eggs.

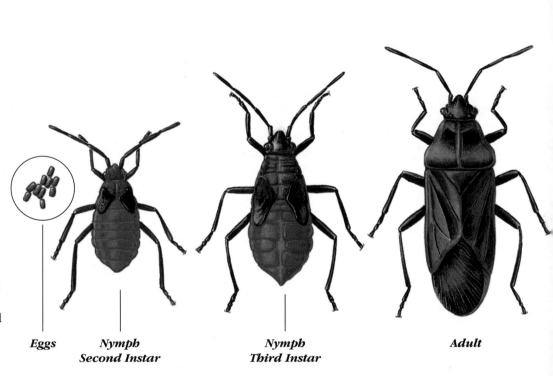

Eggs   **Nymph**   **Nymph**   **Adult**
          Second Instar   **Third Instar**

Some insects, like the box elder bug shown above, develop by simple metamorphosis, changing little as they grow. Emerging from near microscopic eggs laid on leaves or in small crevices in the ground, the immature insects, or nymphs, are each covered with a rigid shell, or exoskeleton. As a nymph grows, its exoskeleton becomes too tight, forcing the nymph to shed, or molt, its outer layer and grow a larger one. Immediately after a molt, the insect is soft bodied and pale, but within a couple of hours, the new exoskeleton hardens and begins to take on color. Typically, an insect's development involves four to eight molts, or instars. A box elder bug undergoes five instars during its early life.

16

hornworm are both larval stages of moths, and feed on grass and tomato plants, respectively. These pest species and some others inflict damage only as larvae; in other species, the adult is the pest, and in a few species, the insect is damaging in all of its life stages.

Knowing the life-cycle stages in which a pest feeds on your plants will help you spot a troublemaker more quickly, because you'll know what kind of creature—adult or larva—to be looking for. Complete identification of your pest will also help you apply the most effective control at the life stage dormant, larval, or adult—when the pest is most susceptible to attack. The encyclopedia of insect pests beginning on page 101 details when in each pest's life cycle the insect does its damage and when to apply controls.

Insect Relatives

Insects are often grouped with certain other garden pests and beneficials that seem related but belong to no insect order. These include spiders and mites—known by their four pairs of legs—as well as centipedes, millipedes, slugs, snails, and roundworms. These so-called insect relatives have feeding habits similar to those of the insects inhabiting your garden. As with insects, you'll want to take care not to eliminate them indiscriminately, since not all are harmful. (Mammal pests, such as gophers, moles, and deer, which can devastate a garden within hours, obviously call for different methods of identification and control. See pages 36-41.)

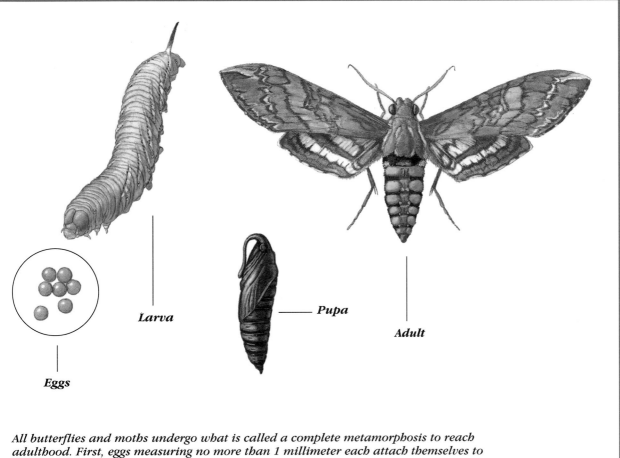

Larva

Eggs

Pupa

Adult

All butterflies and moths undergo what is called a complete metamorphosis to reach adulthood. First, eggs measuring no more than 1 millimeter each attach themselves to the undersides of leaves, where they take about a week to hatch. Each emerging larva, or caterpillar, feeds voraciously for 2 to 4 weeks, shedding its skin several times, until it is fully grown. To advance to the next stage and become a pupa, the mature caterpillar attaches itself to a plant or other object and spins a cocoon around its body. Inside the cocoon, the pupa's body changes dramatically over the next 10 to 15 days into a winged, six-legged adult. The adult butterfly or moth breaks out of the cocoon and, by mating to produce eggs, perpetuates the life cycle.

Graceful Adult, Voracious Larva

Butterflies are among the most spectacular and colorful creatures in your garden. In their larval state, however, many of these elusive beauties can munch your plants down to nubs. By growing species that the larvae prefer *(below, left)*, you can nourish these soon-to-be butterflies while minimizing the damage to your other plants.

To keep your garden attractive to the adult butterflies as they emerge from their cocoons, grow plants of various heights with colorful, nectar-bearing flowers from which butterflies can sip *(below, right)*. Butterflies also need to bask in sunlight to keep their body temperatures up, so be sure to locate these plants in a sunny spot. Forgo pesticides; the chemicals will turn all butterflies away from your garden, no matter how many attractive plantings you provide.

Plants to Nourish Larvae

Anethum graveolens
(dill)
Artemisia spp.
(wormwood)
Barbarea
(winter cress)
Cirsium spp.
(thistle)
Daucus carota
(Queen Anne's lace)
Dicentra spp.
(bleeding heart)
Foeniculum vulgare
(sweet fennel)
Nasturtium
(nasturtium)
Pastinaca sativa
(parsnip)
Petroselinum crispum
(parsley)
Populus spp.
(poplar, aspen, cottonwood)
Ruta graveolens
(common rue)
Sedum spp.
(stonecrop)

Note: The abbreviation "spp." stands for the plural of "species"; where used in lists it means that many, but not all, of the species in a genus meet the criterion of the list.

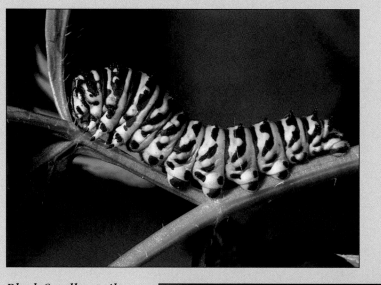

Black Swallowtail Butterfly Larva

Black Swallowtail Butterfly

Plants to Attract Butterflies

Artemisia spp.
(wormwood)
Asclepias spp.
(milkweed)
Aster spp.
(aster)
Buddleia spp.
(butterfly bush)
Centaurea spp.
(knapweed)
Cephalanthus spp.
(buttonbush)
Coreopsis spp.
(tickseed)
Echinacea purpurea
(purple coneflower)
Lantana spp.
(lantana)
Lonicera spp.
(honeysuckle)
Mentha spp.
(mint)
Rudbeckia hirta
(black-eyed Susan)
Salix spp.
(willow)

Note: The abbreviation "spp." stands for the plural of "species"; where used in lists it means that many, but not all, of the species in a genus meet the criterion of the list.

Dealing with Pests on the Spot

For the gardener who wants to avoid overkill, a simple physical control is the first line of defense when a pest threatens to do serious damage. Most of these measures—barriers, traps, and the like—rely on common sense and traditional techniques of good gardening. However, discoveries in insect behavior and reproduction have provided several technological twists in the area of physical controls that have proven to be enormous boons.

As a rule, physical controls pose no environmental hazards and are inexpensive. Put to use singly or in combination, they offer you sensible options for managing pest problems.

Protecting Seedlings

An obvious way of heading off trouble is to erect a barrier that stops pests from getting to your plants. Seedlings are especially vulnerable to attack. Because of their small size, they can be chewed to the ground in no time and have little or nothing in the way of food reserves to help them replace shoots or leaves.

Plant collars and row covers are two easy ways of protecting seedlings until they are established. Collars, which are slipped around individual seedlings as shown in the illustration at right, keep crawling pests like cutworms from reaching tender stems and foliage. Row covers, made of transparent fabric that allows a full complement of sunlight to reach young plants, are most often used in the vegetable garden as barriers against birds and flying insects. The covers' edges are buried in the soil to keep crawling insects from wiggling underneath them.

Blocking Pests on Trees

Tree bands, a variation of the plant-collar idea, can be used to block gypsy moth caterpillars, webworms, root weevils, and other crawling pests that make their way up a tree trunk to feed on the foliage. Garden centers and mail-order catalogs carry bands, but it's easy and much less expensive to make them yourself.

Barriers and Traps

This seedling is shielded from crawling pests with a plant collar, here an inverted paper cup. You can also use sections cut from the cardboard tube of a roll of paper towels. At left, a length of burlap tied around the tree and folded down over the string stops gypsy moth larvae and other pests from climbing the trunk to feed on foliage. Sticky glue painted above the burlap catches any pests that elude the barrier.

Placed near plants that would otherwise be attacked, the sticky trap at right lures aphids and several other flying pests that share a strong attraction to yellow objects. Insects landing on the surface of the trap become mired in its adhesive coating and suffocate. White and blue traps are effective with other species of pests.

Using burlap or another sturdy fabric, cut a strip 8 to 12 inches wide and several inches longer than the tree trunk's circumference. Cut a piece of heavy string a foot or so longer than the circumference. At a point several feet above the ground, wrap the strip of fabric around the trunk. Center the string on the fabric and tie it firmly in place. Then fold the top portion of the fabric down over the string to make a flap.

Some of the pests that blunder into this dead end will find their way out and crawl back down the trunk. Others will remain trapped, and some, such as gypsy moths, may enjoy the shelter from sun and rain and pupate there. Check the bands about once a week, or more frequently in the case of heavy infestation. Wearing gloves, pick off any trapped pests and drop them into a bucket of soapy water to kill them.

Leaf-eating pests are especially hard on young trees, but established trees can also be vulnerable in years when a pest's population explodes. Install bands before the threatened trees put forth new foliage in the spring.

Mulching for Pest Control

Among its many virtues, mulch helps combat pests in a variety of ways. A coarse organic mulch such as cocoa hulls discourages slugs and snails because their bodies are soft and scratch easily *(pages 22-23)*. A thick layer of shredded bark or other mulch prevents overwintering pests like beetle grubs from finding food as they emerge from the soil. And black plastic, which is impenetrable as long as it isn't torn, disrupts the life cycles of thrips, leaf miners, and other pests that lay their eggs in soil or overwinter in a dormant stage. A newspaper mulch works much the same way but is effective for only one season since it is biodegradable.

Aluminum to Foil Flying Pests

The light rays bouncing off a reflective mulch confuse aphids, thrips, and other flying pests and keep them from locating their target plants. You can buy aluminum-coated kraft paper insulation or aluminized plastic at garden and home centers, but ordinary aluminum foil works just as well. Given the utilitarian appearance of these materials, they are best reserved for the vegetable garden or a nursery bed tucked out of sight.

Lay strips of the reflective mulch under the leaf canopy, leaving spaces between the strips and near the plant's stem so that water can reach the soil. Since the aluminum reflects enough heat to scorch plants, especially tender seedlings, it should be removed before the weather becomes hot. A good practice is to remove the mulch as soon as young plants have become established.

Traps for Flying Pests

Along with barriers and mulches, traps are one of the most effective physical controls for the home garden. There are many types of traps on the market, almost all of them designed to catch flying insects of a specific kind. Be sure to identify the pest you're targeting so that you'll select the right kind of trap. In addition to drawing pests away from your plants, the traps help you monitor changes in the size of a particular pest population. If the number of pests trapped begins to rise sharply, you can take defensive measures before a lot of plant damage is done.

Avoid using any type of electric-light trap. None of these traps discriminates between victims, killing all insects, pests and beneficials alike. Moreover, they are expensive.

Luring Pests with Scent

One popular type of trap uses a scented lure, which, in most cases, is designed to catch a particular insect. For apple maggot flies, for example, the traps contain fruit and floral scents. The traps that attract adult Japanese beetles use two different lures—a floral scent for the females and, for the males, a synthetic scent that mimics a sex pheromone females produce to attract a mate. (For more about pheromone traps, see the next page.)

Unless it is used properly, a Japanese beetle trap can be counterproductive, actually attracting more insects to the plants you are trying to protect than would have appeared had you done nothing at all. Be sure to position the traps on nonhost plants such as pines, or on a structure like a fence post, at least 20 to 30 yards away and downwind from vulnerable plantings. If your area is suffering from an un-

Luring Pests with Sex Chemicals

During mating season, some insect pests release a pheromone—an airborne chemical signal that lets the opposite sex of the species know where to find them. Each species has its own unique pheromone, and its members have a remarkable ability to detect it, even at extremely low concentrations and over a distance of several miles. Insects are indifferent to alien pheromones.

The ability to produce synthetic versions of insect pheromones has resulted in a highly targeted technique of pest control. A trap impregnated with a pheromone catches males of one species only, eliminating them from the mating game and thus reducing the size of the next generation.

The traps come in a number of different shapes; the triangular or delta trap and the wing trap are shown at right. These two traps have sticky inner surfaces that hold insects fast. Other traps have a funnel-shaped entrance that prevents escape.

In addition to being control devices, some pheromone traps are used for monitoring changes in a given pest population. If the number of pests captured begins to rise sharply, the gardener can take an appropriate measure to short-circuit trouble, perhaps by using physical controls more diligently or by taking advantage of one of the biological controls described on pages 24-29.

Before you buy a pheromone trap, make certain the pest attacking your garden belongs to the species for which the trap was designed. Follow the directions for replacing the pheronome lure and cleaning the trap.

usually large influx of Japanese beetles, it is probably better not to use the traps at all, lest the pests swarm to your garden from neighboring yards.

To protect a quarter-acre garden, set out at least one trap; a half-acre will need two or more. The smell of accummulated dead beetles keeps live ones from entering traps, so it's important to empty them at least twice a week. A trap that lets rainwater drain away quickly minimizes the odor. After a month or 6 weeks, if the influx of pests has not diminished, renew the trap's effectiveness by installing a fresh lure.

Luring Pests with Color

Some traps, like the one shown on page 19, combine an alluring color with a sticky surface. Different insects are drawn to different colors—aphids, leafhoppers, and whiteflies are partial to yellow, for instance, whereas tarnished plant bugs, flea beetles, and rose chafers prefer white, and most thrips flock to blue. When the pest lands on the trap's colored panel, it becomes entangled in the coating of glue covering the surface. Unlike Japanese beetle traps, these sticky traps, as they are called, should be placed near the plants you want to protect, and at about the same height as the plants.

Homemade Sticky Traps

Although sticky traps can be bought through many mail-order catalogs or at any well-stocked garden center, you can make one easily at home. Cut scrap wood into rectangles measuring about 6 by 6 inches and paint them yellow, white, or blue, depending on the pest. You can either buy a weather-resistant adhesive designed for coating traps or make the glue yourself. Simply combine equal parts of petroleum jelly or mineral oil and liquid dishwashing soap or laundry detergent and mix well. Spread the glue on the painted rectangles and hang them in the garden. In an exposed place, homemade glue should last about 2 weeks. When it is no longer sticky, remove the old glue and pest remnants with a paint scraper and apply a fresh coat.

In addition to spreading it on traps, you

Coping with Slugs and Snails

Snails and slugs are elusive pests, feeding at night and taking refuge during the day under rocks, boards, leaves, or dense ground cover, or in other moist, shaded spots. Their presence in the garden is betrayed by the silvery trails of mucus they leave behind and the large ragged holes they chew in stems, bulbs, fruits, and leaves. Hosta, iris, and succulents are among their favorite plants, and in the vegetable garden, they nibble tomatoes, lettuce, strawberries, and the pungent leaves of onions.

Gardeners have a number of effective options for fighting snails and slugs, including those illustrated at right—two kinds of traps and a barrier that exploits these pests' aversion to copper. Your level of squeamishness will influence which of the following methods to try:

- Handpicking is most productive at night, when snails and slugs are actively feeding. Equip yourself with a flashlight and a pail of soapy water for disposing of the pests as you find them. Since their mucus is difficult to wash off, you may want to wear thin surgical gloves or use large tongs to pick the pests up.
- Salt sprinkled on slugs kills them by drawing fluid out of their bodies. However, repeated use of this technique carries the risk of making your soil salty enough to injure plants. This method is less successful with snails because their shells shield them from the salt.
- Place inverted flower pots or melon or grapefruit rinds in a shady spot to trap slugs or snails seeking daytime shelter.
- Sink a shallow can or pie tin to its rim in soil and fill with beer or other yeasty liquid. Empty every few days and replace liquid.
- Spread a band of an abrasive material around plants as a deterrent; diatomaceous earth, sand, sawdust, and wood ashes are effective, but only when dry.

COPPER BARRIERS
The most reliable barriers against slugs and snails are made of copper, which is toxic to these mollusks. Thin sheets of copper, available at hardware stores, are easily cut in strips to use as barriers. For a raised bed, fasten strips at least 4 to 5 inches wide to each side (above). To edge a bed, cut strips 4 to 6 inches wide and install them with the top 2 inches above the soil line. As an extra deterrent, bend the strip's upper edge outward to form a lip.

can paint a stripe of glue around a tree trunk to catch crawling insects. If you've put a fabric trap on the tree *(page 19),* apply the sticky glue just above it.

Catching Pests in the Act

With traps, the need to actually handle pests is kept to a minimum. But if you're a gardener who doesn't mind the closer contact required, handpicking crawling creatures such as hornworms, cutworms, and Colorado potato beetles off leaves and stems is a very effective method of control. There are only a few plant pests that will cause you any discomfort if they come into contact with bare skin, and even then it is usually temporary. These include blister beetles, whose body fluids can irritate skin; caterpillars with stinging hairs; and black flies, which inflict bites like those of a mosquito. As a precaution, you should always wear garden gloves when handpicking pests. You can also use kitchen tongs instead of your fingers to grasp them. To kill handpicked pests, drop them into a container filled with soapy water. Dispose of them in the trash or your compost heap.

Techniques for Dislodging Pests

If you prefer to place a bit of distance between you and your garden pests, a stream of water from a hose is often sufficient to remove invaders from plants. Be sure to spray the underside of the foliage, where aphids, whiteflies, mites, and other pests frequently feed, as well as the upper surfaces. If a plant's stems are fragile, hold them firmly with one hand as you wash the pests off.

BAITED TRAPS
Designed for use with bait, the plastic trap illustrated below has a removable lid and a small, lightweight door that swings inward only, preventing the snails and slugs that crawl in from escaping. If you use a poison bait, a trap with a tightfitting lid like this one reduces the risk of harm to pets. The lid also makes it easy to dump out the dead snails and slugs and to clean the trap's interior. The trap is partially buried to make it easier for the pests to enter.

AN UNBAITED BOARD TRAP
Nail two strips of wood about an inch thick to one side of a board. Set the board strip-side down on the ground. After a night of feeding, snails and slugs will collect in the dark, moist space beneath the board to escape drying heat and sunlight. Check the trap early each morning. Pick or scrape off any slugs and snails you find, disposing of them in a pail of soapy water.

Make sure, however, not to turn the water on so high that the jet rips off leaves or damages new shoots.

If stems and branches are strong and resilient, vigorous shaking is enough to make many kinds of pests, including leaf-eating beetles and black vine weevils, fall to the ground. Place an old sheet or a tarpaulin around the base of the plant to collect the falling pests. When you are finished, shake the pests into a pail of soapy water.

Vacuuming pests off plants is another option, but only when it's done with a machine that has been made specifically for this purpose and has a gentle sucking action. Don't use a household vacuum, which is powerful enough to cause damage to the plant. Since the vacuum will pick up any insect in its path, this is a technique that calls for distinguishing pests from harmless or beneficial insects and wielding the machine accordingly.

Pruning Infested Plants

The best way to deal with some pests is to prune off the part of the plant that is afflicted. Fall webworm caterpillars, for example, hatch inside a gauzy-looking nest the female spins in susceptible trees. To rid the tree of the pests, crush the caterpillars or tear the bag open to expose the larvae to the elements. Then use sharp, well-made shears or a pruning saw and sever the infested stem or branch cleanly with a slanting cut about a quarter inch above a bud, as shown on page 54.

Insect-egg masses on foliage or stems can be pruned off, and when you see leaf-miner trails on such a susceptible plant as columbine, pinch off the infested leaves promptly. Add them to a hot compost pile—one that reaches at least 140°F—or put them in a tightly sealed plastic bag and place it in the trash.

Exploiting Natural Checks and Balances

In nature, the predator-prey system does a good job of keeping the size of pest populations within safe bounds. Even though a garden is an artificial environment, in which planting and cultivation practices can tip the balance in favor of pests, the checks and balances that operate in the wild can be adapted as a powerful and environmentally sound weapon against them.

The arsenal borrowed from nature includes predatory vertebrates, insects, insect relatives such as spiders and mites, beneficial nematodes, and bacteria that attack garden pests. Organisms that benefit the garden by feeding on pests are referred to as biological controls.

By encouraging the beneficial predators that already inhabit your garden and introducing others to augment its defenses, you can keep the pest population at a level that doesn't threaten the health or good looks of your plants. Moreover, this defensive system may become largely self-perpetuating, requiring little more of you than occasional tinkering. It is important to recognize, however, that biological controls are not overnight solutions to pest problems. Nor are they always complete solutions by themselves. An excellent way to apply them is in conjunction with many of the physical and cultural controls described on pages 8-12 and 19-23.

You must also recognize that biological controls function properly only if you minimize or even abandon the use of broad-spectrum pesticides. These products, which include most synthetic chemical pesticides as well as certain natural ones, such as pyrethrum and rotenone, kill many kinds of insects, including beneficials. At best, such pesticides provide you with a short-term solution to your pest problem.

Creating a Hospitable Environment

Just as there are conditions that make your garden attractive to pests, there are things you can do to attract and keep pest predators. A steady source of water such as a small pool is sure to draw beneficial vertebrates including frogs, toads, snakes, lizards, and birds. Toads also appreciate shelter in the garden—perhaps an overturned flower pot with an opening chipped from the rim. Fruiting shrubs and trees will be magnets for birds, providing both shelter and food. The species that are mainly fruit or seed eaters in maturity will catch prodigious numbers of insects to feed to their young.

Insects, spiders, and other small predators will also be drawn to your garden by water and shelter; some types will gravitate to shrubs, others to tall herbaceous plants or to a moist, cool layer of organic mulch. The

A LADYBIRD BEETLE AT WORK
An insatiable predator, this convergent ladybird beetle eats its way along an aphid-infested plant stem. An adult beetle of this species can consume more than 30 of the insects a day; during its 3-week larval stage, the predator's intake can total 400 aphids. Other species of ladybird beetles, which are also known as ladybugs, feast on scale insects, mealybugs, whiteflies, and mites.

How a Parasitoid Destroys a Pest

The body of an insect selected by a parasitoid is both a protected habitat and a food supply for developing offspring. The drawings below illustrate this sequence in the life of a typical parasitoid, the braconid wasp. At far left, the female wasp injects an egg into its victim through a tube called an ovipositor **(A)**. The egg-laying process usually paralyzes the host but does not kill it immediately.

The egg quickly develops into a larva **(B)**. By the end of this life stage, which lasts 8 to 10 days, the larva's feeding activity has killed the host aphid. The larva metamorphoses into a pupa **(C)**, which continues to develop within the aphid's dry shell. At the end of pupation, the braconid wasp has attained its adult form and cuts a neat escape hatch to emerge from the host's remains **(D)**.

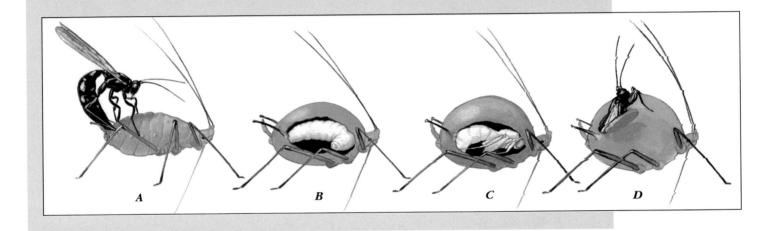

A   B   C   D

more varied your landscape, the greater the chance that these creatures will find appropriate niches.

Spiders have an undeservedly bad reputation, for only a few species are dangerous to humans and none to plants. The wise gardener suppresses the impulse to kill spiders, since they are among the most efficient biological controls in the garden, consuming a wide variety of common garden pests. They are also present in great numbers in most areas: According to one study, a typical 1-acre suburban plot has more than 60,000 spiders.

Purchasing Biological Controls

If the naturally occurring population of beneficials in your garden doesn't adequately contain pest outbreaks, it may be because they are too few in number or because they don't prey on the particular species of pest causing the trouble. In such cases, you can buy beneficials from a mail-order insectary for release in your garden. The information on the following pages and in the encyclopedia that begins on page 94 will help you choose the beneficials you need.

Predatory Insects

Beneficial insects can be divided into two groups according to their feeding habits—predators and parasitoids. A predator's diet consists of other, usually smaller, insects. Green lacewings, ground beetles, ladybird beetles, rove beetles, and praying mantises are typical of these hunters. Some indiscriminately feed on a wide range of pests including aphids, whiteflies, flea beetles, and spider mites. Others are very specific about their food choices. Aphid midges, for example, feast only on aphids.

Most predators are voracious eaters. In its larval stage, the green lacewing can devour a hundred aphids in a day. But a shortcoming of predatory insects is that they also prey on other beneficials. Praying mantises, for instance, hunt down and devour their own kind.

Predators for Sale

Many beneficial insects and other predators are available from mail-order insectaries. Before placing an order, identify your target pest. If you're uncertain of its type, send a specimen to your local Cooperative Extension Service. You can also talk to a customer-service representative at a reputable insectary.

When your shipment of predators arrives, attend to it promptly. All need careful handling, and most must be released at a certain time. Read and follow all instructions. Three common mail-order predators are shown below in various life stages; since they'll be garden friends, you'll want to recognize them in all their various forms.

The convergent ladybird beetle, *shown as a larva above left and as a pupa at center, is sold in its adult form (above, right).*

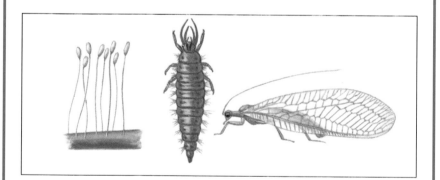

Green lacewings *are typically sold as eggs (above, left). The larva is at center and the adult appears at right.*

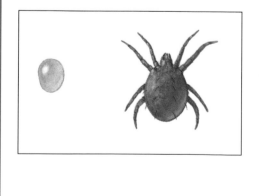

Predatory mites, *which have eight legs like other arachnids, arrive as adults (left). The egg stage appears at far left.*

Parasitoid Insects

Parasitoids, whose name means parasite-like, lay their eggs on or in a living insect host. After hatching, the larvae feed on the host, usually remaining attached to it until they have developed into adults *(diagram, page 25)*. Unlike a true parasite, which feeds on its host but doesn't kill it, hosts of parasitoids die.

Most parasitoid species target a particular type of pest and often only at one life-cycle stage. The trichogramma wasp, for instance, lays its eggs exclusively inside the eggs of specific butterfly and moth pests, thereby preventing the host eggs from hatching into troublesome caterpillars. Other pests controlled by parasitoids include aphids, whiteflies, and scale insects. Because the para-

How to Release Beneficial Nematodes

Because of their ability to destroy more than 400 different soil-borne pests, beneficial nematodes are a popular biological control. The wormlike creatures are easy to handle and easy to apply to the soil. They arrive on sponges that usually measure about 5 by 7 inches, each of which has been saturated with a solution containing nearly 1 million nematodes—an amount sufficient to treat three to four large patio pots or window boxes. Before you can know how many nematodes to order, you'll need to determine the severity of your infestation and the size of the area to be treated. For a quarter-acre garden with a moderate infestation, you'll need around 25 to 30 million nematodes.

When the nematodes are delivered, immediately remove them from their packaging and inspect them *(Step 1, right)*. Apply them only during warm months, when temperatures range between 65° and 78° F. Wait until after sunset to release them into the garden; otherwise ultraviolet rays from the sun can kill them. Nematodes work best in moist, loamy soil. If applying to turf that has a thick mat of thatch, dethatch the lawn *(page 81)* so that the nematodes can easily penetrate the soil.

sitoids are so selective, they are useful only when their chosen host infests your garden; without the host, the beneficial won't survive. This underscores the importance of learning to recognize garden pests, so that you'll be able to pick an appropriate control.

At least a dozen different parasitoids are widely available for purchase through the mail. Some species are shipped as adults, others in earlier stages of development. In the case of trichogramma wasps, the package you receive may contain a 1-inch-square card that holds up to 5,000 wasp eggs. Be sure to read fully all instructions for unpacking, handling, and dispersing parasitoids. For further information and details on specific parasitoids available commercially, see the chart on page 29.

Predatory Mites

Like spiders, mites are arachnids rather than insects. The mite family includes several species of beneficials that prey on pests such as thrips and pest mites, including the spider mites and cyclamen mites that frequently cause serious damage to vegetables, herbaceous ornamentals, trees, and shrubs.

Measuring less than 1/50 inch in length, the predatory mite species are often smaller than their prey, which can include adult mites as well as mite eggs, larvae, and nymphs. Under optimal environmental conditions, the beneficials can go from egg hatching to egg laying in a week, outstripping the reproductive rate of the pests. Because their population can in-

2. Fill a bucket with 1 gallon of lukewarm distilled water or rainwater. Do not use chlorinated water, which can kill the nematodes. Wearing gloves, rinse the sponges in the water for a few minutes to release the nematodes into the water. Lightly squeeze the sponges, then dispose of them in the trash.

1. Look over the sponges. They should feel damp and, to the naked eye, should appear to be coated with a cream-colored film. Using a magnifying glass, look to see if the nematodes are alive (they'll be wriggling). Proceed to Step 2, or reseal the sponges in their original plastic bag and store for no longer than 1 week in a refrigerator set at 40° to 50°F. (Caution: Because food refrigerators must be set lower than this to keep food from spoiling, do not store nematodes in them.)

3. Pour the nematode solution into a watering can and apply evenly to the soil. Saturate the area but do not overwater—excess water can deplete the oxygen in the soil and kill the nematodes.

crease so rapidly, predatory mites are a particularly effective biological control. They do not attack beneficial insects or insect relatives and, because they are harmless to humans and so tiny as to be no annoyance at all, they can be used indoors safely and conveniently to control houseplant pests.

A Benevolent Snail

The decollate snail is a Mediterranean native that appeared in this country over a century ago and has since become widespread in the southern states and in California. A nocturnal hunter, the predator feeds voraciously on pest snails, egg and adult alike. The decollate snail is especially important in controlling the common brown garden snail, which chews holes in a wide variety of plants, especially those that grow in warm, moist climates.

This benevolent creature does have its drawbacks, however. It feeds on the seedlings of a wide variety of plant species and can do serious damage to several succulents and other low-growing plants. You should also check local ordinances before ordering a supply of decollate snails. In some parts of California, buying these predators for release in the garden is illegal because they can pose a threat to benign native mollusk species.

Beneficial Nematodes

Barely large enough to be seen with the naked eye, beneficial nematodes are microscopic roundworms that live in the soil. Unlike pest nematodes *(pages 44-46)*, which cause lesions and galls as they feed on plant stems and roots, beneficial nematodes destroy certain species of caterpillars, cutworms, borers, grubs, and beetle larvae. Like the parasitoids, beneficial nematodes are specialists: Certain species target certain pests. They do not damage plants; nor do they attack earthworms, which are essential as natural aerators of the soil.

Applied to the soil *(page 27)*, beneficial nematodes locate their prey by following the trail of carbon dioxide released by the pest as it moves through the ground. The nematodes then invade the pest's body. One species has a dorsal "tooth" that it uses to pierce the epidermis of a pest; the creatures can then enter the host through its vascular system. Once in-

side, nematodes release fast-multiplying bacteria that can kill the host within 24 to 48 hours. The nematodes feed on the host and also eat the lethal bacteria, then lay hundreds to thousands of eggs inside the host. When the food supply is exhausted, the new generation of nematodes begin searching out insect hosts on their own. As long as the soil remains moist and the temperature is between about 65° to 78°F, the reproductive cycle continues uninterrupted; thus a single application of nematodes may be effective for up to a year. If soil-borne pests are a persistent problem in your area, however, you may need to replenish the nematodes once or twice a year. The nematodes will die out once the pests have been eradicated.

Beneficial Microbes

Microorganisms even smaller than nematodes are also being exploited as pesticides. The most popular of these are two bacteria strains that are extremely effective against particular target insects. Virtually nontoxic to other insects, animals, or humans, these controls are easy to mass-produce, inexpensive, and easy to apply.

Bacillus thuringiensis (Bt) is lethal to leaf-eating caterpillars. There are 30 different strains of Bt, each of which infects only one host species. Other serious garden pests controlled by a strain of Bt include the elm leaf beetle and the larvae of the Colorado potato beetle. Given the specificity of Bt, correctly identifying the type of pest that is causing damage in your garden is essential. Bt can be purchased in a variety of forms—dusts, powders, liquids, and sprays—at most garden or home centers and from mail-order companies. As with all pest-control agents, read the instructions before use.

The second bacterium widely used to control pests causes an infection called milky spore disease, which attacks Japanese beetle grubs, or pupae. Japanese beetles commonly lay their eggs just below the surface of a lawn. As the grubs develop there they feed on the roots of the grass or on thatch, a matted accumulation of grass debris. When the bacterial spores are dusted onto the lawn, they attack the grubs and multiply inside their bodies. The grubs die, releasing the spores into the soil and keeping the cycle of infection going.

BENEFICIAL INSECTS AND THEIR TARGETS

Beneficials	Target Pests	Comments
Braconid wasps	Aphids, beetle larvae, moth larvae	Overwinter as newly hatched larvae inside living hosts. Adults feed on nectar and pollen.
Flower flies, hover flies	Aphids, mealybugs, mites, thrips	Black-and-yellow-banded bodies resemble bees or hornets. Adults feed on nectar and pollen of daisylike flowers.
Green lacewings, brown lacewings	Aphids, thrips, mealybugs, scales, moth eggs, mites, small caterpillars, soft-bodied insects	Eggs overwinter on plants. Adults feed on nectar and pollen. To prevent cannibalism in larvae, distribute purchased eggs widely.
Ladybeetles, ladybugs	Aphids, whiteflies, mealybugs, spider mites, scales	Adults overwinter in leaf litter. The migratory convergent ladybeetle overwinters in large groups.
Praying mantises	Aphids, beetles, bugs, caterpillars, flies, leafhoppers, wasps. Mantises also prey on butterflies, bees, and other desirable insects and on one another.	Eggs overwinter in a frothy gray case attached to stems or twigs. Mantises are highly territorial and feed mostly on large insects.
Predatory bugs: assassin bug, ambush bug, big-eyed bug, minute pirate bug, spined soldier bug	Aphids, beetle larvae, leafhopper nymphs, spider mites, thrips	Prefer permanent beds and garden litter for shelter.
Predatory mites	Citrus red mites, cyclamen mites, European red mites, rust mites, two-spotted spider mites, thrips	Found in soil, moss, humus, manure, and on plants. Thrive in high humidity; cannot survive at low humidity. Low temperature slows reproduction rate.
Rove beetles	Aphids, fly eggs, maggots, mites, nematodes, slugs, snails, springtails	Found in a wide variety of habitats. Prefer permanent beds for overwintering.
Soldier beetles	Aphids, beetle larvae, butterfly larvae, caterpillars, grasshopper eggs, moth larvae	Adults are nectar and pollen feeders; prefer goldenrod. Eggs laid in soil or ground cover. Both larvae and adults are predators.
Trichogramma wasps	Cabbage worms, cutworms, eggs of 200 moth species, leaf-roller caterpillars	Larvae parasitize and kill pest eggs. Adults feed on nectar; prefer the daisy family and Queen Anne's lace, other members of the carrot family.

Earth-Friendly Pesticides

Buying Pesticides

Confronting the myriad bottles and containers in the pesticide aisle of the local garden center can be a bewildering experience for a gardener. Your first impulse may be to reach for the familiar package with the well-known manufacturer's name. But before you purchase your next pesticide, take a moment to consider the differences between an organic pesticide and a synthetic one.

Organic pesticides, as the name implies, are made from naturally occurring ingredients. They are effective against a wide range of pests and break down easily, leaving little residual effects on the environment. Although some organic pesticides have harmful effects on humans, bees, ladybird beetles, and other benign creatures, the danger is short-lived and can be minimized by proper handling. The chart on page 35 lists eight organic pesticides, the pests they target, and any cautions to follow in using the pesticide.

Synthetic pesticides are derived from both naturally occurring and manufactured materials. They are similar in chemistry to what are called persistent insecticides, which have been banned because of their damaging residual effects to the environment and all life forms. Synthetic pesticides can be highly toxic and tend to remain active for much longer periods of time than organics.

The product label will not tell you straight out whether the pesticide is organic or synthetic; you'll need to know the names of the botanical insecticides and the chemical names of the various synthetic products. Three groups of synthetics are widely available—organochlorines, organophosphates, and carbamates. Organochlorines contain carbon, chlorine, and hydrogen, in addition to pesticides such as chlordane and methoxychlor. Both chemicals are toxic to aquatic life if released into the water supply. Organophosphates, the most common of the synthetic pesticides, are derived from phosphoric acid and control a wide variety of garden pests. Although toxic to vertebrates, organophosphates break down quickly and have little residual effect. This group includes malathion, trichlorfon, and diazinon. Carbamates are derived from carbamic acid; one of the best known is carbaryl, which is used to control lawn and garden pests as well as ticks and cockroaches. Carbaryl is highly toxic to natural predators, bees, and aquatic invertebrates, and moderately toxic to fish.

With both organic and synthetic pesticide products, it is imperative that you read the label and follow all instructions for applying the pesticide and disposing of it.

If you've given milder pest-control measures a fair trial and been disappointed with the results, you may decide to opt for a chemical control. As with other techniques, the prudent approach is always to use the pesticide least likely to harm humans, pets, or the environment. In practice, this means giving preference to pesticides derived from natural materials—principally minerals, plants, soaps, and oils—over the more toxic synthetics.

The reason that natural pesticides are relatively benign is that they target specific insects. These pesticides also break down into harmless substances shortly after being applied; synthetic pesticides, on the other hand, may remain toxic far longer.

The fact that natural pesticides lose their potency quickly shouldn't mislead the gardener into underestimating their lethal capabilities. For instance, two of the most venerable botanicals—rotenone and pyrethrins—are powerful broad-spectrum poisons, killing a wide range of insects that includes aphids, spider mites, and other serious pests—as well as some beneficials, such as honeybees, lacewings, spiders, and braconid wasps.

Nor are higher animals, including humans, immune to natural pesticides. Carelessly handled, they can make a gardener very ill. And different creatures have peculiar sensitivities. While pyrethrins earn good marks for doing little harm to most mammals, cats are highly susceptible to pyrethrin poisoning.

Judging a Product's Safety

Many pesticides have not been fully tested, and being registered with the Environmental Protection Agency (EPA) does not necessarily mean they are safe. In fact, no pesticide on the market is designated "safe" on its label. Even the chemicals of low to moderate toxicity must be labeled with the word "caution" because they have the potential for doing serious harm to humans. Ingesting even a fraction of an ounce of one of the milder pesticides can be fatal, and long-term exposure also has been known to kill.

A pesticide's label spells out the product's appropriate uses, its toxic effects, methods of application, and other critical information. The guide on page 34 will help you interpret this information so you'll get full benefit from the pesticide with the least possible harm.

How Natural Pesticides Work

If you decide to use a pesticide, identify the pest first, then choose a chemical that targets your problem. There is no one cure-all; your natural arsenal will have a range of weapons. Some of them, including Bt, are stomach poisons and work only when an insect ingests a bit of a treated plant. As a group, chewing insects—beetles, caterpillars, and the like—are more vulnerable to stomach poisons than sucking insects, which may not be affected at all because they pierce the leaf surface and suck out the sap rather than eat the pesticide-coated surface itself.

Contact poisons, as their name suggests, must make direct contact with the pest. They are best sprayed onto the pest—a technique that is easiest to carry out on eggs, pupae, slow-moving crawling insects, and insects such as scale, whiteflies, larvae, and aphids. Flying insects can be felled unintentionally by drifting spray, and creeping or crawling pests can pick up a poison on their feet or antennae as they make their way over the surface of a treated plant. When you apply a contact pesticide, don't neglect crevices and the undersides of stems or foliage, where many pests prefer to congregate and feed *(pages 32-33)*.

Using Soap Sprays

Insecticidal soap sprays are contact poisons that are absorbed through the cuticle covering the pest's body. Once inside, they make cell membranes leaky, causing severe dehydration. Most vulnerable to soap sprays are aphids, scales, mites, and other soft-cuticled pests. Beetles, grasshoppers, and other pests with hard cuticles are much less susceptible.

The soap sprays remain potent only as long as they are wet, so spray in the early morning or in the evening, when lower temperatures and higher humidity slow the rate of evaporation. To avoid killing beneficials, keep the pesticide narrowly aimed at problem species.

TIPS FROM THE PROS

A Unique Pesticide

Diatomaceous earth (DE) is unlike any other pesticide in its makeup and mode of action. The substance is not a poison but a mineral obtained from deposits of fossil diatoms, a kind of tiny plankton that inhabited lakes and oceans over 20 million years ago. The deposits are ground to a fine powder that, when it comes into contact with a crawling pest, absorbs the oil in the pest's protective outer cuticle, rather like sand absorbing motor oil spilled on a driveway. When the waterproofing oil is removed, the pest dies of desiccation. Most vulnerable to diatomaceous earth are pests with thin, soft cuticles such as snails, slugs, mites, cutworms, and moth larvae.

When you apply DE, wear a mask to protect your lungs. Dust the powder onto a plant's leaves or spread it on the soil to form a barrier around the plant, in a continuous band 2 inches wide and a quarter inch deep.

Diatomaceous earth works well only as long as it remains dry. Rain and hot, humid weather can reduce its capacity to absorb a pest's vital oil. When buying diatomaceous earth, be sure it is labeled as a pesticide. A different form is sold for use as a swimming-pool filter and offers no protection against pests.

Also, test-spray a few leaves and inspect them for yellowing or other symptoms of injury before treating the entire plant.

Horticultural Oils

These pesticides are sprayed on infested plants, smothering pests in a fine film. Eggs are especially vulnerable, as are soft-bodied mites and insects, including scales, mealybugs, and whiteflies. Beneficials coated by the spray may also be killed, but once the treated plant dries, beneficials aren't in danger. The oils are available as dormant oil, for use when plants are dormant, and as superior oil, for use during the growing season. Avoid using any oils when temperatures exceed 90° F, and spray in early morning or late evening when the sun is at its weakest.

A Pesticide from Seeds

A remarkably versatile botanical insecticide extracted from the seeds of the neem tree and first registered by the EPA in the 1980s, neem has been found to combat more than 200 species of pests including gypsy moths, whiteflies, mealybugs, Japanese beetles, leaf miners, and the Colorado potato beetle. For some leaf-eating insects, it is a repellent so powerful that they completely shun plants they would otherwise defoliate. Other leaf eaters may begin to feed but stop immediately. Neem can also halt a larva's metamorphosis to the pupal stage. Since fewer individuals mature and reproduce, the population declines.

Neem is available as a foliar spray and as a soil drench. When taken up by a plant's roots and transported throughout its tissues, neem protects the plant from voracious insects for as long as 2 months. Judged safe for use on vegetables and fruits by the EPA, neem has an extremely low toxicity rating for humans and other mammals. It does not harm butterflies, honeybees, or ladybird beetles, and it does not accummulate in soil or water.

A Variety of Pesticide Forms

Pesticides are available in a number of different forms—liquid, granular, or dust. Whatever a pesticide's formulation, use a delivery device that allows the maximum possible precision to protect yourself from exposure and the environment from contamination.

An aerosol can filled with a premixed pesticide is an easy-to-use, surefire applicator (and also the most expensive). More important, it eliminates the risk of accidental spills. Equally convenient and somewhat more economical are the small trigger sprayers that contain premixed pesticide. At a still lower cost, you can mix a small quantity of liquid concentrate or wettable powder with water in a small pail reserved for the purpose. Carefully pour the mixture into a trigger sprayer for application.

When you have a large job to do—spraying a lawn, for instance, or a number of trees or shrubs—the best device for applying a liquid pesticide is a compressed-air sprayer (below). On a well-designed sprayer, the trigger that controls the spray is far enough from the nozzle that there is little danger of pesticide dripping onto your hand.

That's not the case with hose-end sprayers, which are notorious drippers and splashers. Not only is it difficult to calibrate them to get the right proportion of pesticide to water, but if the sprayer lacks a backflow-prevention filter the pesticide may flow backward into the

How to Use Horticultural Oils

Horticultural oils are safe and effective pesticides if you observe the following guidelines:

- Use either dormant oil or superior oil on plants that are in dormancy. In spring and summer, when plants are in active growth, use superior oil only.
- Choose the right strength. A 3 percent solution for dormant plants and a 2 percent solution in spring and summer are safe for the majority of plants. If the oil makes leaves burn or blister, try a 1 percent solution.
- Shake the sprayer occasionally to keep the oil and water solution well mixed.
- Apply horticultural oil early in the day in sunny, dry conditions so the oil will dry quickly.
- Spray each plant until every exposed surface is wet—trunk, stems, branches, both sides of the leaves, and flowers.
- Allow at least 2 weeks between applications, and longer when plants are stressed by drought. Most species can be sprayed up to four times a year.

1. Before mixing or spraying horticultural oil, put on a face mask and goggles to prevent oil particles from getting into your lungs and eyes. Wearing rubber gloves, unscrew the top of a 1-gallon compression sprayer. Measure the amount of oil according to the strength of the solution needed and pour it into the sprayer (left). Recap the bottle of oil. Fill the sprayer with water.

hose—or even into the domestic water supply. For all of these reasons, you should avoid hose-end sprayers.

Soil infested with pests is commonly treated with granular pesticides, which can be applied with a drop spreader or sprinkled directly from the container onto the soil. However, birds can be killed by eating granules. A better dry pesticide choice is a dust, which can be safely spread with either a bulb duster or a crank duster.

Applying a Pesticide

A critical first step to working with a pesticide is to read the label thoroughly, even for a product that you have used before. Then, though it may be inconvenient, wait for a day when there is no wind to apply the pesticide. If it is imperative to go ahead with the job and no more than a slight breeze is stirring the air, proceed with caution, making sure that you keep your back squarely to the wind while you work; otherwise, you risk exposing yourself to the chemical.

In addition to being windless, the weather should be mild; low temperatures slow the

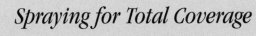

Spraying for Total Coverage

To ensure that a contact poison hits all target pests on a plant, begin spraying at its base and work up to the top, aiming the sprayer at the undersides of the leaves, as shown at left. Spray each surface, including stems and leaf axils, until the pesticide just begins to drip off. Next, spray the upper surfaces of the leaves, working from the top of the plant down.

3. Spray an even coat of the oil solution on the entire plant (left). Shake the container occasionally to mix the oil and water. When you have finished, release the pressure valve on your sprayer, or carefully unscrew the sprayer's top. Dispose of any unused solution according to the pesticide label directions.

2. Replace the top of the sprayer and screw it on tightly. Hold the container steady with one hand and pump the handle until you cannot pump it any more (left). Shake the sprayer vigorously to make sure the oil and water are thoroughly mixed.

Reading Pesticide Labels

The label on a pesticide container is your most complete source of information about a product. Although the words may be in microscopic type, it is important to read them before you buy. Each label has certain information required by law. It will inform you of the relative hazards of the material as well as how it may legally be used, along with any precautions you should take. Below are explanations for some of the most important components of a pesticide label.

- SIGNAL WORD: This is the most critical word—and the largest one—on the label. It reveals the relative acute toxicity of the pesticide, which is the measure of damage done if a product is ingested, inhaled, or absorbed through the skin. The least toxic materials are labeled with the word "Caution." The word "Warning" means the pesticide is moderately toxic. "Danger" or "Poison" on the label means the pesticide is highly toxic; this designation may also be accompanied by a skull-and-crossbones symbol. If there is no signal word on the package, the pesticide is relatively nontoxic. These signal words refer only to immediate damage sustained from a single exposure to the pesticide; they reveal nothing about possible chronic effects.
- PRECAUTIONARY STATEMENTS: These are the possible chronic effects, if any, including the chemical's ability to poison components of the nervous system (neurotoxicity), cause cancer (carcinogenicity), have adverse effects on the reproductive process, and create mutations in genetic structure (mutagenicity). Also under this heading are precautions that should be taken when applying the pesticide, such as protective clothing that must be worn. The amount of time that must pass before you harvest food crops that have been sprayed with the product, sometimes listed as "reentry times required," are also included here.
- ACTIVE INGREDIENT: The pesticide's chemical composition and the percentage of it contained in the mixture.
- INERTS: A general term for all fillers and inactive ingredients, listed by percentage.
- STATEMENT OF PRACTICAL TREATMENT: Emergency first-aid measures if you are exposed to the pesticide.
- ENVIRONMENTAL HAZARDS: Includes effect on beneficial insects such as bees, waterfowl, and other wildlife.
- DIRECTIONS FOR USE: How to mix the pesticide and when and how to apply it. You are required by law to follow these directions to the letter.
- STORAGE AND DISPOSAL: Whether the material must be kept from heat or freezing, and how to dispose of packaging and unused material.
- CROPS AND INSECTS CONTROLLED: Includes a list of plants this pesticide may be used on and pests for which it has been approved. By law, the product may not be used on any crop or against any pest not listed on the label.

breakdown process and pesticides remain toxic for a longer time. If the pesticide you are using is toxic to bees, apply it early in the morning or in the evening when they aren't active. Never apply a pesticide where it can run off into a drain, storm sewer, or stream. Treat only the plants or the parts of plants that are troubled by the pest and use the lowest recommended dose. Because many natural pesticides are slow acting, you should give them several days to work before reapplying.

Dressing for the Job

The label of every pesticide describes any special protective equipment you will need, so read it carefully before you begin and follow the directions scrupulously. With even the least toxic pesticide, you should wear a long-sleeved, loose-fitting shirt; long pants; rubber work gloves (dishwashing gloves are not adequate); and nonporous shoes or boots (pesticides can soak into leather or fabric). As insurance against eye or lung irritation, you may want to add a mask and goggles. For more toxic chemicals, goggles and a respirator that has been specially designed for the chemical you are using are necessities.

Once you begin handling a pesticide, do not smoke, drink, eat, or use the bathroom until the job is completed and you have washed your hands thoroughly. When you are preparing a mixture for spraying, measure out precisely the prescribed amount of pesticide. Be careful not to splash the material on yourself, your clothes, or the ground.

To avoid disposal or storage problems, mix only as much pesticide as you need for a single spraying. Should there be any left over at the end of the job, spray out the excess on other plants that can be treated or on an open grassy area.

Cleaning Up

Wash the sprayer and mixing implements thoroughly with soap and water, rinse, and repeat. Store pesticides and any implements used with them in a cool, dry place, preferably a toolshed or garage rather than in the house. They should be out of a child's reach. Finally, wash your clothes separately from the rest of the laundry; dry them on high heat or outdoors in the sun.

CHOOSING A BOTANICAL PESTICIDE

Pesticide	Target Pests	Comments
Citrus oils	Spider mites, aphids	Relatively nontoxic to humans and other mammals. May cause an allergic reaction.
False hellebore	Beetles, caterpillars, grasshoppers, sawflies	Highly toxic if ingested.
Neem	Aphids, flea beetles, gypsy moths, leaf miners, thrips, whiteflies	Relatively nontoxic to humans and other mammals and to beneficial insects.
Pyrethrins	Aphids, leafhoppers, spider mites, thrips, whiteflies	Toxic to fish, aquatic insects and ladybeetles. Moderately toxic to bees and mammals. Pest insects may appear dead but revive after metabolizing pyrethrin.
Quassia	Aphids, caterpillars, sawflies	One of the safest botanical insecticides. Nontoxic to ladybeetles and bees.
Rotenone	Aphids; flea beetles, leafhoppers, spider mites, whiteflies, and other chewing insects	Highly toxic to fish, aquatic insects, and birds. Moderately toxic to humans and other mammals. May cause an allergic reaction.
Ryania	Aphids; Japanese beetles, ledidopterous larvae including codling moths, painted lady butterflies, and sunflower moths	Low toxicity to humans and other mammals and to beneficial insects.
Sabadilla	Aphids, blister beetles, chinch bugs, citrus thrips, grasshoppers, harlequin bugs, tarnished plant bugs, webworms	Toxic to humans and other mammals and to bees. May cause an allergic reaction.

Nuisance Mammals

Wildlife in the garden is a mixed blessing. Many gardeners enjoy having chipmunks and cottontail rabbits around; they are fun to watch, and the damage they do, although it can be annoying, is almost always minor. Moreover, fences and and chemical repellents do a good job of minimizing their impact.

On the other hand are the animals that do so much harm to the garden even the kindliest of gardeners cannot tolerate their presence. Although it isn't easy, it is possible to rid a garden of such pests by depriving them of food and water and eliminating their access to shelter. They can also be captured in live traps or, more drastically, in lethal traps.

Ten mammals are especially notorious for damaging American gardens. Moles dig underground burrows that disturb plant roots and disfigure lawns. Voles, pocket gophers, ground squirrels, and woodchucks also tunnel extensively, feeding underground on roots and bulbs and making aboveground forays for leaves and stems. Jack rabbits, hares, rats, mice, and deer graze on shrubby ornamentals, fruit trees, and perennials. Skunks pockmark lawns in search of grubs and insects, and tree squirrels eat bulbs, fruits, and nuts.

Moles

Members of the shrew family, the seven species of moles found in the United States are torpedo-shaped creatures weighing about 4 ounces. Outfitted for digging with strong forepaws splayed outward, they can tunnel as far as 200 feet a day. Gardeners rarely see moles, which emerge from their network of burrows and feeding tunnels only to gather nesting materials. Active day and night year

A RARE APPEARANCE ABOVE GROUND
The star-nosed mole pictured here has 22 fleshy pink appendages around its nostrils that it uses like fingers to explore the soil for grubs and insects. Like all moles, this species has large-toed, spade-shaped forepaws that are well adapted for efficient digging.

round, moles search constantly for the insects, slugs, and grubs that make up their diet; after only a few hours without food they starve to death. They use their snouts, which have a highly developed sense of touch, to locate their prey.

Moles make their presence known by the small cone of loose soil—or molehill—around the openings to their burrows and by the telltale ridges made by shallow tunnels. The ridges are primarily an aesthetic problem, as are the molehills, although they can be high enough to damage a lawn mower.

Since moles devour soil pests such as cutworms and white grubs in large numbers and don't feed on plants at all, it makes sense to be as tolerant of their objectionable habits as possible. You can minimize the impact of their tunneling by tamping down raised strips of soil and watering them well to ensure disturbed plant roots don't dry out.

Moles have hearing so acute that you may be able to get rid of them with what to human ears is a tolerable level of noise. A simple technique is to push the shaft of a plastic pinwheel down into a tunnel until you feel it touch the tunnel's floor. As it turns in the wind, the pinwheel may transmit vibrations strong enough to force the moles to abandon the tunnel. Partially buried bottles, which whistle and vibrate in the wind, may also do the trick.

Lethal traps are undoubtedly the most effective means of managing moles. Harpoon, scissor-jaw, or choker-loop traps should be set over frequently traveled tunnels in early spring or early fall. These devices kill quickly and are considered more humane than a live trap, since a mole could easily starve to death before the well-meaning gardener has a chance to check the trap.

Bury a dead mole where you trap it. Its remains will discourage other moles from reinfesting that part of your garden.

Voles and Pocket Gophers

Voles and pocket gophers are small rodents that deface lawns and beds with mounds of soil and feed on the entire range of plant materials. Voles, also called meadow or field mice, are found across the northern tier of the United States and as far south as northern Florida. About 6 inches long including their tails, they live in abandoned mole burrows, thick blankets of mulch, dense weeds, or

A VORACIOUS HERBIVORE
The meadow vole (left) feeds on strawberries and other fruits, seeds, and grasses, and in winter it strips bark from trees and shrubs. The lawn shown below has been ruined by the maze of runways made by voles.

grassy areas. They eat seeds, fruits, grasses, tender bark, and other soft plant materials, digging 1- to 2-inch-wide surface runways in which they feed on roots. These runways crisscross a lawn like a brown maze. A vole eats twice its weight every day but destroys much more than it eats.

Reproducing at a rate of 10 litters of five offspring per year, voles tend to be so numerous that a gardener's options for control are few. A house cat that is a diligent mouser is a help, but traps scarcely make a dent in the population. Modifying the garden habitat by weeding, mowing the lawn often, and removing

PEST OF THE WEST
A pocket gopher emerging from its tunnel displays the sickle-shaped claws it uses for digging. On its aboveground feeding forays the pocket gopher fills its expandable cheek pouches with food and nesting materials.

thick mulches deprives voles of favorite habitats. You can erase their runways by tilling the soil and replanting the area. You will likely kill some of the population in the process.

Pocket gophers, unlike voles, lead solitary lives. Named for the pocketlike cheek pouches in which they carry vegetation for food and nesting, pocket gophers are common throughout the West and Midwest. Like moles, they are active at all hours and in all seasons, and tunnel underground. You can easily distinguish the entrance of a pocket gopher's tunnel from the opening of a mole's burrow: Instead of a cone, the soil is arranged in a fan-shaped mound.

Pocket gophers feed above ground and below. If you see a plant wiggle, then disappear beneath the soil's surface, a pocket gopher is at work. Besides destroying vegetation, these animals also chew through plastic irrigation lines.

Fumigating a pocket gopher's tunnel with smoke or gas cartridges, flooding it with water, dumping used kitty litter into it, or placing a few tablespoons of strychnine-laced bait in the tunnel are sometimes suggested as controls, but none of them is completely reliable. If you have a severe infestation, you may have to resort to a lethal trap. The best type for pocket gophers is the two-pronged pincher trap. Always wear gloves when checking traps, since pocket gophers are hosts to lice and external parasites. Stuffing a dead pocket gopher into the tunnel will discourage reinfestation.

Rats, Mice, and Squirrels

Together, these three groups of rodents account for nearly 40 percent of all mammalian species. They breed prolifically, can be found in all climates except the polar regions, and continuously compete with people for food and space.

Rats and mice dig up seeds and eat seedlings and fruits. Ground squirrels, which live in underground burrows, are omnivores. They eat seeds, fruits, grasses, insects, and lizards, and raid

A LONG-DISTANCE DEFENSE
Found in most parts of the United States, the striped skunk (above) digs holes and damages garden plants in its search for insects and grubs. When alarmed, the noxious, malodorous liquid it sprays to a distance of 10 feet or more can cause temporary blindness.

A HUSKY CHISEL-TOOTHED HERBIVORE
Adopting an erect posture meant to intimidate an enemy, the woodchuck at right may eat more than 1½ pounds of vegetation a day, including leaves, blossoms, and tougher fare such as woody stems. To make up for the wear and tear on the woodchuck's sharp incisors, these teeth grow at a rate of 14 inches a year to replace the portions worn away by incessant gnawing.

Commonly Used Controls

Prevention is the best way to control animal pests. Choose shrubs and perennials animals shun. To prevent burrowing, lay down wire mesh before spreading topsoil and planting. Use fencing in your design. When damage occurs, identify the animal causing it. The chart at right shows management options for 10 common pests. If possible, first make changes in the garden's habitats—remove brush piles, control weeds, fill in boggy areas, store firewood on pallets—to eliminate sources of food, water, and shelter. If this doesn't work, choose controls from the chart at right. The following controls exclude animals, manipulate their behavior, or reduce their population:

- Fences and plant guards: The height of a fence and whether it should extend underground depend on the ability of the pest to jump or burrow. Guards include metal flashing, wire mesh, and netting.
- Repellents: Chemical taste and odor repellents such as thiram, ammonium salts, and putrescent egg solids sprayed directly on plants can be effective if applied weekly.
- Scare tactics: Noise, the scent of natural predators (including people), and lifelike owl, snake, and cat decoys can ward off pests.
- Live and lethal traps: Live traps include baited cages and boxes. Spring-loaded snap, skewer, scissors, and choke traps kill the animal.

PESTS	CONTROLS					
	Habitat Alteration	Fences/Protective Guards	Repellents	Scare Tactics	Live Traps	Lethal Traps
DEER		✔	✔			
GROUND SQUIRRELS			✔	✔		✔
JACK RABBITS/HARES		✔	✔	✔	✔	
MEADOW VOLES	✔	✔				✔
MOLES		✔	✔	✔		✔
POCKET GOPHERS	✔					✔
RATS/MICE	✔			✔		✔
SKUNKS	✔	✔	✔		✔	
TREE SQUIRRELS		✔	✔		✔	
WOODCHUCKS	✔	✔		✔	✔	

birds' nests for both eggs and hatchlings. Tree squirrels, which have long, bushy tails and usually nest in trees, feed on buds, nuts, fruits, and the tender stems of woody plants. They strip bark from trees and gnaw through irrigation lines and telephone cables.

The yard cleanup recommended for discouraging voles may also work with rats and mice. Spread mothballs around the bases of shrubs and trees to repel both ground and tree squirrels. Two types of lethal traps—snap traps and jaw traps—are effective against ground squirrels, mice, and rats.

Using a Live Trap

You can also catch mice, rats, and squirrels in a live trap, either a box or a cage type. Special caution is called for, however, since these rodents can transmit viral diseases to humans.

THE UBIQUITOUS TREE SQUIRREL
At home in rural, suburban, and urban areas, the highly adaptable American gray squirrel (left) eats buds, seeds, nuts, and fruits of ornamental plants, gnaws through the bark of trees to reach the edible inner layers, and chews holes in irrigation lines.

Deer-Resistant Plants

While only a handful of ornamentals are truly deer-proof, there are many that deer shun unless preferred food sources are scarce. Characteristics likely to make a plant deer resistant are thorns, tough or fuzzy leaves or stems, and strong flavors and aromas.

GROUND COVERS

Ajuga reptans
(carpet bugle)
Asperula odorata
(sweet woodruff)
Convallaria majalis
(lily of the valley)
Lamium 'Beacon Silver'
(dead nettle)
Pachysandra
(pachysandra)
Vinca minor
(periwinkle)

PERENNIALS

***Achillea* spp.**
(yarrow)
***Astilbe* spp.**
(false spirea)
***Coreopsis* spp.**
(tickseed)
***Dianthus* spp.**
(garden pink)
***Echinacea* spp.**
(purple coneflower)
Eupatorium purpureum
(Joe-Pye weed)

***Geranium* spp.**
(cranesbill)
***Helleborus* spp.**
(hellebore)
***Iberis* spp.**
(candytuft)
Liatris spicata
(spike gay-feather)
***Linaria* spp.**
(toadflax)
Lychnis coronaria
(rose campion)
Perovskia atriplicifolia
(Russian sage)
***Rudbeckia* spp.**
(coneflower)
***Solidago* spp.**
(goldenrod)
Veronica officinalis
(speedwell)

VINES

***Celastrus* spp.**
(bittersweet)
***Clematis* spp.**
(clematis)
Hedera helix
(English ivy)
***Lonicera* spp.**
(honeysuckle)

***Wisteria* spp.**
(wisteria)

SHRUBS

Buddleia davidii
(butterfly bush)
Buxus sempervirens
(common boxwood)
Calycanthus occidentalis
(sweet shrub)
Ceanothus sanguineus
(wild lilac)
Cephalotaxus fortunei
(Chinese plum yew)
Cornus stolonifera
(red-osier dogwood)
Corylus americana
(American hazelnut)
Enkianthus campanulatus
(enkianthus)
Hibiscus syriacus
(rose of Sharon)
Ilex x meserveae
(blue holly)
Ilex glabra
(inkberry)
Leucothoe fontanesiana
(leucothoe)
Mahonia bealei

White-Tailed Deer Fawn

Decide beforehand where you will release any animal you catch and check the trap at least once a day. When you catch an animal, calm it by covering the trap with a tarpaulin or blanket before moving it; wear heavy gloves and keep children away from the trap. When you are ready to release the animal, back away from the trap as soon as you open it.

Skunks can also be controlled with live traps, but because of their offensive smell when alarmed this is a job best left to a pest-control professional. Besides doing damage with their digging, skunks are undesirable because they carry the rabies virus.

The Rabbit Family

Jack rabbits and snowshoe hares are far more destructive than cottontail rabbits because of their greater size and fecundity: The average female produces four litters of eight kits annually. These pests consume up to 1 pound of vegetation each day, feasting on flowers, turf grass, foliage, shoots, stems, and the tender bark of young trees and shrubs.

Physical barriers and repellents are effective against jack rabbits and hares. They are stopped by a 3-foot-high fence of ¾-inch wire mesh, which need not extend underground since these pests do not normally burrow. You can also protect a tree with a collar of sheet-metal flashing that extends 2 feet above the snow line. Commercial repellents containing thiram, ammonium soaps, putrescent egg solids, lime sulfur, copper carbonate, or asphalt must be reapplied to plants weekly or after a heavy rain.

Woodchucks

Although woodchucks are far less numerous per acre than the animals described so far, their size—as much as 20 pounds—and voracious appetite create a serious problem for

(leatherleaf mahonia)
Philadelphus spp.
(mock orange)
Spiraea spp.
(bridal wreath)
Syringa vulgaris
(common lilac)
Viburnum carlesii
(Koreanspice viburnum)
Viburnum opulus
(snowball bush)
Yucca filamentosa
(yucca)

TREES

Acer platanoides
(Norway maple)

Acer saccharinum
(silver maple)
Betula papyrifera
(white birch)
Crataegus spp.
(hawthorn)
Cryptomeria japonica
(Japanese cedar)
Lithocarpus densiflorus
(tanbark oak)
Metasequoia
glyptostroboides
(dawn redwood)
Parrotia persica
(Persian parrotia)
Picea abies
(Norway spruce)
Picea glauca

(white spruce)
Pinus sylvestris
(Scotch pine)
Pinus thunbergii
(black pine)
Tsuga canadensis
(Canadian hemlock)

Note: The abbreviation "spp." stands for the plural of "species"; where used in lists it means that many, but not all, of the species in a genus meet the criterion of the list.

Clematis sp. (clematis)

Rudbeckia hirta (black-eyed Susan)

Syringa vulgaris (common lilac)

Betula papyrifera (paper birch)

the gardener: These rodents can devastate new plantings in a few hours. They dig burrows up to 50 feet long on two or more levels. The apron of dirt at each of the two or three entrances serves as a sentry post and a safe spot for sunning and grooming. Slow-moving and easily frightened, woodchucks rarely venture far from their homes.

Because of their timidity, woodchucks prefer the protection of tall grass or undergrowth, so clearing away such vegetation may effectively discourage them. If this tactic fails, a sturdy fence that extends 3 feet above ground level and at least 2 feet below will keep a woodchuck out of a garden plot. You can also capture the animal in a baited box or cage trap. Release it more than 5 miles from its burrow; otherwise, it may find its way back home. A lethal trap can be used, of course, but you may not want to handle a dead mammal of this size.

Deer

Deer can pillage a garden even faster than woodchucks. The two species common to the United States—the white-tailed deer in the East and the mule deer in the West—strip shrubs and trees of foliage and devour perennials and vegetables in record time. While deer usually live at the edge of woodlands, they also roam suburban areas.

The same commercial repellents that succeed with jack rabbits and hares work with deer if plants are sprayed at the first sign of new growth in spring and at weekly intervals thereafter. Fences must be at least 7 feet high to prevent deer from leaping over them, and it is preferable for them to slant outward from the protected area at a 45° angle. Another tactic is to fill your garden with plants that deer generally ignore; a list of these appears above. Keep in mind, though, that when the deer population in an area outstrips the available food, the hungry animals will eat virtually any kind of vegetation.

CHAPTER TWO

Disease in the Garden

At one time or another even the most conscientious gardener is likely to discover in her yard a plant with signs of disease. The outdoors is teeming with billions of microorganisms, and although most of them are beneficial, a few, called plant pathogens, feed upon and damage living plants. Fortunately, the mere presence of a pathogen does not mean that disease is inevitable. Two other factors must be present for disease to occur—a susceptible plant host and an environment in which the pathogen thrives. In addition, the three factors must exist simultaneously for a period of time long enough for disease to develop. Together, the pathogen, host, environment, and time make up what is called the disease pyramid. If any piece of the pyramid is lacking or is removed too soon, disease will not take hold.

Instead of relying primarily on synthetic chemicals to prevent disease or restore plants to health, many gardeners have begun to adopt a more sophisticated, environmentally friendly strategy that is founded on the disease pyramid. It calls for selecting disease-resistant plants suitable to a garden's particular environment and keeping the soil in good condition. Cultural, physical, and biological means of preventing and controlling disease are the gardener's first choice. Chemical controls aren't ruled out, but they are reserved for use only when simpler, safer methods are ineffective.

SUBTLE SIGNS OF DISEASE
Blemished petals and leaves on the red tulips at left betray the presence of botrytis blight. Wider spacing to ensure good air circulation might have prevented the fungal disease, as would planting a blight-resistant variety.

Identifying Diseases

It is impossible to predict when disease will strike the garden. A plant that grew vigorously one year may have wilting leaves or inferior blooms the next, for no apparent reason. With a little knowledge, however, the gardener can learn to detect signs of disease early on and may be able to prevent a small problem from burgeoning into a large one.

An essential first step to knowing your garden is identifying your plants. Since different genera and species are vulnerable to different diseases, a plant's botanical name is an important diagnostic clue. Keep a list of your plants in a diary and update it with each acquisition. In addition, use the diary to note such events as the date you set out a new plant or transplanted an old one, and how a new disease-resistant cultivar is performing. Also note any periods of unusual weather and the application of fertilizers or other chemicals.

The more observant you are in the garden, the more likely you'll be to notice when your plants deviate from the norm. Make it a habit to stroll through the garden once a week to examine your plants, looking at the undersides of leaves and checking stems. A 10-power hand lens will help you inspect them more closely. Keep track of your observations, recording any unusual symptoms you may find. Some common symptoms of disease are illustrated on page 47. Typically, diseases are seasonal, so if there's an outbreak one year, your diary will remind you when to be on the alert in coming years for a recurrence.

If you have difficulty pinning down a plant's problem, ask the local Cooperative Extension Service or a reputable nursery for help. Your diary, along with a fresh specimen of the plant, will provide the expert with information needed to make a diagnosis.

The Varieties of Diseases

Plant diseases are divided into two broad categories—infectious and noninfectious. Among the agents responsible for infectious diseases are a number of invasive, parasitic pathogens that include certain fungi, bacteria, viruses, and even a few plants. Noninfectious diseases, on the other hand, arise from environmental problems such as mineral deficiencies, severe weather, and overwatering. Understanding these causes should be the first line of defense for your garden.

Fungi

About 80 percent of the infectious diseases you are likely to encounter in your garden are caused by fungi. Most fungi are beneficial: They live off dead leaves and other organic matter, decomposing it in the process. Disease-causing fungi, by contrast, feed on living plants and release toxins as they spread over the plant's surface or invade its tissue. Some fungal infections, such as powdery mildew, are mainly a cosmetic problem, but others, such as root rot, are likely to kill the plant.

Fungi reproduce by releasing spores, which can be spread by water, wind, insects, birds, animals, and humans. Some spores can survive a trip of hundreds of miles, then germinate within minutes when deposited in a hospitable place. Spores need moisture to germinate, so dry weather will suppress fresh outbreaks of fungal disease.

Bacteria

As with fungi, most species of bacteria in the garden are valuable organisms, releasing nitrogen into the soil and breaking down dead plant and animal tissue. The species that cause plant diseases are most frequently transmitted by water, but can also be carried by foraging insects and wind and on gardening tools.

Some bacteria enter a plant by penetrating cells on its surface, whereas others invade through pores or other natural openings, or through wounds in stems or bark. An insect carrying a bacterium can inject it directly as it feeds. Once inside, bacteria may clog a plant's water-conducting system or drain nutrients from its cells. The symptoms of a bacterial disease often resemble those produced by a fungus, such as rotting tissue. If the rotted portion is slimy and smells foul, however, the cause can only be a bacterium; fungi don't produce either symptom.

Viruses

A plant that has stunted foliage, abnormal leaf curling, mosaic-like patterns on its foliage, or color changes such as yellow rings or lines may be infected with a virus. Most viruses travel among plants in the saliva of insects, but nematodes—microscopic, wormlike creatures—are also carriers. In addition, a gardener can transmit viruses via hands, shoes, and tools, especially those used for cutting.

Thus pruning, grafting, dividing, and taking cuttings all carry a risk, however minimal, of exposing plants to viruses.

Viral diseases are the hardest to diagnose. A single virus may have a variety of symptoms, which often closely resemble those produced by a nutrient deficiency. The only sure way to diagnose a virus is to have the plant analyzed at a laboratory. The simpler course is to maintain an adequate supply of nutrients in your soil. If the problem persists despite the addition of amendments to the soil, assume that a

LIMITING DISEASE NATURALLY
The owner of this lush Chapel Hill, North Carolina, garden shuns chemicals. She credits the garden's health to well-prepared soil and to disease-resistant shrubs, grasses, and perennials such as the Joe-Pye weed blooming at right.

Detecting Tree Decline

A simple annual examination will allow you to detect early signs of decline by comparing a tree's most recent rate of growth with that of earlier years. If there's been a change for the worse, you may be able to reverse the decline before it claims your tree.

To check a deciduous tree, examine a 2-foot section at the end of a branch like the one shown below, right. Working back from the tip, look for a groove, or sometimes several closely spaced grooves, encircling the branch. This scar marks the position of the bud that, in the preceding year, produced the branch's newest wood. (In an evergreen tree, a whorl of lateral branches marks the beginning of the preceding year's growth.)

Compare this year-old wood with the wood on the other side of the scar or whorl: The newer wood is smaller in diameter, and on some kinds of trees its bark will be smoother, paler, or greenish. Compare the length of the newer growth with the wood of previous years.

Most healthy older trees put out at least 4 to 6 inches of new growth a year. If the growth for any year measures less than 2 inches, the tree was under great stress. A bad year is probably nothing to worry about if the tree stepped up its rate of growth the following year. On the other hand, the tree needs attention if there is a continuing pattern of poor growth. An undiagnosed disease or an infestation of insects such as borers may be responsible. Other possible causes of decline include construction that has severed roots or compacted the soil, exposure to salt or chemicals, bad drainage, or a lack of nutrients.

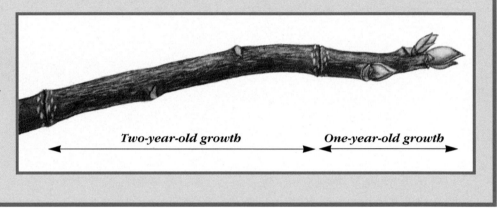

Two-year-old growth   **One-year-old growth**

---

virus is the cause. Since there is no known cure of any kind for viral diseases, the prudent move is to destroy the plant.

Nematodes

Although most species of nematodes are harmless or even beneficial to plants *(page 27),* some are destructive. Most parasitic nematodes feed on roots, stunting the plant and causing wilting and yellowing. A few species feed inside stems, while others mar leaves and sometimes blossoms. The damage done by nematodes, viruses, and cultural disorders can look very similar, but laboratory analysis of a soil sample or a plant can pinpoint the cause.

Cultural Problems

Mineral deficiencies, unsuitable light conditions, bad drainage, too much or too little water, air pollution, and injury can also be responsible for plant disorders. It can be hard to distinguish from infectious diseases, but one helpful clue is the way a problem is distributed in the garden. If all of the plants in one area share the same symptom, an environmental factor is likely to be at fault; infectious diseases tend to be randomly distributed or to attack one plant at first, then spread to others. Here again, noting the pattern of distribution in a garden diary can be an invaluable diagnostic tool.

Keeping an Eye on Trees

Many gardeners assume that trees can take care of themselves. In reality, the unnatural conditions of the garden, such as the lack of accumulated leaf litter, soil compaction, and inept pruning, are hazardous to trees, and for this reason the plants should be examined from time to time for signs of environmental stress or disease. This is especially important for a tree beyond the sapling stage. A tree slows its growth rate as it ages, but a slowdown that is too abrupt is a sign of declining health. A technique for tracking a tree's health from year to year is described above.

Disease Families and Their Symptoms

Plant diseases are commonly grouped by the kinds of symptoms they produce. Illustrated here are the eight symptoms that appear most frequently in home gardens, and the popular terms for the diseases in which they figure. However, no single pathogen is responsible for each symptom. For instance, the wartlike swellings known as galls may be caused by a bacterium or by fungi.

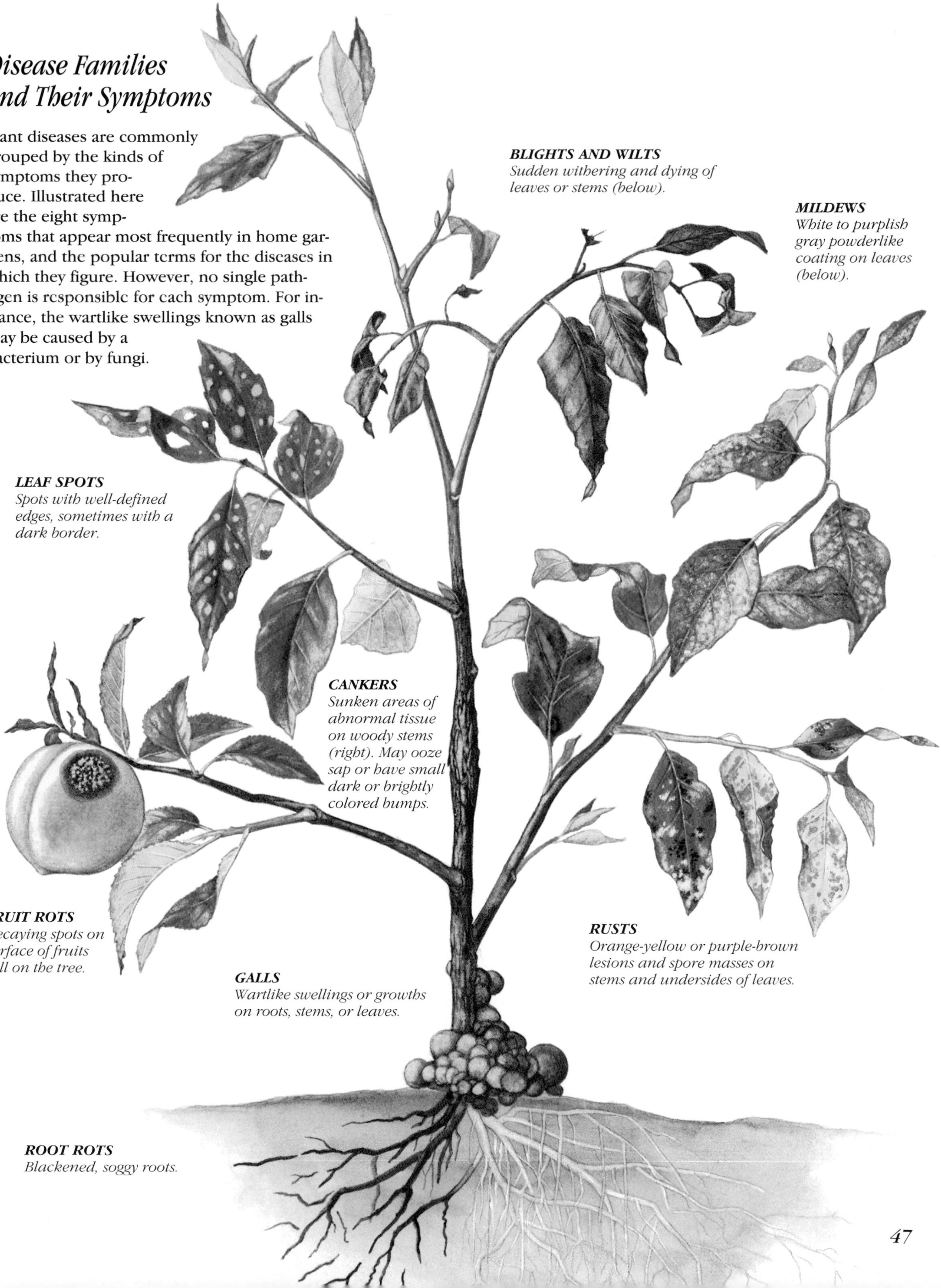

BLIGHTS AND WILTS
Sudden withering and dying of leaves or stems (below).

MILDEWS
White to purplish gray powderlike coating on leaves (below).

LEAF SPOTS
Spots with well-defined edges, sometimes with a dark border.

CANKERS
Sunken areas of abnormal tissue on woody stems (right). May ooze sap or have small dark or brightly colored bumps.

FRUIT ROTS
Decaying spots on surface of fruits still on the tree.

GALLS
Wartlike swellings or growths on roots, stems, or leaves.

RUSTS
Orange-yellow or purple-brown lesions and spore masses on stems and undersides of leaves.

ROOT ROTS
Blackened, soggy roots.

Preventive Medicine for Plants

Every day, plant pathogens find their way into your garden and within striking distance of your favorite plants. But a well-planned garden—one that optimizes growing conditions for plants and discourages the presence of pathogens—has a much better chance of avoiding infection. Gardening defensively is a much more effective way of managing plant diseases than attempting to cure them. The techniques and approaches described here will help keep your garden disease free, and they can also prevent the recurrence of diseases that have been troublesome in the past.

The Right Plants

Plants have evolved to adapt to particular environments, and a gardener should strive to make a suitable match between the physical needs of plants and the physical conditions of the garden. Trying to fight the environment is a losing battle for gardener and plant alike, so make sure before you buy that your garden will offer a plant what it needs to grow vigorously. If you are replacing a plant that has died, do not get an identical variety; chances are strong that the same problem would beset the replacement plant, creating unnecessary work and expense for you.

Shopping for Disease-Resistant Plants

Some plants are naturally resistant to infection, possessing toxic compounds or physical features such as a thick, impenetrable outer coating to repel pathogens. Other resistant plants are the product of crossbreeding pro-

Disease-Resistant Species and Cultivars of Popular Shrubs

The following shrubs are resistant to one or more diseases—listed after the plant's common name—that typically attack other members of the genus:

Chamaecyparis lawsoniana 'Ellwoodii' (false cypress)—armillaria
Cotoneaster adpressus, C. apiculatus, C. praecox (cotoneaster)—fire blight
Euonymus alata (euonymus)— crown gall, scale
Juniperus chinensis 'Femina', 'Keteleeri'; J. communis 'Aureo-spica', 'Depressa', 'Suecia'; J. conferta; J. sabina 'Broadmoor', Knap Hill, 'Skandia' (juniper)—phomopsis, cedar-apple rust
Pyracantha 'Apache', 'Fiery Cascade', 'Mohave', 'Navaho', 'Pueblo', 'Rutgers', 'Shawnee', 'Teton' (firethorn)—scab, fire blight
Rhododendron 'Copperman', 'Fashion', 'Pink Gumpo' (azalea)—phomopsis; *R. poukhanense, 'Corrine', 'Fakir', 'Formosa', 'Fred Cochran', 'Glacier',* 'Hampton Beauty', 'Higasa', 'Merlin', 'Polar Seas' (azalea)—phytophthora; *R. delavayi; R. occidentale; R. sanctum; R. simsii, 'Caroline', 'Martha Isaacson', 'Pink Trumpet', 'Red Head'* (rhododendron)—phytophthora; *R. 'Boursault', 'Cunningham's White', 'English Roseum', 'Le Bar's Red', 'Roseum 2'* (rhododendron)—botryosphaeria
Rosa 'All That Jazz', 'Carefree Wonder', 'Pascali', 'Peace', 'Queen Elizabeth', 'Sutter's Gold', 'The Fairy', 'Tropicana' (rose)—black spot
Thuja occidentalis 'Ellwangeriana', 'Lutescens' (arborvitae)—phomopsis, tip blight
Viburnum burkwoodii 'Mohawk'; V. carlcephalum 'Cayuga' (viburnum)— bacterial leaf spot, powdery mildew

Euonymus alata (winged euonymus)

grams that seek to combine naturally occurring protective chemicals with outstanding ornamental features.

More and more attractive cultivars of virtually every kind of plant are being bred for disease resistance. Before you undertake a planting project, find out whether there are resistant varieties that would work well in your garden. Below are lists of some desirable species and cultivars of shrubs and trees that will outperform their unimproved relatives where the diseases indicated are a problem. Check with your Cooperative Extension Service agent for a list of diseases that commonly occur in your area.

When you are shopping at a nursery, read plant labels to see if they contain information about the plant's resistance to disease. This often takes the form of coded abbreviations —for example, "DMPM" means that the plant is resistant to downy mildew and powdery mildew. Also desirable, although their level of natural protection is somewhat less, are plants described as "tolerant" of a certain disease. This means that although the plant may become infected, it won't be significantly damaged.

Immunity vs. Resistance

A plant that is resistant is just that—it is unlikely to be infected by a pathogen, but it isn't totally immune. If a serious disease is widespread in your area, you may want to play it safe by restricting yourself to plants that are never harmed by that particular pathogen. For instance, where flowering crab apples are plagued by apple scab, which defaces foliage and makes leaves and fruit drop prematurely, you might choose instead a redbud, a Kousa dogwood, or a serviceberry if you want a small ornamental tree that flowers in spring.

Choosing a Healthy Specimen

When you have decided what kind of plant to buy, select the individual specimen carefully. Use the guidelines on page 8 to examine a nursery plant for diseases and pests. If possible, check the root system by gently lifting the plant out of the pot. If the roots are dark, soggy, or malodorous, choose another plant. Also

Disease-Resistant Species and Cultivars of Popular Trees

The following trees are resistant to one or more diseases—listed after the plant's common name—that typically attack other members of the genus:

Acer platanoides 'Jade Glen', 'Parkway' (maple)—verticillium wilt
Cornus kousa; C. florida x kousa hybrids (dogwood)—Discula anthracnose
Ficus carica 'Kadota', 'Mission' (fig)—armillaria
Fraxinus pennsylvanica (ash)—anthracnose; *F. velutina 'Modesto'*—armillaria
Ilex cornuta, 'Meserve', 'Blue Prince', 'China Boy', 'China Girl' (holly)—black root rot; *I. aquifolium*—armillaria
Lagerstroemia 'Acoma', 'Apalachee', 'Biloxi', 'Choctaw', 'Comanche', 'Hopi', 'Lipan', 'Miami', 'Natchez', 'Osage', 'Pecos', 'Sioux', 'Tonto', 'Tuskegee', 'Wichita', 'Zuma', 'Zuni' (crape myrtle)—powdery mildew
Malus 'Beverly', 'Dolgo', 'Donald Wyman', 'Liset', 'Naragansett', 'Red Jewel', 'Snowdrift' (crab apple)—gymnosporangium rust, fire blight, frogeye leaf spot, rust, scab
Pinus nigra (Austrian pine)—armillaria; *P. palustris* (longleaf pine)—fusiform rust
Platanus 'Columbia', 'Liberty' (plane tree)—anthracnose
Populus 'Assiniboine' (poplar)—canker, rust
Quercus coccinea; Q. palustris; Q. rubra; Q. velutina (oak)—anthracnose

Malus 'Donald Wyman'
('Donald Wyman' crab apple)

reject a plant that has a wound on it: Nicked or torn bark or a broken branch provides an entry point for disease.

Some nurseries sell plants labeled "certified disease-free." These plants have been grown under carefully controlled conditions, protected from insects, and determined by a plant pathologist to be free of infection. Although such certification adds to the price of the plant, the expense may be well worth it in the long run.

Optimizing Growing Conditions

Relying heavily on resistant and tolerant cultivars is an essential tactic in creating a garden as free of disease as possible. Equally important is maintaining the health of your plants with proper cultural and physical practices, for the more vigorous they are the less likely they'll be to succumb to disease.

Observing Good Planting Practices

Resist the temptation to crowd your plants together to achieve the effect of dense foliage and lush blooms. Instead, space them generously, following the recommended planting distances. This reduces competition for nutrients, water, and sunlight, and it permits air to circulate freely around stems and leaves. Good air circulation is especially vital for relieving the humid conditions in which fungi

thrive. The spores of botrytis blights and powdery mildews, for instance, are present in air, soil, or plant debris in most gardens, but they can't infect plants unless the environment is warm and moist.

Amending the Soil

Healthy soil leads to healthy plants that can fend off all but the most persistent diseases. If the soil has a proper balance of nutrients, a hospitable pH range, and is well drained, plants will develop good root systems and make efficient use of nutrients and water.

You will need to amend the soil every year to replenish nutrients consumed by growing plants. Compost is the most effective all-round amendment; you can make it yourself or buy it in bags. In the fall, spread a 2-inch layer over the soil and dig it in.

Overall soil fertility can also be enhanced with fertilizer. You can choose an inorganic, chemical-based fertilizer or one made from natural materials such as dehydrated manure, cottonseed meal, dried blood, bone meal, or rock phosphate. Chemical fertilizers are often less expensive to use and may act more quickly, but they will burn a plant's roots if applied too heavily. An organic fertilizer, on the other hand, may take a little longer to work but has less chance of burning plant roots. Also, it won't harm the soil microbes that help control plant diseases.

If the soil has been well prepared, an application of fertilizer before the growing season begins will probably be sufficient for the year.

The Art of Watering

The following techniques will keep your plants well watered while making the garden less hospitable to disease organisms:

- When planning a garden, group plants according to their water needs.
- Most gardens need 1 to 1½ inches of water every 7 to 10 days. Install a rain gauge so you can measure how much rainfall your garden receives. If it is insufficient, make up the deficit with a single, slow soaking.
- Use soaker hoses or install an underground drip-irrigation system. Unlike sprinkling, these watering methods keep foliage dry and eliminate splashing, reducing the likelihood of fungal infections.
- If you do use a sprinkler, water early in the day so that the sun can quickly evaporate the moisture on the leaves. If your system is automated, be sure it does not automatically water when it's raining.
- After watering, use a trowel or a soil auger to check that the water has penetrated to a depth of 8 to 12 inches. If it hasn't, apply the water at a slower rate.
- Between waterings, dig down 6 to 8 inches with a spade or trowel to check the soil moisture. Don't water again until the top 1½ to 2 inches of soil begin to dry out.
- If the soil in one area is much slower to dry out, test the drainage *(page 52)* and, if necessary, take steps to improve it.

Be moderate, though, especially when applying nitrogen. Too much of this element can promote rapid leaf and stem growth, which is often soft and susceptible to pathogens.

Plants grown in a soil that lacks one or more nutrients will eventually show symptoms of deficiency, usually stunted growth and yellowing leaves. Included in the encyclopedia that begins on page 94 are descriptions of four of the most frequently encountered deficiencies—iron, magnesium, nitrogen, and potassium. If you suspect a nutrient imbalance, have your soil tested. Your local Cooperative Extension Service can recommend a kit you can use to administer the test yourself or, if you prefer, a laboratory where you can send a soil sample for analysis. Ask the laboratory to recommend the appropriate organic fertilizer and the rate at which it should be applied if there is a nutrient imbalance.

The Plant's Restorative: Manure Tea

Another environmentally safe way to give plants a mild dose of nutrients is by spraying them with manure tea. This homemade brew is easy to concoct: Just wrap 1 gallon of manure-based compost or well-rotted manure in burlap or some other coarse cloth and secure it at the top. Place the bag in a 5-gallon bucket and fill it with water. Leave the mixture in a warm place for at least 3 days, but preferably for a week. Then fill a spray applicator with the liquid and spray the plants well. Repeat every 3 to 4 days. You can also use manure tea for watering plants and to provide some protection against fungal diseases. For example, soaking seeds overnight in manure tea has been found to reduce the incidence of damping-off *(right)*.

Finding the Correct Soil pH

Most plants absorb nutrients and grow best in slightly acid soil, with a pH of around 6.5. There are a few exceptions to this rule—azaleas, for instance, prefer a more acidic soil—so you'll need to find out whether any of your plants have different pH requirements. Some soil-borne pathogens such as pythium, a fungus that causes damping-off and root rot, are very sensitive to minor fluctuations of pH lev-

TIPS FROM THE PROS

Protecting Seedlings from Damping-Off

Many gardeners have experienced the disappointment of sowing seeds, watching them germinate, and carefully tending the tiny, apparently healthy seedlings only to find them one morning keeled over dead and rotting. The cause is an attack of damping-off fungi. These pathogens can kill seedlings even before they emerge from the soil.

Damping-off fungi are present in most gardens, and virtually every kind of seedling is vulnerable; no resistant cultivars have been developed. Nevertheless, the disease can be prevented if you take a few simple precautions. The most important step, of course, is to minimize the risk of exposure to the fungus itself. It is also critical to avoid high nitrogen levels and excess moisture in the soil and to ensure adequate light, whether natural or artificial. Poor light results in spindly seedlings that are more vulnerable to infection. Below are some tips for starting healthy seedlings:

Starting Seed Outdoors. Sow seeds directly in the garden only in places where the drainage and air circulation are good. Plant seeds of heat-loving annuals only after night temperatures are reliably warm so that the seedlings will grow out of their vulnerable stage quickly. Cover seeds with vermiculite or perlite, both of which are free of pathogens and drain quickly. Space the seeds generously, and thin the seedlings early on so that air can circulate around them freely. Do not fertilize with nitrogen until the seedlings begin to produce true leaves—these follow the first growth of leaves to sprout, which are called seed leaves. Keep the soil moist, but let the surface dry out slightly between waterings.

Starting Seed Indoors. Wash a container and disinfect it with a 10 percent bleach solution. Fill it with a commercial sterile seedling mix; do not substitute houseplant potting soil, since it may contain damping-off fungi. Follow the same watering, thinning, and fertilizing techniques used for seed started outdoors.

els. These pathogens can be controlled simply by lowering the pH level with additions of lime or raising it with sulfur. If your plants have been infected by a soil-borne pathogen in the past, ask the Extension agent if it would make sense to adjust the pH.

Rotating Annuals and Vegetables

Despite your best efforts at controlling soil-borne pathogens, they will thrive as long as a preferred food supply is present. In a fairly short time, they can multiply from negligible numbers to a population capable of launching a devastating attack. For instance, vinca is highly susceptible to root rot, which is caused by a fungus found in small numbers in most soils. If allowed to feed on vinca for several years in a row, however, the fungus will become rampant. To eliminate a pathogen that is partial to only one or a few species, try rotating your plants. This solution isn't practical for perennials and other plants in permanent locations, but it is easily accomplished with annuals and vegetables. Instead of planting them in the same spot year after year, skip at least 2 years before repeating an annual or vegetable in a site.

The Importance of Soil Drainage

Many fungi flourish in waterlogged soil, so it's wise to test how well your soil drains, especially if it is largely composed of clay. Dig a hole 10 inches deep and 12 inches in diameter and pour in 1 gallon of water. If any remains in the hole after 10 minutes, the drainage needs to be improved. You may be able to correct the problem merely by digging in generous amounts of organic matter and coarse sand. Other solutions to try when simpler ones are inadequate are building a raised bed or installing drainage pipes below the soil surface.

Watering to Promote Garden Health

How and when one waters also plays an important role in whether disease takes hold in your garden. The powerful stream of a hose, for instance, can splash pathogens that are on or near the soil's surface onto leaves and stems. When humidity is high, overhead watering with a sprinkler can leave foliage wet for long periods, providing a favorable environment for fungi to germinate. The method that best discourages disease is ground-level watering, whether through soaker hoses or through an underground system. For more tips on acquiring good watering habits, see the box on page 50.

Since pathogens spread most easily in moist environments, it is important to avoid working in the garden soon after a rainfall or a watering. You could inadvertently pick up the pathogens on your hands, shoes, clothing, or tools and transport them to other parts of the garden.

The Benefits of Mulching

Another way to keep soil-borne pathogens away from plant stems and leaves is to lay down a protective barrier of mulch. A 2- to 4-inch layer of compost, shredded bark, or other organic material will not only block disease-causing pathogens, it will also introduce into the soil various kinds of microorganisms that promote a healthy garden. Composted pine bark, for example, is particularly rich in beneficial nematodes and bacteria that prey on parasitic nematodes and other pathogens. Other microorganisms keep down the pathogen population by outcompeting them for food and habitat.

Mulch also helps keep plants in good health by conserving moisture and adding nutrients as it decays. And a circle of mulch at least 4 feet in diameter around the trunk of a tree will prevent the lawn mower from inflicting nicks and cuts that would expose the inner layers of living tissue to disease organisms. (When spreading the mulch, remember to keep it a few inches away from the trunk—it should surround the trunk but not touch it.) The tree will be even better protected if all of its roots that protrude above the soil are mulched.

Biological and Chemical Preventives

The microorganisms in decaying mulch are an example of biological disease control, which lets living organisms destroy harmful ones either by eating them or by appropriating their food and territory.

Besides the biological controls that are naturally present in a garden, there are also a handful of commercial fungicides and bactericides; Galltrol-A and Norbac 84-C, for example, kill the bacterium responsible for crown gall. If you have had trouble with a disease in the past, check with your local nursery to see if a biological fungicide or bactericide has been developed for home gardens. Apply the control to all susceptible plants to prevent a recurrence, following the instructions on the label.

Controlling Diseases

Once you've diagnosed a plant disease, there are often several ways to get rid of it or prevent a recurrence. Some of these methods, such as pruning, involve virtually no risk to your plants or to the environment. Earth-friendly sprays and dusts of low or no toxicity *(pages 55-56)* offer another avenue of attack. For truly stubborn and serious diseases, you may decide to use one of the more toxic chemical controls *(pages 56-57)*.

But before you do anything, keep in mind that many diseases are merely cosmetic problems and will run their natural course without doing serious damage to the infected plant. If you feel you must take action in such instances, limit yourself to cultural or physical controls; these diseases don't warrant the use of toxic chemicals.

Destroying Pathogens with Sunlight

Solarization is a reliable, environmentally safe way to rid a garden plot of soil-borne diseases as well as weeds. Clear plastic is spread on the

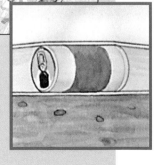

Solarizing Soil Pathogens

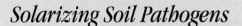

1. Clear a sunny plot of existing vegetation, rocks, and other debris, and dig in any soil amendments needed. *Rake the soil smooth and dig a trench a few inches deep around the plot. Water the soil to a depth of at least 12 inches. Next, using clear plastic measuring 3 to 4 mils thick, cut two sheets large enough to cover the plot.*

2. Spread one sheet smoothly on the soil. *Lay empty soda cans about 2 feet apart on the sheet, then spread the second sheet over the cans (above and inset). Tuck the edges of the plastic sheets into the trench and pile soil on them to make a seal; this will trap heat and moisture in the air space between the sheets. After a rain, sweep off any water.*

3. To check soil temperature, *fold back a corner of the plastic and insert a soil thermometer; reseal the sheets afterward. Leave the sheets in place for several days after the temperature maintains 120°F or above; it may take 4 to 8 weeks for the bed to heat to this point.*

Pruning Diseased Wood

Stems showing signs of disease should be pruned back promptly to healthy tissue to prevent further infection. (However, if the weather is rainy, wait for a dry day, since pathogens are easily transmitted by water.) To remove a stem completely, make the cut at its base flush with the parent stem so there won't be a stub. If you are shortening a stem rather than removing it, prune back to a healthy bud. Cut the stem at a 45° angle in the same direction that the bud points, so that water will drain away from the bud.

Remove a stem's diseased portion plus 6 inches of healthy-looking wood, cutting ¼ inch above a bud (above) or at a juncture. If the cut surface has discolored tissue (right), prune back to pale, healthy wood.

Pruning Large Branches

The bulge at the base of a tree branch, called the branch collar, is a protective zone that helps heal the wound created when the branch is removed, whether naturally or by pruning. This specialized tissue produces a callus that seals the wound's surface, preventing wood-decay fungi from infecting the trunk.

When you prune, be very careful to leave the branch collar intact so that healing will take place. For the same reason, never cut into a callus, even to remove a rotted or diseased section of a trunk. The tree itself will seal off the dead tissue.

A single pruning cut made flush with the trunk (A) removes the branch's collar and tears bark, exposing wood to infection. Cutting too far from the trunk leaves a disease-prone stub (B). For good healing (C), use a series of three cuts (D). First, saw halfway through the branch from the underside 8 to 12 inches from the collar (1). Then saw through the branch from above, a few inches beyond the first cut (2). Saw off the resulting stub just forward of the collar, following its natural angle (3).

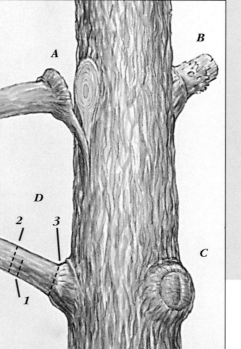

ground to trap the sun's heat, which raises the temperature of the top 3 to 5 inches of soil to 120°F or more, roasting microorganisms and weed seeds buried in it. The technique must be carried out in the hottest, sunniest season and is suitable only for plots that are in direct sun for most of the day. Also, the soil must be bare—that is, unplanted.

How long the process takes depends on weather and climate. Solarization is complete in about 4 weeks when daytime temperatures average 90°F; it can take up to 8 weeks if temperatures average in the 70s. Fungi, nematodes, and weed seeds are killed when the soil temperature exceeds 120°F. At 160°F and above, some viruses and bacteria will also be destroyed. Unfortunately, solarization kills beneficial microbes as well, so be sure to dig a microbe-rich material such as aged manure or compost into the plot later to repopulate it. Earthworms survive the process by tunneling deeper into the soil.

After solarization, take care to cultivate the soil very shallowly; if you dig too deep, you may reinfest the plot with pathogens and seeds that survived in the cooler soil below.

Pruning

Some tree diseases, such as fire blight and twig canker, can be controlled by pruning out infected branches. You can also use pruning as a method of prevention. Thinning a plant—that is, removing some stems or branches from its center—discourages diseases that thrive in stagnant conditions by improving air circulation and reducing humidity.

When pruning, take care not to inadvertently increase a shrub's or tree's vulnerability to disease with badly executed cuts *(opposite, below)*. Use a high-quality tool that is large enough to cleanly cut the wood you're working on. To keep from spreading disease as you work, some horticulturists recommend carrying along a pail containing a solution of one part household bleach and nine parts water so that you can disinfect your clippers after each cut. Leave the clippers in the solution for 15 seconds. When you are finished pruning, sterilize them again, rinse in clean water, and dry, then coat the metal parts with a light oil to prevent rusting.

When to Prune a Tree

The timing of tree pruning is very important. Done in the wrong season, it can actually increase problems. Trees respond to pruning either by releasing sap or by quickly producing a burst of new growth, both of which attract pests and diseases. Most trees do best when pruned during their dormant stage, so if the job can be postponed until then, you should do so. Pruning diseased wood is an exception to this rule. It should be removed as soon as you notice it unless the weather is wet, since pathogens spread easily in water.

Horticulturists now advise against using tree paint on pruning cuts. Not only does it have no known benefit, it may actually promote some wood rots by preventing the wound from drying, which is a natural protection against infection.

Removing Diseased Plants

For some diseases, there is no known cure. In these cases, the plant should be pulled up and disposed of as soon as possible. If the plant has a soil-borne disease such as nematodes or crown rot, dig it out roots and all, being careful not to knock any soil off the rootball. Put everything in a plastic garbage bag and seal tightly. Replace the diseased plant with a resistant variety. Once the pathogens have lost their hosts, they will eventually die out.

Handling diseased plant material properly is crucial in preventing the further spread of pathogens. Keep a plastic bag with you when you garden for collecting clippings and other material. Fungus spores can spread in the garden as quickly as dandelion seeds in the breeze. Dispose of the bagged plant material with your household trash, or bury it in an out-of-the-way place. You can also compost it, but only if you are certain that your pile will heat up to a minimum of 140°F.

A Safe, Simple Spray

Baking soda is a natural fungicide that is nontoxic to the environment. When sprayed on plants, it prevents fungal spores from penetrating plant tissue. In addition, it can halt the spread of an established infection. The box on page 56 gives directions for making and using baking soda spray.

DISEASES OF VARYING DESTRUCTION
Although spot anthracnose can spoil the looks of a flowering dogwood's blossoms, as shown here, the tree suffers no serious or long-lasting effects. However, another fungal disease with similar symptoms, Discula anthracnose, is fatal to this species of dogwood.

Horticultural Oils

Spraying infected trees and shrubs with horticultural oils prevents the fungi responsible for rusts and mildews from germinating. These oils are even more widely used to control pests such as mites, plant bugs, and psyllids. The sprays aren't toxic to mammals.

Horticultural oils are applied in two different concentrations depending on the season. The stronger of the two is applied in winter, while plants are dormant. For warmer weather, when plants are in active growth, a diluted solution is used, to avoid damaging foliage.

Chemical Controls

When milder measures prove to be useless, the gardener must weigh the risks posed by a more potent chemical method of control. If the disease's only effect on the plant is a less than perfect appearance, you may feel that a fungicide, most of which kill beneficial microorganisms along with plant pathogens, is not warranted. Moreover, many fungicides harm wildlife, especially fish. Fortunately, the question of whether or not to spray rarely if ever arises with most ornamentals. For a handful, however, such as hybrid tea roses, chemicals are essential for the plant to grow and bloom well. In such cases, you'll have to decide whether the plant is worth the risks, the expense, and the effort of spraying.

Baking Soda Spray

1 tablespoon baking soda
1 gallon water
⅛ to ¼ teaspoon insecticidal soap

Dissolve the baking soda in the water, then add the soap, which helps the solution spread and stick to the foliage. Fill a spray can or bottle with the solution and spray all of the leaves on both sides. Repeat every 5 to 7 days until the symptoms disappear.

To prevent another outbreak the following year, begin spraying in spring and continue until the fall. This spray is effective against powdery mildews, leaf blights, and leaf spots.

If disease symptoms are far advanced, it's probably too late for a spray to be effective, at least during the current season. If so, wait until the following year, then spray shortly before the season and the conditions—muggy, hot weather, for instance—are ripe for a renewed outbreak. In short, think in terms of prevention, and plan ahead.

Fungicides

Since fungi cause about 80 percent of the diseases that affect ornamental plants, most of the chemicals available for treating plant diseases are fungicides. Fungicides work in two ways. Most of them are surface protectants, which means they keep spores from germinating on or penetrating a plant. These fungicides prevent disease, but they cannot cure it. Apply these sprays when conditions favor infection: For example, in the case of garden phlox, which is susceptible to powdery mildew, spray shortly before the days turn warm and sunny but when nights are still cool.

The second group of fungicides are the systemics, which prevent disease and also cure it. A systemic penetrates a plant's tissue, where it interferes with the growth of the pathogen. Unlike most surface protectants, which prevent a wide range of diseases, systemics generally have a narrow spectrum, making accurate diagnosis especially important. Systemics are much less likely than surface protectants to injure plant tissues, and they seldom leave a visible residue.

The chart at right lists the most common fungicides available to home gardeners in ascending order of toxicity, with the safest one appearing first. Pick the least toxic product for your disease problem. All of these fungicides are considered organic because they are active for only one day instead of persisting in the environment, as some other fungicides do.

Taking Precautions

Before you buy a fungicide, and again when you are preparing to use it, read the label carefully to make sure it is an appropriate chemical for the plant and the disease you are treating. Follow all instructions to the letter, and handle the fungicide with as much care as you would a pesticide or a herbicide *(pages 30 and 68-69)*.

RECOMMENDED FUNGICIDES

Type	Diseases Controlled	Precautions and Hazards
Fungicidal soap. Surface protectant.	Black spot, brown canker, leaf spot, powdery mildews, and rust.	Before treating a plant, test a few leaves for browning or other symptoms of sensitivity.
Copper hydroxide, copper tanate. Surface protectants.	Many fungal and some bacterial leaf spots, botrytis, downy mildews, and powdery mildews.	Spray early on a dry, sunny day. Copper hydroxide is less expensive than copper tanate but may burn foliage in damp weather and leaves a visible residue. Both are eye irritants and toxic to wildlife.
Copper sulfate and hydrated lime (Bordeaux mixture). Surface protectant.	Many fungal and some bacterial diseases, including anthracnose, bacterial leaf spots, black rot, blights, fruit scab, septoria leaf spot, and wilts.	Spray on a windless evening, when no bees are active. Do not use in damp or humid weather if the temperature is below 50°F. Never use with other pesticides or fungicides.
Sulfur. Surface protectant.	Black spot, brown rot, powdery mildews, rusts, scabs, and other fungi. Also controls mites.	To avoid damaging foliage do not apply when the temperature exceeds 85°F. Do not apply to open flowers, because bees will be harmed. Wait a month to use after applying horticultural oil.
Lime sulfur. Surface protectant.	Anthracnose, powdery mildews, rusts, and scabs.	Use only in cold weather on dormant plants. Lime sulfur is more caustic and thus more likely to damage plants than plain sulfur. Toxic to fish.
Horticultural oils. Surface protectant.	Powdery mildews, puccinia rust, and septoria leaf spot.	Do not use when temperatures exceed 90°F or when plants are water stressed. Do not use if a fungicide containing sulfur has been applied within the last month.
Captan. Surface protectant.	Damping-off fungi (used on seed).	Leaves visible residue. Causes spotting, yellowing, or defoliation if used in cool, moist weather on young leaves of roses and stone fruits. Eye irritant; wear goggles. Toxic to soil microorganisms.
Chlorothalonil. Surface protectant.	Blights, botrytis, leaf spots, and powdery mildews.	Eye irritant; wear goggles. Slightly toxic to wildlife and soil microorganisms.
Mancozeb. Surface protectant.	Blights, botrytis, downy mildews, and leaf spots.	Use sparingly on foliage only. Store in a cool, dry location in an airtight container; heat and moisture may decompose it. Toxic to soil microorganisms.
Propiconazole. Systemic.	Many diseases of ornamentals and turf grasses including Discula anthracnose of dogwood, blights, leaf spots, powdery mildews, and rusts.	Severe eye irritant; always wear goggles and rubber gloves. Toxic to soil organisms.
Thiophanate-methyl. Systemic.	Many blights, black spot, Discula anthracnose of dogwood, and leaf and fruit spots.	Irritant to eyes, nose, and throat; always wear respirator, goggles, rubber gloves, and rubber boots.
Triadimefon. Systemic.	Powdery mildews, rusts, and a variety of leaf spots and blights.	Avoid contact with powder when mixing. Toxic to soil organisms.
Triforine. Systemic.	Powdery mildews and a variety of leaf spots and blights, including brown rot of stone fruit.	Resistance to this fungicide has appeared in some strains of fungi that cause black spot on roses. Toxic to soil organisms.

CHAPTER THREE

Coping with Weeds

Weeds are the most diverse of all plant groups—inch-high creepers, 40-foot-tall trees, perennials with beguiling flowers, rangy thistles with finger-pricking spines. Their common trait is not a fixed one, like color or size. Instead, it is a matter of definition: If a plant is growing in the wrong place, it is a weed. In the various ecological niches in which they evolved, these plants may be singled out for their desirable traits, such as exceptional hardiness, adaptability, and successful reproduction. In the artificial plant communities we call gardens, however, the same traits can turn a plant into an overbearing competitor among ornamentals— that is, it becomes a weed, something to be eliminated.

With concern for the environment on the rise, chemical methods of controlling weeds have given way to nonchemical ones wherever feasible. Among the most basic of earth-friendly defensive measures are designing your garden to thwart weeds and understanding a weed's life cycle so you'll know when it is most vulnerable to attack. Techniques such as mulching and hoeing can also help limit the weed population safely.

For the times when herbicides are the only answer to a weed problem, you'll need to learn the proper methods for handling the chemicals and how to apply them in special situations (pages 68-69). By using the photo gallery on pages 70-73, which describes 24 weeds widely distributed across the United States, you'll be able to identify the irksome plants before routing them becomes an arduous task.

BEGUILING PLANT, DEVILISH WEED
Queen Anne's lace, a Eurasian native that has colonized American fields and roadsides, mingles demurely with red valerian in this informal garden. However, the plant has another name that suggests how hard it is to eradicate: devil's plague.

Defending the Garden against Weeds

As a gardener, you can view weeds in two ways: as benefactors in some situations and as opponents in others. Paradoxically, the very traits that make a plant a headache in a garden often make it valuable in a natural plant community.

When fire, flood, or some other disturbance strips away vegetation in the wild, weeds are among the pioneers that recolonize the denuded soil. Those with long taproots pull up nutrients from below the surface—a Canada thistle's roots, for instance, grow down as far as 20 feet. When the weed dies and decomposes, the nutrients enrich the soil, and the remains of the foliage and stems increase its organic content. Also, taproots break through the underlying hardpan that, in many areas of the United States, prevents water from sinking deep into the soil. Once the weeds have cracked the hardpan, other plants can flourish there. Ragweed, annual morning glory, and clover—all weeds, to gardeners—are known to agronomists as soil improvers. Purslane spreads its rooting stems across eroded hillsides, netting organic particles and rebuilding soil.

The weeds that take root in your garden say something about the characteristics of its soil and can therefore point the way to the steps that should be taken to amend it. Sorrel, knapweed, coltsfoot, and hawkweed, for instance, are sure indicators of acidic soil, and Joe-Pye weed, buttercups, moss, and dock spring up where drainage is poor. A flourishing crop of mustard, bindweed, or quack grass may be evidence of a thin, hard surface crust or of a hardpan lying below the surface that will discourage other plants.

Weeds as the Gardener's Enemy

Whatever their usefulness in some situations, weeds must nevertheless be viewed as the enemy, and for several excellent reasons that have to do both with aesthetics and with the health of the plantings. First, their straggly or obtrusive shapes spoil the look of the garden. Second, their vigorous roots spread rapidly, depriving ornamental plants and vegetables of soil nutrients and moisture and competing with them for space and light. Third, weeds may harbor plant diseases that destroy cultivated plants, and they also attract pests to the garden. Sorrel, dock, and groundsel, for example, are favorite breeding grounds of the tarnished plant bug, which does serious damage to hundreds of different species, including most vegetables and many perennials, trees, and shrubs.

Life Cycles of Herbaceous Weeds

Weeds fall into many of the same categories as ornamentals—woody plants, vines, and herbaceous annuals, biennials, and perennials. Annual weeds, which account for about 80 percent of common garden weeds, germinate, grow, bloom, set seed, and die in one growing season. Most of these are shallow-rooted sun lovers that set vast numbers of seeds. A single redroot pigweed, for instance, may scatter more than 100,000 seeds, whereas one witchweed plant can produce five times that number.

Just as impressive as the sheer number of weed seeds is the length of time they can remain dormant when conditions are unfavorable, then germinate and produce healthy plants when conditions improve. Lamb's-quarters seeds unearthed at an archaeological site, for example, sprouted after 1,700 years. In view of their prodigality, the main strategy for combating annual weeds is to get rid of them early in the season, before they bloom and drop those enduring seeds.

A few weed species, such as Queen Anne's lace, are biennials, which means that they begin growth one year, then flower, set seed, and die the next. Like annuals, these plants can be prodigious seed producers—a biennial mullein may scatter 223,000 seeds. Handle biennials as you would annuals: Cut or pull them the first season and you won't have to look for them again.

SELECTING A WEED-CONTROL STRATEGY

Weed Habitat	Solution	Comments
Ground cover	Mulch; hand pull or hoe; apply herbicide.	Lay mulch only 2 inches deep to allow ground cover to spread. Shield the ground cover from herbicide as shown on page 69.
Lawn	Hand pull or hoe; raise blade of mower.	Close mowing and a constantly moist soil encourage weeds.
New garden area	Plant cover crop; solarize *(pages 53-54)*; till repeatedly.	Plant the area promptly so weeds won't recolonize it. Control any that appear with hand pulling or cultivation. Mulch the newly installed plants.
Perennial or annual bed	Mulch; hand pull or hoe; install an edging.	If the area has poor drainage, underplant with ground cover or mulch with stone.
Rose bed	Mulch; cultivate shallowly.	Do not use an organic mulch if the area is prone to black spot or mildew.
Tree set in lawn	Mulch; plant ground cover.	Keep mulch several inches away from tree trunks.
Under shrubs	Mulch; plant ground cover.	Keep mulch several inches from stems; use a coarse mulch on slopes to prevent washing; use easily controlled species such as ice plant or ajuga.
Terraces, walks	Pour boiling water on weeds; install pavers over landscape fabric or tarpaper block; plant low-growing plants between pavers; spray with herbicide.	Use herbicide sparingly to minimize runoff.

Designing Defenses against Weeds

Your garden will be far easier to maintain if you take principles of weed control into account when you are laying out beds and borders, selecting and siting plants, and choosing mulches. Several methods of prevention that are not only utilitarian but aesthetically pleasing have been incorporated into the garden shown at right:

- The fence surrounding the garden and the dense shrubs planted at the perimeter block many airborne seeds.
- Where the perennial bed in the foreground abuts the lawn, plastic edging keeps grass rhizomes from creeping into the bed. Such a barrier must extend at least 4 inches underground to prevent frost from heaving it out of place.
- The woodchip mulch covering the planting bed discourages weed seeds that need light to germinate. The mulch also keeps soil moist, making it easier to pluck out unwanted seedlings.

The Tenacious Perennials

While not as common in the garden as their annual counterparts, the perennial weeds that pop up among your plantings are potentially even more of a nuisance because they may live and reproduce for many years. Poison ivy, dandelion, and pokeweed send roots deep into the soil. Cutting their tops off early in the season keeps them from blooming and spreading, but the roots will send up foliage repeatedly. Many other perennial species, including quack grass, henbit, and comfrey, sprout anew from even small fragments of root or stem. To get rid of these weeds, you must destroy them roots and all. With repeated cutting or heavy mulching, you may be able to starve the roots, since a plant deprived of either leaves or sunlight can't manufacture food.

Keeping Weeds Out

The most satisfactory way to deal with weeds of any type is to keep them out of your garden in the first place or, if they do find their way in, to make their stay less agreeable. Although it is easiest to do this when you're working with a new garden, there are reliable techniques for reducing or eliminating the weed population in mature gardens.

One proven way to prevent weeds is to choose plants well suited to your garden's climate and its various microclimates, soil conditions, and drainage patterns. Vigorous plantings resist competition from stray weeds and are less likely to succumb to the pests they attract. For instance, a rugosa rose planted on a dry, windy slope can spread quickly and shade out weeds. A rhododendron planted in the same spot will be a much poorer competitor because it needs more moisture and shade to thrive. Weed seedlings will flourish around and beneath it.

Getting Rid of Weed Seeds

When you create a new flower bed or lawn, allow the extra time it takes to give the soil a weedless start. If your garden has only a thin layer of topsoil, spend a season digging in organic materials to enrich it. Resist the quick but risky alternative of buying merchandise that's advertised as topsoil. Far too often such an offering is a poor substitute at best, lacking the nutrients, organic content, and microorganisms that characterize genuine topsoil. Soil you buy may also be full of weed seeds waiting to germinate on your property. At the same time, be wary of soil said to be weed free: It may have been heavily treated with herbicides that will allow nothing at all to grow for years. Either way, it's a bad bargain.

Once the organic content of the soil has been boosted, the second step is to eliminate any weed seeds. One way of doing this is by solarization *(pages 53-54),* a process that takes several weeks. Alternatively, if you are so fortunate as to be able to reserve an entire growing season for preparation, you can remove the weeds and greatly improve the soil at the same time by tilling the ground and sowing what is called a cover crop.

A Clean Start with Cover Crops

Begin the process in early spring, sowing the tilled ground with buckwheat, hairy vetch, or another cover crop recommended for your area. If you are using buckwheat or vetch, apply seed at the rate of 4 pounds per 1,000 square feet. As the crop sprouts and grows, so do the weeds, but most of them get shaded out before they set seed. Before the crop flowers, till it under completely—the decaying plants now act as "green manure"—then plant another batch of seed. Again, till the crop under before it flowers. For the third and last crop of the year, use annual ryegrass to carry on the weed-shading work from late in the growing season until the following spring. Once more, till the crop under before it flowers. These cover-crop cycles will eliminate nearly all the weeds on the site, both annual

and perennial, and after the last tilling, your garden or lawn is ready to plant.

A cover crop is feasible for virtually any size plot. In a small area, you won't need a rototiller to break up the soil. Simply spade the ground and rake it before seeding, then, when the time comes, use a garden fork to turn the crop under. Whether you till by hand or by machine, the relatively weed-free condition of the soil plus the nutrients and organic matter furnished by the cover crop will give a new bed or lawn a wonderful boost.

Barring Weeds from Entry

Even if you've eliminated weeds from your soil, the wind, birds, wild animals, and roving pets can carry seeds from neighboring properties and deposit them in your yard. Fences, walls, and hedges are effective barriers against airborne seeds and those carried by animals. Among fences, a solid, stockade type is best, but even lattice fencing offers significant protection. A row of closely planted shrubs with dense foliage will also intercept would-be weed invaders. Such barrier plantings can even be seasonal: A strip of tall annuals or perennials, for instance, will protect your vegetable garden but will disappear when frost arrives, leaving the way clear for you to do cleanup chores.

Weed seeds sometimes stow away in the containers and rootballs of plants you buy at garden centers. Examine your purchases carefully lest you inadvertently transport weeds home to your garden. And if you go camping or hiking, look over your gear and brush yourself off on the way back, so that wilderness weed seeds won't come home with you.

Mulches for Weed Control

In addition to the many other benefits mulch provides a garden, it acts as a ground-level barrier against weeds. By restricting the amount of light reaching the soil surface, mulch prevents many weed seeds from germinating. In addition, it can smother any seedlings that do get started before they become large enough to be troublesome. Both organic materials such as leaves, bark, or newspaper and inorganic materials such as stone and landscape fabric are effective weed blockers.

Using an Organic Mulch

Plant-material mulches, such as leaves, shredded bark, buckwheat hulls, wheat or oat straw or salt hay, and woodchips, are widely available and convenient to use. They also have the added advantage of improving the soil as they decay. Plan on replenishing the mulch occasionally to replace material that has decomposed. Most leaf and shredded-bark mulches must be renewed annually; bark chips and pine needles last longer. *(Caution: Orchard grass should never be used because it contains seeds that will sprout into hummocks that are very difficult to get rid of.)*

The depth of the mulch depends on the size of its particles. A layer 2 to 3 inches deep for a finely textured mulch, such as compost, or 4 to 6 inches deep for a bulkier one, such as pine bark, is usually sufficient for weed control; laid deeper, the mulch may keep oxygen, water, and nutrients from reaching roots. Lay mulch thickest in areas between plants. Avoid piling it directly against the stems, as this encourages disease. Mulch piled against the base of a tree or shrub is a favorite nesting place for rodents, so leave a bare ring of soil around those plants. If you are mulching with fresh woodchips, scatter a slow-release nitrogen fertilizer over the soil before spreading the chips; otherwise, microorganisms breaking down the wood will draw nitrogen from the soil.

Inorganic Mulches

Gravel, marble chips, lava rock, and other stone mulches are good choices for small formal areas, desert gardens, and rock gardens. In areas where slugs, snails, or mildews and other fungus diseases are a serious problem, stone is preferable to organic materials, which foster the moist conditions these pests and diseases require.

For maximum protection against weeds, you can combine a top layer of stone with an underlay of woven landscape fabric, black plastic sheeting, or newspaper spread several sheets thick (don't use colored pages, however—the inks can be toxic). Some gardeners use these materials alone, but aside from the fact that they're uniformly unattractive, they have some practical drawbacks. Black plastic and landscape fabric deteriorate when they are exposed to sunlight, and newspaper and

TIPS FROM THE PROS

Weedproofing Terraces and Walkways

Because it's often difficult or impossible to uproot weeds growing in the cracks of unmortared terraces and walkways, even gardeners who are loath to use herbicides feel they don't have an alternative. Here are two ways to keep a paved area both well groomed and chemical free:

- When you are installing a new area of paving, use several layers of roofing felt under the pavers to stop roots from penetrating the soil. Weeds sprouting in the spaces between pavers will remain shallow rooted and easy to pull up.
- Where foot traffic is light, use the spaces between pavers

as miniature beds for low-growing perennials or herbs with a horizontal growth habit. Fill the spaces with a fast-draining sandy soil, then sow seeds or set out rooted slips of low-growing plants. Varieties that do well in these conditions include woolly or creeping thyme, prostrate sedum, alyssum, pennyroyal, miniature veronica, and portulaca. These tiny plants grow fast, shading out weeds and giving you the bonus of colorful flowers. Treading on thyme or pennyroyal, which is a kind of mint, releases a delightful fragrance as well. Any of these plants can easily be cut back if necessary.

plastic especially are prone to being blown out of place unless they're weighted down.

Landscape fabric is the most expensive of the underlays, but it can last 5 years or more. Water and nutrients easily pass through it, and its rough texture helps keep the overlaid mulch in place. Newspaper and black plastic excel at blocking weeds, but they also block the downward movement of moisture and fertilizers. If you use such an underlay, you'll need to punch several holes through it where it surrounds each plant.

With any of the underlays, pile on at least 2 inches of decorative mulch. If the layer is too thin, you'll have to spend gardening time tweaking it back into place over the bare patches that will inevitably appear.

Ground Covers for Weed Control

If you'd prefer to suppress weeds with an attractive blanket of plants rather than one of woodchips or stone, consider a perennial ground cover with dense foliage. Just make sure you don't plant one that will become a weed itself. English ivy has this potential,

CREEPING PLANTS THAT OUTCOMPETE WEEDS
Mother-of-thyme in full rosy purple bloom fills the crevices of this northern California terrace and spills down the steps between billowy white mounds of snow-in-summer. Both of these plants grow densely enough to outcompete weeds.

especially in the warmer parts of the country. Play it safe by choosing shallow-rooted, easily controlled ground covers such as periwinkle, hypericum, sedum, moneywort, plumbago, and creeping phlox. When you plant a ground cover, remember that until it spreads and fills out, it's a good idea to mulch the bare spaces between plants to discourage weeds. With ground covers like periwinkle that colonize by runners or rooting stems, lay mulch no more than 2 inches deep; a thicker layer will prevent the plant from spreading.

Once your ground cover becomes established, hand pulling or digging should take care of the few weeds that come up. If stubborn perennial weeds make it necessary for you to use a herbicide spray, protect the plants carefully, as shown on page 69.

A Temporary Ground Cover

A creative way to keep weeds from sprouting before the ornamentals in your garden have filled out and can shade the soil is to set out a temporary ground cover of fast-growing leaf lettuce, radicchio, or other early-season salad greens. By the time you've harvested and enjoyed the last of your crop, the perennials will have grown large enough to minimize late-appearing weeds.

Kudzu vine (Pueraria lobata)

Invasive Exotic Plants

Some plants that are harmless in their native habitats can be disastrous when introduced into a new area. There are many instances of plants from abroad that have become all-but-invincible weeds in the American landscape, overrunning gardens and escaping into the countryside because they've been freed from the factors such as climate or pests that had kept them within bounds. A well-known example is the kudzu vine *(right),* native to China and Japan, which can grow stems up to 60 feet long in a single season.

Unfortunately, many nurseries continue to market troublesome exotics without any cautionary advice, even though experience has shown how ill suited the plants are for certain parts of the United States, or even the entire country. Watch out for claims of so-called "miracle plants" touted for their rapid growth; the weedy Japanese rose, for example, has become naturalized in much of the country.

At right is a list of exotic plants that you should investigate carefully before planting. A reputable local nursery, horticulturists at nearby public gardens, or your Cooperative Extension Service agent are good sources of information about a plant's weed potential in your area.

Exotic Plants to Beware Of

Aegopodium podagraria
(goutweed, bishop's weed)
Ailanthus altissima
(tree-of-heaven)
Celastrus orbiculatus
(Oriental bittersweet)
Eichhornia crassipes
(water hyacinth)
Hedera helix
(English ivy)
Houttuynia cordata

(houttuynia)
Lathyrus latifolius
(perennial pea)
Lonicera japonica
(Japanese honeysuckle)
Lythrum salicaria
(purple loosestrife)
Morus spp.
(mulberry)
Phyllostachys spp.
(running bamboo)
Pueraria lobata
(kudzu vine)

Rosa multiflora
(Japanese rose)

Note: The abbreviation "spp." stands for the plural of "species"; where used in lists it means that many, but not all, of the species in a genus meet the criterion of the list.

Combating Weeds

Despite the best preventive measures, weeds will inevitably appear in a garden. Hand pulling, digging, hoeing, and mowing are, in environmental terms, the safest means of eliminating the pesky plants. If you keep an eye out for seedlings and attack them before they develop extensive root systems, weeding won't be an onerous, back-straining chore, and you can reserve herbicides for otherwise intractable problems.

The Best Time to Weed and How to Do It

Pulling or digging weeds is easiest when the soil is moist. The roots are more likely to come up intact, with fewer fragments left behind to resprout. If you have just watered the garden or if you've had heavy rain, however, wait a day or two before you weed to give the soil surface time to dry out. Walking on wet soil compacts it, and you run a greater risk of transferring disease organisms from one plant to another when foliage is wet.

For small weeds, you'll need a trowel and a hand fork. For dandelions and other weeds with taproots, use a dandelion weeder (also called an asparagus knife). There are short-handled and long-handled versions of this tool; if you get one with a long handle, you won't have to kneel to do your weeding. For larger weeds or weed-infested areas, useful tools include hoes and long-handled garden forks to dig the weeds, and lawn mowers and power trimmers with whipping filaments to cut off weeds before they go to seed.

Cultivating the garden with a hoe—that is, working the soil to destroy weeds—is an art that becomes easier with practice. Hold the hoe so that the blade, kept well sharpened as shown at right, cuts through the soil in a shallow arc and goes no deeper than about 1 to 1½ inches below the surface. Avoid turning over clods of soil, as this may expose buried weed seeds and encourage sprouting. And above all, hoe regularly. Annual weeds may be killed on your first pass, but perennial weeds may take repeated cutting. When confronted with a large weed, the garden fork is the best tool for the job. Thrust the tines deep into the

soil beside the weed, and rock the fork back and forth. When the roots are well loosened, lift them out and shake off the soil. Gather up and discard any root fragments.

A filament trimmer works well in tight spots a lawn mower can't reach, such as along the bottom of a fence, around a mailbox post, or along the edge of a bed or border. Be extremely careful when using this tool, lest you cut down a favorite ornamental by accident. And never use a filament trimmer on a weed growing against a tree trunk; the filament can cut the bark, opening a pathway for disease organisms and pests. Mowing larger expanses of weeds before they go to seed will keep them in check. This may not kill them but will prevent most of them from spreading further.

Proper disposal of weeds is vital, since they have remarkable powers of regeneration. Try to gather up everything—foliage, seed heads, bits of stems and roots. Compost weeds only if your pile heats up to 160°F at its center and is turned regularly. Otherwise, dispose of weeds in accordance with local ordinances for green trash.

Selecting and Maintaining a Hoe

When shopping for a new hoe, look for one with a blade and shaft, which fits onto the wooden handle, that are cast from a single piece of metal. If the two parts are cast separately and welded together, they are likely to break at the weld. Make sure the blade's bevel runs along the inner side, as shown below.

Keeping your hoe sharp greatly reduces the time and effort you spend on weeding. Use a bastard mill file to sharpen it; although a whetstone is faster, it produces an edge that is too fine and brittle and so is easily chipped. File across the bevel in one direction only, from the edge of the blade toward the shaft.

The Prudent Use of Herbicides

When mechanical methods of weed control fail despite your best efforts, you may decide the problem is severe enough to warrant using a herbicide. If you do, be sure to choose the right product and use it responsibly, for your own sake and for the sake of the environment.

Choosing a Herbicide. There are two basic types of herbicides for the home garden—preemergent herbicides, which prevent seeds from germinating, and postemergent herbicides, which kill plants that are actively growing. Postemergents work in one of two ways. One kind kill foliage on contact and are a good choice for annual weeds. The other kind, called systemics, are drawn into the plant's tissues, disrupting natural functions and destroying the plant from within. Use systemics on herbaceous perennial weeds or woody weeds; a contact herbicide may cause damage but fail to kill them.

The Importance of Labels. A herbicide label indicates the types of plants for which the product is formulated, when and how to apply it, and the period of effectiveness. Such information is vital. For instance, if you sow seeds in a bed recently treated with a preemergent herbicide that persists in the soil for months, the seeds won't germinate and you will have wasted your time and money. (See the guide to reading herbicide labels below).

Taking Site and Weather into Account. If a weed is growing among ornamental plants, you'll need to protect them from the chemical *(opposite)*. Don't use a granular herbicide on a slope, since it is likely to wash downhill and do unintended damage. Be especially cautious with herbicides near a vegetable garden, drainage field, wetland, stream, or garden pool. The chemicals can drift or wash onto other plants, kill fish, or pollute water supplies. You also need to exercise care in the root zone of a tree or shrub, which can be harmed if the roots absorb a systemic herbicide.

Never apply herbicide when it is rainy or windy; wait until a dry, calm day.

Heeding Precautions. While working with herbicides, don't drink, smoke, eat, touch your face, or use the bathroom. Keep pets and children away from treatment areas. (Follow this precaution if a neighbor's property is sprayed, whether by the homeowner or by a commercial service.)

Before you fill a sprayer with herbicide, test the nozzle's spray pattern with plain water so you'll know how to aim; for a ready-mixed spray product, spray newspaper to check the pattern. For liquids that are diluted before application, avoid disposal problems by preparing only a small quantity; if necessary, mix a second batch to finish the job. The herbicide should wet the foliage and stems well without dripping; using an excessive amount increases the risk of environmental damage.

To check a granular herbicide spreader's rate of application, mark out a measured area on a driveway or sidewalk and run the spreader over it. Sweep up and measure the herbicide and adjust the spreader if necessary.

When finished, rinse all equipment with three changes of water. Wash your clothes and take a shower. Store the herbicide in its original container, preferably under lock and key.

Reading a Herbicide Label

Herbicide labels, which are regulated by the Environmental Protection Agency, contain information that will help you choose the right product for the job and use it properly. For the best results, read the entire label and follow the instructions to the letter. A typical label includes the following kinds of information:

- **Uses.** Plants that the herbicide controls; may also list plants on which the herbicide should *not* be used. Areas where the product can safely be used; others where it should not be used, such as near vegetable gardens or water sources.
- **Cautions and Hazards.** Specific dangers to users and the environment; emergency procedures to follow in case of accidents with the herbicide.
- **Directions for Use.** Dilution formulas as necessary; amount to use per unit area; details of application, such as appropriate methods and equipment and weather conditions not conducive to safe use; clothing and safety wear, such as goggles for users.
- **Contents.** The product's chemical name and its chemical formula; the common name; percentages of ingredients in the formulation.
- **Storage and Disposal.** Specific directions for correct handling of the container and any unused contents.

Protecting Ornamentals from Herbicides

Many postemergent herbicides are so potent that even a small amount will kill any plant tissue it touches. Easy ways to protect ornamentals with newspaper and cardboard are shown below, along with a method for applying the herbicide to woody weeds with a brush instead of a spray. Even if you are spraying just a single weed, don't neglect to shield valuable plantings, and be sure to wear sturdy waterproof gloves. When the job is finished, leave the newspaper or cardboard in place until it is dry. Handle it carefully when you remove it; dropping it spray-side down on a plant could kill it. Be equally careful with a chemical-laden brush.

Since they are contaminated with herbicide, store shields or brushes in a secure, dry place. Be scrupulous about following any local regulations when you dispose of them.

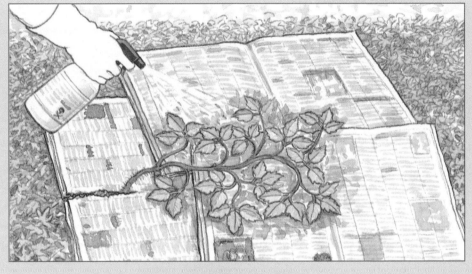

PROTECTING LOW-GROWING PLANTS
To spray a weed surrounded by low-growing plants, cover all the plants you want to save with three layers of newspaper and weight down their edges. Stretch a vining weed out across the paper; hold an erect weed against the paper with a stick. Spray the foliage and stems until they are barely wet. Remove the paper when it dries; remove the weed when it withers, in a week or so.

SPRAYING WEEDS NEAR LARGE ORNAMENTALS
Lay newspaper three sheets deep around the weed. Put a large piece of cardboard cut from a carton between the weed and the ornamental, then spray. Make sure the cardboard screen is tall enough to shield the ornamental's top growth.

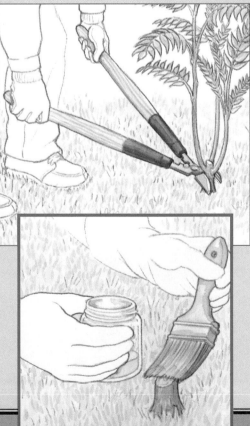

GETTING RID OF AN UNWANTED SHRUB OR SAPLING
1. Cut the plant's stems or trunk off as close to the ground as possible.

2. Choose a herbicide, such as a triclopyr, that is licensed for application with a brush. Pour a very small quantity into a glass container with a wide mouth. Dip a brush into the herbicide, barely moistening it to avoid drips, and brush the cut surfaces. When you're finished, wash the brush well in a bucket of soapy water. Empty the bucket into an outdoor drain or a hole dug in an unplanted spot in your garden. Reserve the brush for herbicide use only.

Guide to Common Garden Weeds

1. AMARANTHUS RETROFLEXUS (Redroot Pigweed)
This annual produces as many as 200,000 seeds per plant. Some western pigweeds break loose from their roots and roll like tumbleweeds across the land, scattering their seeds as they go. Control pigweed by uprooting young plants or cutting the stems off at ground level early.

2. AMBROSIA ARTEMISIIFOLIA (Common Ragweed)
Although its seed is a favorite food of birds, ragweed pollen is the bane of hay fever sufferers. The seeds need light for germination, so a layer of mulch is a good preventive. The shade cast by larger plants will also discourage growth. Mow or cut plants down before they go to seed.

3. BRASSICA KABER (Wild Mustard)
Introduced to the Americas as a seasoning, wild mustard has spread to become a pest species. Dig out or cut plants to the ground before they flower to prevent seeds from forming. The seeds are numerous and remain viable for years.

4. CENCHRUS SPECIES (Sandbur)
The spiny seeds of these annual or biennial grasses are painful for humans and animals alike and, if plentiful enough, can make a yard unusable. As the name implies, sandburs prefer sandy soils. When they invade a lawn, their blades are camouflaged and hard to see. Hand pull or dig, taking care not to touch the seeds.

5. CENTAUREA SOLSTITIALIS (Star Thistle)
Fast becoming a serious pest in California, Washington, and Oregon, star thistle usually grows as an annual but sometimes acts like a biennial. Cut it down before the flowers form; the bracts around the flowers bear sharp spines.

6. CERASTIUM ARVENSE (Field Chickweed)
This perennial weed grows in gardens throughout the United States. Destroy it with shallow cultivation before it can flower and go to seed. Gather up all the stems you've cut, since each one can form roots and develop into a new plant.

7. CHENOPODIUM ALBUM
(Lamb's-Quarters)

An annual that appears early in the season, lamb's-quarters grows in gardens all over the United States. Mulch beds to discourage germination, and pull out or cut down any plants that appear before they flower.

8. CIRSIUM ARVENSE
(Canada Thistle)

Despite its name, this perennial weed is a Eurasian native. A single plant can extend its root system over a large area, sending up numerous stems to create a massive stand. Cut stems down but don't hoe the plants, since root pieces start new plants. Treat persistent stands with a systemic herbicide.

9. CONVOLVULUS ARVENSIS
(Field Bindweed)

This perennial has a huge root system that makes an established plant almost impossible to get rid of. Avoid tilling near the roots, since severed pieces will produce new plants. Control bindweed with regular hoeing. Never allow plants to go to seed. Thick mulches help suppress germination.

10. CYPERUS ESCULENTUS
(Nut Sedge, Nut Grass)

Nut sedge, a perennial, is usually found in moist or poorly drained soil. Its roots send up new shoots whenever the main stem is cut. Dig up the roots or cut off new growth as it appears; this will eventually kill the plants. Use landscape fabric, not woodchips or other organic mulches, to block the foliage.

11. DATURA STRAMONIUM
(Jimson Weed)

All parts of this annual are poisonous, so remove it as soon as you see it. Most herbicides don't affect it; hoe it or hand pull it, wearing gloves to protect against the spines that form on the flower capsules. Because of its poisons, jimson weed should be disposed of according to local ordinances for green trash.

12. DIGITARIA ISCHAEMUM,
D. SANGUINALIS (Crab Grass)

Crab grass, an annual, is well known for its unsightly, sprawling presence in lawns, especially in places where the soil is compacted. Aerate the lawn and let turf grass grow taller than usual so it can shade out crab grass. In flower beds, dig it out before it sets seed; mulch to prevent seeds from sprouting.

Guide to Common Garden Weeds

13. ELEUSINE INDICA
(Goose Grass)

Goose grass is an annual that commonly takes hold in a sparse lawn growing in compacted, nutrient-poor soil. Aerating the soil, fertilizing, and mowing the lawn higher all help to control the weed. Remove plants from the lawn by hand before they flower, and mulch beds to discourage seedlings.

14. EUPHORBIA MACULATA
(Spotted Spurge)

This annual, which often takes root in pavement cracks, grows so low that the blades of a lawn mower pass above it, leaving the weed intact. Pull it out by the roots before it produces its tiny, pink-white flowers and thousands of seeds.

15. HORDEUM JUBATUM
(Foxtail Barley, Wild Barley)

Foxtail barley grows to about 2 feet and has sharp bristles, or awns, on its seed heads that pose a danger to animals, since they can lodge in the ears, mouth, and eyes or be drawn into the lungs. Mow this perennial low or dig it out. Don't compost it, since the awns may not decompose completely.

16. OXALIS STRICTA
(Wood Sorrel, Sourgrass)

This annual weed and its look-alike relative, the perennial O. corniculata, have seed capsules that explode and shoot seeds as far as 6 feet from the mother plant. Mulch to smother seed or dig out the taproots.

17. PHYTOLACCA AMERICANA
(Pokeweed)

Most pokeweed plants are seeded by birds, which relish poke berries. If you can dig up this perennial's long taproot, do so. Otherwise, keep the stems cut to the ground. This will eventually starve out the plant.

18. POLYGONUM PERFOLIATUM
(Mile-a-Minute)

A native of Asia, this fast-spreading vine thrives in many different habitats in the United States. If you discover no more than a plant or two in your garden, dig them out, taking care to avoid the sharp thorns. If the vines are more numerous, treat them with a systemic herbicide.

19. PORTULACA OLERACEA (Purslane)

Purslane lives on such a compressed schedule that there can be several generations of this drought-tolerant annual in a single growing season. Hoe regularly to destroy new plants, or pull them up by hand. Dispose of purslane promptly; left lying on the ground, it can go to seed or reroot weeks later.

20. RHUS DIVERSILOBA (Poison Oak)

This West Coast native produces an oil that causes a bad rash in most people. It may grow as a shrub or a vine. Dig out by the roots or use a systemic herbicide if the site allows, following the precautions recommended for poison ivy (right). Handle eastern poison oak (R. toxicodendron) in the same way.

21. RHUS RADICANS (Poison Ivy)

Another cause of nasty rashes, poison ivy varies in form but generally has leaves arranged in threes. Dig out the roots or use a systemic herbicide if other plants will not be harmed. Wear protective clothing, and wash it and tools well afterward. Never compost or burn poison oak or poison ivy; inhaling the smoke is dangerous.

22. ROSA MULTIFLORA (Multiflora Rose)

Once sold as a decorative hedge plant, this tough perennial spreads by seeds and rooting stems, and takes hold tenaciously in uncultivated areas. Dig small plants up by the roots. Cut larger ones to the ground and treat the stubs with a systemic herbicide.

23. RUBUS SPECIES (Wild Bramble)

In time, the thorny canes of brambles such as raspberry, dewberry, and blackberry create impassable thickets. If you get at a plant when it is still young, however, digging out as much of the roots as you can and cutting new shoots to the ground, it will eventually die. This may take more than a year.

24. TARAXACUM OFFICINALE (Dandelion)

Dandelion's long taproots nourish it through many a beheading, so for effective removal dig out the root. Try to get it all: New shoots spring from root pieces left in the ground.

CHAPTER FOUR

Growing a Healthy Lawn

The perfectly manicured lawn is an American institution. Nowhere else in the world do people devote so much effort to maintaining a large expanse of smooth green turf. But the lawn as we know it is a relatively recent invention; in its early days it was a low-maintenance item. Before the advent of the lawn mower in the 19th century, grass could be shorn only by sheep or scythes. Weeds, because they had to be removed by hand, were usually tolerated. Rubber watering hoses did not exist. Herbicides and pesticides weren't available, and the only fertilizer was manure.

Today, in an effort to cultivate an unblemished carpet of grass, many homeowners put higher concentrations of chemicals on their lawns than American farmers apply to their crops. And yet, all that pampering doesn't necessarily improve the lawn's appearance. Large chemical doses can kill useful creatures such as earthworms and beneficial insects and microorganisms. Frequent fertilizing and watering makes the grass grow faster, leading to more mowing, and close mowing encourages weeds, pests, and disease.

The good news is that you can create a lawn that is beautiful and at the same time undemanding. On the following pages you'll learn how to choose the right grass for your site's conditions, how to care properly for your soil as well as your grass to keep the plants green and vigorous, and how to spot trouble and manage it in ways that are not only effective but also kind to the environment.

THE NEW AMERICAN LAWN
This Baltimore lawn is healthy and lush without the aid of chemical fertilizers or pesticides. Contributing to its ease of care is its small size: Instead of turf, much of the yard is taken up by low-maintenance ornamental plantings.

Lawn-Care Basics and Preventive Measures

The most important component of a healthy lawn is the grass itself. Traditionally, American lawns have been made up of old varieties of grass that require considerable care to keep healthy. Recently, however, breeders have created improved grasses that need much less maintenance. A number are disease resistant, many are drought tolerant, and some even repel insects. Other varieties require less fertilizer and less frequent mowing.

Whether you are starting a new lawn, overseeding an existing one, or simply want to make the most of what's now growing on your property, it helps to know something about the different types of grasses that are available, what their particular needs are, and which variety best suits your area.

What Is Turf Grass?

Unlike most other plants, which grow from the tips, turf grasses grow from the base—a feature that endows a lawn with the durability to survive heavy foot traffic and frequent mowing. Turf grasses are usually classified by the season and the part of the country in which they grow best, as indicated in the chart at right. Perennial ryegrass and Kentucky bluegrass, for example, are known as cool-season grasses; they are planted primarily in northern areas and grow most vigorously in spring and fall. Warm-season grasses—Bermuda and St. Augustine, for instance—grow actively in the hot summer temperatures of the South before going dormant in the fall and turning brown.

Turf grasses are also classified by their growth habits, which can be either creeping or bunching. Creeping varieties—also known as sod-forming—spread relatively quickly by sending out horizontal shoots, called stolons when above ground and rhizomes when underneath the soil. Bunching grasses send up blades, called tillers, from a single crown, forming clumps and spreading slowly. If you live in the North, it's best to mix creeping and bunching grasses or two bunching varieties rather than plant a single species. Combining cool-season species with different habits makes your lawn hardier and more resistant to stress *(box, page 78)*. Warm-season grasses don't mix well, however, because they grow more aggressively; southern lawns are usually a single species.

GRASSES		CHARACTERISTICS				
		Texture & Appearance	Growth Habit	Drought Tolerance	Heat Tolerance	
Cool Season	**Bent grass**	Very fine bladed; bright green	Bunching	Very low	Low	
	Kentucky bluegrass	Medium- to fine-bladed; medium to dark green	Creeping, rhizomes	Moderate	Moderate	
	Fine fescue	Very fine bladed; medium to deep green	Bunching or creeping, rhizomes	Moderate to high	Moderate	
	Tall fescue	Medium- to coarse-bladed; light to medium green	Bunching	High	High	
	Perennial ryegrass	Medium-bladed; shiny; medium to dark green	Bunching	Moderate to low	Moderate to low	
Warm Season	**Bahia grass**	Tough, coarse-bladed; light green	Creeping, rhizomes	High	High	
	Bermuda grass	Fine- to medium-bladed; medium to dark green	Creeping, rhizomes and stolons	High	High	
	Blue grama grass	Medium-bladed; grayish green	Bunching	Very high	High	
	Buffalo grass	Fine-bladed; light green to grayish green	Creeping, stolons	Very high	High	
	Centipede grass	Medium- to coarse-bladed; light green	Creeping, stolons	Moderate	High	
	St. Augustine grass	Coarse-bladed; bluish green to medium green	Creeping, stolons	Moderate	High	
	Zoysia	Coarse- to medium-bladed; medium green	Creeping, rhizomes and stolons	Moderate to high	High	

Know Your Turf Grass

The chart below describes 12 common lawn grasses—five cool-season varieties, which thrive in spring and fall, and seven warm-season grasses, which perform best in summer. The growing zones recommended for each grass appear on the map at right. At zone borders, you can grow both cool- and warm-season grasses.

	Cold Tolerance	Light Requirements	Propagation & Rate of Establishment	Lateral & Top Growth Rate	Soil Requirements	Fertilizer Needs	Wear Tolerance	Thatching Potential	Disease Susceptibility	Zones
	Very high; thrives in cool, humid climates	Full sun; tolerates some light shade	Seed (germinates 5-12 days); moderate to slow	Fast; mow often to ¾ inch	Moist, fertile; compaction-intolerant; pH 4.5-6.7	High; 4-6 lbs. N per 1,000 sq. ft. per year	Moderate to low	High	Very high	A, northern parts of C
	High	Full sun; some cultivars tolerate some shade	Seed (germinates 14-21 days), sod; moderate to slow	Moderate	Moist, fertile, well-drained; compaction-tolerant; pH 6 to 7	Moderate to high; 3-5 lbs. N per 1,000 sq. ft. per year	Moderate to high	Moderate to high	Moderate	A, B, C
	High	Full sun to medium shade	Seed (germinates 10-14 days); moderate	Moderate	Silt, clay; tolerates sandy, infertile; compaction-intolerant; pH 5.5-6.5	Low; 0-2 lbs. N per 1,000 sq. ft. per year	Low	High	Moderate to high	A, B, C
	Moderate	Full sun to medium shade	Seed (germinates 7-10 days) or sod; moderate	Very fast top growth	Silt, clay; tolerates sand, heavy clay, compaction; pH 4.7-8.5	Low to moderate; 2-4 lbs. N per 1,000 sq. ft. per year	Moderate	Low	Moderate	A, B, C, western parts of D
	Moderate	Full sun to light shade	Seed (germinates 5-7 days); very fast	Fast	Fertile; tolerates moderately compacted; pH 6-7	High; 4-5 lbs. N per 1,000 sq. ft. per year	High	Low	High	Northern parts of D and E, southern parts of B and C
	Low	Full sun to part shade	Seed (germinates 21-28 days); moderate to slow	Slow	Tolerates sand to clay, infertile, coastal areas; pH 6.5-7.5	Moderate; 2-4 lbs. N per 1,000 sq. ft. per year	Moderate to low	Low	Low	F, southern parts of E
	Moderate to low	Full sun	Seed (germinates 10-14 days), sod, sprigs, plugs; all fast	Fast; invasive	Sand, silt; tolerates clay, compacted; pH 5.5-7.5	Moderate to high; 3-6 lbs. N per 1,000 sq. ft. per year	High	High	Moderate	D, E, F
	High	Full sun	Seed (germinates 15-30 days); moderate to fast	Moderate	Tolerates all conditions but acidity and compaction; pH 7-8	Very low; 0-1 lb. N per 1,000 sq. ft. per year	Moderate to low	Low	Low	B, D, western parts of C and E
	Moderate to high	Full sun; some hybrid cultivars tolerate light shade	Seed, sod, plugs; slow to moderate from seed, fast from plugs	Fast; invasive	Tolerates silt, clay, sand; alkaline, compacted; pH 6-7.5	Low; 0-2 lbs. N per 1,000 sq. ft. per year	Moderate to low	Low	Moderate	B, D
	Moderate to low	Full sun to part shade	Seed (germinates 14-20 days), sod, sprigs, plugs; slow to moderate	Slow	High tolerance; prefers infertile, acid; salt-intolerant	Low; 0-2 lbs. N per 1,000 sq. ft. per year; may need iron	Moderate to low	Moderate; avoid overfertilizing	Low	F, southern parts of E
	Very low	Full sun to part shade	Sprigs, plugs, sod; all fast	Fast	Well-drained, fertile, sandy; tolerates salt, compaction; pH 6-7.5	Moderate to high; 3-5 lbs. N per 1,000 sq. ft. per year	Moderate to low	High	Moderate	D and F, southern parts of E
	Moderate to high	Full sun to part shade	Sprigs, plugs, sod; slow	Slow lateral; moderate top	High tolerance; prefers well-drained, fine-textured; pH 5-7	Low; 0-3 lbs. N per 1,000 sq. ft. per year	Very high	Moderate; high if too much nitrogen	Low	D, E, F

Growth Habits

Creeping grasses spread by sending out lateral shoots: either aboveground stolons, underground rhizomes, or both. The thick, spreading turf they create is particularly good at crowding out weeds, although it is more prone to thatching than is a bunch-ing-grass turf. Bunching grasses grow in clumps and spread by means of new upright shoots called tillers. These grasses create a dense, wear-resistant turf. In northern zones, mixing the two types makes for an especially resilient lawn.

Bunching

Creeping with stolons

Creeping with rhizomes

Different species of grass vary in their appearance by blade width and color. In the American sensibility, the narrower the blade and the deeper the green, the more elegant the lawn. But the best lawns combine good looks with good growth characteristics. In the North, for example, Kentucky bluegrass makes a very attractive, cold-hardy lawn, but it needs full sun and much tending. Tall fescue is not as fine textured in appearance, but it requires much less fertilizer and resists weeds. A mixture of the two would provide the advantages of both. In a single-species southern lawn, zoysia may be the best choice for areas that experience frequent drought and other difficult weather conditions.

Soil: A Healthy Lawn's Foundation

Turf grass grows best in loamy soil that is well drained, slightly acidic, and rich in organic matter. A soil test will reveal your soil's pH level, the available nutrients, the presence of organic matter, and the soil's texture—determined by the proportions of sand, silt, and clay particles it contains. The chart opposite, which lists the characteristics of different soil types, will help you plan a maintenance strategy for your lawn.

Regardless of soil or turf-grass type, the ground under any established lawn becomes dense and hard over the years, with the result that air, water, and fertilizer cannot reach the plants' roots. Adding to the problem are excessive applications of chemicals, which can kill the beneficial microorganisms that break down the soil and produce humus and earthworms, which are natural soil aerators.

You can restore health to your lawn by aerating the soil yourself. This means removing small soil plugs—about a half-inch in diameter and 3 inches deep—at regularly spaced intervals. If your lawn is small, you can use an aerating fork—a foot-powered tool with hollow tines that pulls up soil plugs. For larger areas, you may want to rent an aerating machine from your local garden center.

Aerate your lawn once a year, while the turf is actively growing, but not in hot weather. And be sure the soil is moist before you begin. Then, after you've removed the soil plugs, spread what is called a top dressing over the lawn and into the holes. The type of top dressing you use will vary according to your soil type. For a fast-draining sandy soil, spread half an inch to an inch of finely screened shredded compost. This will not only help improve the soil's water-holding capacity over time, it will also replenish vital nutrients. For clay soils, which are often compacted and drain poorly, top-dress with sand or compost, or a mixture of both.

Most turf grasses grow best in soil with a slightly acid pH of 6 to 6.8. If your soil tests too acidic, you can correct it—or raise the pH—by adding lime. For an alkaline soil, low-

How Your Soil Affects Your Grass

Soil is the foundation of a lawn's health. The chart at right describes the characteristics of different soil types and will help you determine what amendments you need to incorporate into your soil as part of your lawn's regular maintenance program. If your soil is too acidic or too alkaline, the chart at lower right will guide you in correcting it.

Plant roots are most able to take up essential nutrients in soil that is slightly acidic (pH 6 to 6.8); an improper pH not only impairs your lawn's capacity to extract nourishment, it also leaves it open to any number of problems. Don't make the recommended adjustments all at once, though; instead, gradually apply a fraction of the needed lime or elemental sulfur every 3 to 6 months, during any season and under any condition except on top of snow. Continue adjusting the soil—no more than 1 point in a year—until it has reached the right pH.

SOIL	CHARACTERISTICS						
	Texture	Drainage	Water Retention	Nutrient Retention	Organic Amendment Needs	Spring Warm-Up Rate	Compaction Potential
CLAYEY	Heavy, sticky when wet	Very slow	High	Very high	Compost, peat moss or humus, organic matter; sand for drainage	Slow	High
SILTY	Silty or soapy	Slow	High	Moderate	Well rotted compost or manure, peat humus	Moderate	High
SANDY	Light, dry, gritty	Fast	Low; needs frequent watering	Low; needs frequent fertilizing	Organic matter and fertilizer; peat humus and compost	Fast	Low
LOAMY	Crumbly	Moderate	Moderate to high	Moderate to high	Compost, peat humus, any organic matter	Moderate	Moderate

ADJUSTING YOUR pH LEVEL

To Raise pH					To Lower pH				
Total lbs. of lime (calcium carbonate) needed per 1,000 sq. ft. to raise pH to 6.5					Total lbs. of elemental sulfur needed per 1,000 sq. ft. to lower pH to 6.5				
Soil pH	Clayey	Silty	Sandy	Loamy	Soil pH	Clayey	Silty	Sandy	Loamy
4.5	195	125	100	135	8.5	50	40	35	40
5.0	155	90	75	105	8.0	40	30	25	30
5.5	110	65	50	80	7.5	25	20	15	20
6.0	55	35	25	40					

er the pH with additions of elemental sulfur. Refer to the pH chart above to determine how to adjust your soil's pH.

Fertilizing the Lawn

Turf grass needs a slow and constant supply of nutrients, especially the major elements nitrogen, phosphorus, and potassium. Nitrogen is the most important for steady and vigorous growth of the grass. If plants receive too little, they will look light green or yellow and be vulnerable to pests and diseases. Too much nitrogen weakens the grass, and that too invites trouble. Roots aren't forced to dig deep into the soil for nutrients, and the lawn then becomes dependent on regular doses of fertiliz-

er. Also, because they are stimulated to grow quickly, overfertilized lawns need frequent mowing; this continually stresses the grass.

Lawn fertilizers are either synthetic or natural, or a combination of the two. Synthetics dissolve relatively quickly in the soil, especially the so-called fast-release types. As their name suggests, they work fast but disappear fast as well, subjecting the grass to stressful peaks and valleys of nutrient availability. They should be used only if your lawn needs an immediate dose of nutrients. Slow-release synthetics discharge their nutrients gradually, as do natural fertilizers. Although synthetics are cheaper, natural fertilizers have the additional benefit of adding bulk to the soil in the form of organic matter. There are many blended natural fertilizers on the market,

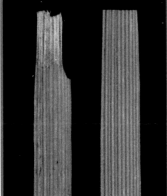

THE IMPORTANCE OF SHARP MOWER BLADES
A lawn mower with dull blades can damage grass tips, causing yellowing and ragged edges (above, left) that are entry points for disease. By contrast, a sharp mower blade makes a clean, straight cut that keeps grass healthy and gives the lawn a trim look (above, right).

THE PROPER MOWING HEIGHT
When grass is continually cut short, root growth slows and may stop entirely (far left). But when it is mowed at the higher end of its preferred range, the plant suffers less shock, allowing the roots to branch and grow deep to make a stronger plant (near left).

which may contain combinations of dried poultry manure, blood meal, cottonseed meal, alfalfa meal, and seaweed. Commercial mixtures of organic and slow-release synthetic fertilizers also work well.

If you live in the northern regions of the United States, you need fertilize only once in early fall and again 6 to 8 weeks later, before the grass goes dormant. Southern lawns require one to three applications a year, depending on the species of grass; they need fertilizing most in late spring and summer. The chart on pages 76-77 lists the needs for each turf species.

If you are applying dry or granular fertilizer to a large lawn, you can quickly cover a lot of ground with a broadcast spreader, which throws out the pellets in 6- to 8-foot swaths. Another device, the drop spreader—which drops the fertilizer in a 2-foot-wide path—can be calibrated to spread the amount recommended on the fertilizer bag. To ensure thorough coverage, first apply half of the recommended amount over the entire lawn, then make a pass in a perpendicular direction to spread the rest. Apply a liquid fertilizer with a hose-end sprayer or with a lawn sprinkler that has been outfitted with a siphon proportioner. This device will siphon fertilizer from a container and direct it to the sprinkler.

How and When to Mow

A lawn needs mowing to stay healthy, not only to keep it neat. Cutting off older growth at the top of the grass plant stimulates root growth and encourages new top growth that fills in bare spots and makes the lawn thicker and more cushiony. There is a right way and a wrong way to mow, however, and improper mowing can actually damage your lawn. Whenever the tips of the grass plants are cut, the roots are weakened to some degree, and if more than 40 percent of the blades' length is removed, root growth is drastically slowed. A rule of thumb is to never remove more than a third of the grass blade at any one time. If the grass gets too tall, don't try to cut it back to its proper height all at once. First, give it a light cut, then let it recover for a few days before cutting again. Continue to alternate cutting with periods of rest until the grass is the proper height. (See the chart opposite for correct mowing heights.)

Tailor your cutting schedule to conform to the growth of the lawn, mowing often when the grass is growing most vigorously and less frequently as growth slows. While you are cutting, make sure to overlap the previous swath by about one-third with each pass so as not to miss any grass blades. Grass blades tend to lean in the direction the mower travels, so vary your pattern every three or four times you mow; this helps the grass stand upright and also keeps ruts from forming in the lawn.

When it comes to lawn mowers, reel mowers, either manual or powered, make the cleanest—and therefore the kindest—cuts. However, they have been eclipsed over the years by the rotary power mower, which is faster and allows you to mow the grass higher. Mulching mowers offer the bonus of chopping up grass clippings and forcing them down to the soil line, thus returning nutrients to the soil. Clippings from any mower, though, will benefit the grass if left in place, although they won't break down quite as fast as those at soil level. Leaving the clippings also eliminates the task of raking and bagging the shorn grass. Do remove the clippings from the first spring mow and the last fall mow, however, to discourage disease. And regardless of what type of mower you use, keep the blades sharp by taking it to a hardware store or other service shop at least once a season.

Watering the Right Way

During its active growing season, turf grass needs 1 to 2 inches of water a week. Much of that may come from rainfall, but in many parts of the country you'll have to provide the water yourself. When lawns are dry, they lose their resiliency: They wilt and are slow to spring back when you walk on them. Also, the blades may look dull and take on a blue tint.

Watering correctly is key. When a lawn is overwatered, the grass blades grow more rapidly than the roots, weakening the whole plant. Not only will you have to mow such a lawn more often, but a constantly moist turf encourages weeds and—worse—fungal diseases. On the other hand, watering too lightly results in shallow root growth. Without adequate root length and branching to anchor the plant and tap into stores of water and nutrients deeper in the soil, the grass has a hard time combating drought, disease, and pests.

The best way to water is slowly and deeply, allowing the fluid to penetrate 6 to 8 inches into the soil. In clay soil, it may take hours for an inch of water to percolate that deeply. In this case it's best to water in cycles of perhaps 10 minutes on and 50 minutes off to allow the soil to take up the water.

GRASSES		MOWING HEIGHTS		
		Cool Weather	Hot Weather	Last Mow
COOL SEASON	BENT GRASS	½" - ¾"	¾" - 1"	½" - ¾"
	KENTUCKY BLUEGRASS	2" - 2½"	3"	2"
	FINE FESCUE	1½" - 2"	2"- 2½"	1½"- 2"
	TALL FESCUE	2" - 2½"	2½"- 4"	2½"
	PERENNIAL RYEGRASS	1½" - 2"	2"- 2½"	1½"- 2"
WARM SEASON	BAHIA GRASS	2" - 3"	3" - 3½"	2½" - 3"
	BERMUDA GRASS	½" - 1½"	¾"- 3"	¾"- 1"
	BLUE GRAMA GRASS	2" - 4"	3" - 4"	2"- 3"
	BUFFALO GRASS	2" - 5"	2" - 5"	2" - 4"
	CENTIPEDE GRASS	1" - 2"	1½" - 2"	1½" - 2"
	ST. AUGUSTINE GRASS	2"- 3"	3"- 3½"	2½"
	ZOYSIA	½ - 1½"	1" - 2"	1" - 1½"

Controlling Thatch

Every lawn eventually accumulates a layer of dead but undecomposed plant material on the soil surface. In a natural system, this material—fibrous roots, stolons, rhizomes, and clippings—is quickly broken down by soil microorganisms. Applications of chemicals slow that process. And some grasses are just naturally thatch builders. While a layer of thatch less than half an inch thick will do no harm, anything more not only blocks the flow of water, air, and nutrients into the soil but also provides a home for pests and diseases. Warm-season lawns should be dethatched once or twice a year, in spring or fall, and cool-season grasses once every 3 years in late spring or summer. If your lawn is small, you can use a metal thatch rake to scratch the matted plant material out. For very large lawns, you may want to rent a gasoline-powered dethatcher. Minimizing your use of chemicals and aerating the lawn will help keep thatch under control.

Identifying and Solving Lawn Problems

TIPS FROM THE PROS

Overseeding for a Better Lawn

You don't have to go to the trouble of digging up your entire lawn and starting over to grow any of the new disease- and insect-resistant or low-maintenance grasses that are now on the market. A technique called overseeding allows you to sow them right over your existing turf. Because the new varieties are more vigorous than the older ones, they will eventually take over the lawn.

You'll get the best results if you overseed at a time when the lawn is not under stress from excessive heat or drought. To start, mow your existing grass to about half the normal mowing height. Then rough up the turf with a garden rake to expose a good deal of soil. Select a seed that is appropriate for your local conditions (consult the chart of turf grasses on pages 76-77), and sow it at one and one-half times the rate that is recommended on the package. Although seed can be sown by hand, for complete, even coverage it's best to use a drop spreader or a broadcast spreader.

Rake the area again, then water well and keep it moist until the new grass begins to sprout. Stay off the area during this period, and don't mow for a few weeks—until the new grass reaches its maximum recommended height, between 2 and 3 inches.

Despite care and attention, any number of things still can go wrong with your lawn, especially if it hasn't been converted to a low-maintenance system. Before assuming that a pest or disease is behind a problem, consider whether environmental or cultural conditions might be responsible. Such problems can often be easily fixed, and doing so promptly may prevent the invasion of pests or diseases.

Recognizing Common Problems

Browning of the grass, though it may be a sign of possible infestation or infection, may also be a symptom of something less troublesome, such as chemical spills, dog-urine damage, or nutrient deficiency (chart, below). Other problems have their own telltale signs. If the lawn appears yellow or grayish, for example, you've probably mowed it with a dull blade. Let it grow out, then mow lightly with a blade that is sharp. Compacted, moist, shady areas often provide the perfect environment for algae, which may appear as a green to black slimy scum on the soil and

ENVIRONMENTAL CAUSES OF DISCOLORED GRASS
Brown spots on the lawn aren't always caused by pests or diseases. The chart at right lists five common environmental causes of such problems—including burns from fertilizer and herbicide spills (above)—and ways you can recognize and treat them.

ENVIRONMENTAL CAUSES OF BROWN SPOTS AND HOW TO FIX THEM

Damage	Problem	Cause	Solution
Salt	Grass slowly turns brown and dies, especially in lowest areas; soil may have white or dark brown crust.	Salt buildup from natural level in soil, or residue from excess fertilizer. Possibly poor drainage.	If drainage is good, water heavily. Aerate soil, add sand. Fill in low spots. Fertilize in correct amounts.
Fertilizer Burn	Patches, stripes, or curves of dead grass that do not spread or enlarge; appear 2-5 days after fertilizing.	High level of nitrogen due to misuse of fast-release synthetic fertilizer, especially in warm weather.	Water thoroughly after fertilizing. Replace soil under spots that are bare after 3-4 weeks and replant.
Dog Urine	Circles of dead or brown grass, surrounded by healthy green grass; may appear as dark green patches.	Nitrogen and salts in dog urine burn or kill grass; especially damaging in hot, dry weather.	Water immediately. If grass dies, allow grass to fill in area, dig up and reseed, or patch with sod.
Drought/Heat	Grass wilts; becomes dull, bluish, or grayish green to brown. Footprints show. Areas thin out.	Symptoms appear first in hottest and driest areas: along sidewalks, driveways, sunny and sandy areas.	Mow cool-season grasses ½" higher. Water; check soil moisture. Overseed with drought-tolerant grass.
Nutrient Deficiencies	Lawn turns slightly yellow, purplish, or reddish brown; grows slowly; leaf tops wither, grass thins.	Lawn needs to be fertilized, or improper soil pH is keeping grass from taking up nutrients.	Have soil tested for nutrient levels; correct with recommended fertilizer. Adjust pH, if necessary.

grass. Spray the area with copper sulfate, aerate the soil, and do what you can to improve drainage and decrease shade. A low pH level may exacerbate the problem; check to be sure your soil pH is in the 6 to 6.8 range.

Moss also settles in shady, infertile, acidic soils. Rake it up and, if necessary, apply iron sulfate at a dose of 3 tablespoons per 1 to 2 gallons of water to cover 1,000 square feet of turf. Afterward, correct your soil by bringing it to the proper pH level and adding the right amount of organic fertilizer to make sure the moss doesn't return. Aerating and improving drainage will also help.

Controlling Weeds

A lawn need not be entirely weed free to be healthy and attractive, so it's up to you to decide how many uninvited guests you'll tolerate. The stricter you are about weeds, the more time and money you'll have to spend to thwart them—and the more likely you'll be to resort to chemical herbicides.

You can rid your lawn of most weeds—and prevent them too—in ways both cultural and mechanical. Turf that is growing vigorously and steadily will on its own crowd out the lion's share of weeds. To that end, light fertilizing at the right time strengthens the grass and allows it to beat out the competition. And don't forget that weeds can be a sign that something else is wrong. Certain weeds

WEEDS THAT MAY SIGNIFY SOIL PROBLEMS
Weeds in a lawn can sometimes serve as warnings of underlying trouble. The perennial weed curly dock (top), for example, with its red-tinged leaves and seeds, is a sign of excessive moisture. Annual bluegrass (bottom), an unwelcome Kentucky bluegrass relative, thrives in compacted, moist soils, especially when the turf is mowed too closely. Good weed control includes correcting those conditions to prevent recurrence.

WEEDS THAT WARN OF TROUBLE	
Name of Weed	**Conditions Indicated**
Annual bluegrass	Compaction; high moisture; shade; infertile soil; low mowing
Black medic	Dry, infertile soil; drought
*Common chickweed	Compaction; thinning turf, excessive moisture; highly fertile or acid soil; moist shade
Clover	Thinning turf; low fertility; drought conditions; compaction
*Crab grass	Thinning turf; frequent, light, shallow watering; low mowing; compaction; low fertility; poor drainage; drought
Curly dock	Poor drainage; excess moisture; turf stressed by hot, dry weather
*Dandelion	Thinning grass; overwatering; low mowing; low fertility; drought; highly opportunistic
*Goose grass	Compaction; high moisture; poor drainage; low mowing; frequent or light watering; highly fertile soil
Ground ivy	Shade; moist soil; poor drainage; highly fertile soil
Henbit	Excessive moisture; highly fertile soil; thinning or new turf
Lespedeza	Dry, infertile, acid soil; drought
Plantain	Dense soil; moisture; low fertility; low mowing
Prostrate knotweed	Compaction, especially in heavily traveled areas; drought; thinning turf
Red sorrel	Low pH (under 5); infertile soil; poor drainage
*Spurge	Sand or gravel soils; dry soil; drought stress; thin, undernourished, infertile turf, also found on well-maintained lawns subject to low mowing
Wild garlic	Thinning turf; tolerates almost any environment in cool seasons, including heavy, wet soil or sandy soil with low humus
Wild onion	Thinning turf; tolerates almost any environment in spring and fall
Wild violet	Shade with cool, moist soil; poor drainage
Wood sorrel	Drought; highly opportunistic in many situations

*See also the weed gallery, pages 70-73.

VISIBLE SIGNS OF TWO COMMON PESTS
When Japanese beetle larvae feed below ground on grass roots, the lawn turns patchy and brown as grass plants die (top). The turf eventually becomes loose and can be lifted from the soil. Mole crickets (above) tunnel about an inch below the surface of the ground, feeding on roots and leaving raised mounds of soil and wilted brown grass.

thrive in compacted soil, for example, while others like wet conditions; the chart on page 83 describes specific weeds and the environmental problems they may indicate.

Lawn weeds may be annual or perennial, broadleaf or grassy, and warm or cool season. Identifying them and understanding their habits can help to control them *(pages 70-73)*. For example, if you cut and remove annual weeds such as crab grass before they set seed, you'll go a long way toward eradicating them. However, perennial weeds, such as dandelion, must be removed root and all to prevent them from spreading. Low-growing, spreading lawn weeds may be discouraged by continued high mowing of the grass.

Sometimes the best way to control lawn weeds is with plain old elbow grease. There are many effective weed knives, diggers, pullers, and poppers on the market. Taking them in hand for an hour or so every week will reduce your weed population dramatically. Pulling weeds can leave bare spots in your lawn, however, and new weeds will move in unless you take steps to foil them. After digging weeds up, fill in any spots with a bit of topsoil, put down some grass seed, and scratch the seeds into the soil with a rake.

If your lawn is more than 25 percent weeds, pulling and cutting won't do the trick. Such a degree of infestation derives from faulty maintenance practices such as improper fertilizing,

or an underlying problem such as the wrong kind of grass, too much shade, or poor soil. Start by overseeding your lawn with an improved grass variety, and consider what maintenance habits or environmental conditions might be allowing weeds to take hold.

As a last resort, you can try a selective herbicide, but be aware that while it may remove the weeds, it won't solve the problem that may be inviting them. In the worst cases, you might consider starting over entirely by removing the lawn, correcting the soil, and replanting with a better turf variety.

The Problem of Pests

Pests are less likely to attack a healthy lawn, but they may show up occasionally, especially when their natural enemies aren't present or when the grass is stressed by harsh weather. Just as with weeds, pests sometimes signal environmental problems, such as poor soil or improper mowing or fertilizing.

The damage often appears as discolored grass or brown and dying patches. You can usually get rid of the pest by using one of several natural insecticides, such as *Bacillus thuringiensis* (Bt). Check with your local Cooperative Extension Service for the right time to apply insecticides, and follow all package directions. Chemical pesticides should be used very carefully and only as a last resort.

Some of the pests most commonly found in lawns are described below:

- Armyworms are serious pests of warm-season grasses, especially Bermuda grass, although they can attack any species. The caterpillars are 1 to 2 inches long, striped, and yellow to brownish green; fall armyworms have an inverted Y on their heads. Active in the heat of summer, they chew grass blades to skeletons, leaving patches of ragged grass. Bt will control them.
- The white grubs of Japanese and other beetles attack the roots of many grasses, including Kentucky bluegrass, bent grass, and fescues. As the grubs feed, the turf loosens from the soil and turns brown. Many grubs can be controlled with neem and beneficial nematodes. Milky spore disease will control Japanese beetle grubs. For complete descriptions of the damage, detection, and control of various species of beetle grubs, see

pages 101-124 of the encyclopedia at the back of the book.

- Adult billbugs are dark, snouted beetles that eat grass leaves and burrow in stems; root-eating grubs are legless and white with yellowish to reddish brown heads. They leave behind yellow or brown patches of turf that can be pulled up from the soil. Early-summer treatment with beneficial nematodes will control these pests.
- Chinch bugs feed on many grass varieties from early spring to late autumn, causing turf to yellow and die in patches. Young nymphs—bright red with a white stripe—cause most of the damage. They prefer hot, sunny lawns during dry weather. See page 104 of the encyclopedia for a comprehensive list of control methods.
- Cutworms are minor pests unless they build up to large populations. The caterpillars are usually smooth and can be brownish, grayish white, or green tinged. They feed at night from spring through summer on grass stems and leaves. Control them with neem.
- Greenbugs are light green aphids that feed on grass blades—especially underwatered or overfertilized Kentucky bluegrass—in early summer and late fall, turning affected areas a rusty color. They can be controlled with insecticidal soap.
- Mites are minute spider relatives that usually attack Bermuda grass or Kentucky bluegrass, sucking the juice out of the blades and turning them yellow. Most active during hot, dry weather, mites can be controlled with insecticidal soap.
- Mole crickets—winged relatives of the grasshopper that are brown and 1½ inches long—cause problems in all types of southern lawns from April to October. They feed on grass roots as they tunnel beneath the lawn, causing the soil to dry out. Control them with *Nosema locustae* or beneficial nematodes.
- Sod webworms attack Kentucky bluegrass, bent grass, fescues, and zoysia. The light brown, spotted caterpillars feed at night in the thatch layer from late spring through summer. For more information on detecting and controlling sod webworms, see page 119 of the encyclopedia.

A surface examination of your lawn may reveal adult or larval insects on the grass, but certain pests—such as sod webworms, cut-

Pest-Resistant Grasses

These cultivated endophytic turf grasses resist attack from many common lawn pests. The percentages given indicate the proportion of the turf that will not be affected if a pest attempts to invade your lawn. Because endophytes are living organisms in the grass seed, the seed must be handled carefully. Be sure to buy fresh seed—the maximum shelf life is 2 years—and store it at 50° to 60° F.

PERENNIAL RYEGRASS
High Endophyte Level
(80-100%):
   'Commander'
   'Pennant'
   'Pinnacle'
   'Repell'
   'Saturn'
   'Saville'

Moderately High Endophyte Level
(60-80%):
   'Accolade'
   'Citation II'
   'Cowboy'
   'Omega II'
   'Stallion'

Moderate Endophyte Level
(30-60%):
   'Caliente'
   'Delray'
   'Palmer'
   'Premier'
   'Vintage'

TALL FESCUE
High Endophyte Level
(80-100%):
   'Bonsai'
   'Shenandoah'
   'SR 8200'

Moderate Endophyte Level
(30-60%):
   'Phoenix'
   'Pixie'

FINE FESCUE
High Endophyte Level
(80-100%):
   'Aurora' with endophytes
   'Discovery'
   'Jamestown II'
   'Reliant' with endophytes
   'Shadow' with endophytes
   'SR 5000'

worms, and chinch bugs—are hard to spot because they live in thatch or at the soil surface. You can force them into the open by thoroughly drenching the soil with a solution containing 2 to 3 tablespoons of liquid dish detergent to every gallon of water.

Other pests, such as beetle grubs, live below the soil surface. If you can roll up the turf like a carpet, you will probably see grubs at work. If the turf doesn't roll but you suspect underground pests, check by digging up a few 1-foot-square, 2-inch-thick slabs of sod and searching the soil. Afterward, replace and thoroughly water the sod, and it will regrow.

If your lawn suffers from chronic problems, consider overseeding with an insect-resistant grass. Many new varieties of perennial ryegrass, tall fescue, and fine fescue resist damage from pests such as sod webworms, armyworms, cutworms, billbug larvae, chinch bugs, and greenbugs. Known as endophytic grasses, they host a beneficial fungus in their leaf and stem tissue that repels or kills these common lawn insects. See the list above for recommendations.

Diseases of Turf Grass

Turf diseases are often a side effect of high-maintenance lawn programs. High temperatures and humidity, inadequate air circulation, poor soil, and too much shade also increase the chance that disease will strike your lawn, especially if your grass variety does not tolerate these conditions.

Most diseases are caused by fungi that live in the soil and the thatch layer. Many are choosy about climate and temperature and will appear only under the right circumstances. Also, some diseases are species specific, targeting only particular types of grass. When disease does strike, diagnosis can be difficult. General symptoms range from striped blades to brown patches of turf to a water-soaked appearance. The most reliable way to identify a disease is to send samples of your turf and soil to your local Cooperative Extension Service or a university's plant pathology lab.

1. BROWN PATCH (Rhizoctonia solani)
This summertime disease strikes most turf grasses at some point. Leaves appear dark and water-soaked, then become dry and brown, creating irregular or circular patches as large as several feet across. It occurs primarily when temperatures and humidity are high; excessive nitrogen exacerbates the problem. Avoid heavy fertilizing, and don't overwater. Raise the mowing height, and apply the beneficial microorganism Trichoderma, neem, fungicidal soap, or garlic oil.

**3. FAIRY RINGS
(Marasmius oreades)**
This disease occurs most often in areas of high rainfall. Dark green circles or arcs of grass appear in spring; later, mushrooms may sprout. Deprived of water and nutrients, the grass within the ring dies. Fertilize with nitrogen, aerate the rings, keep the area watered, and mow frequently. There are no chemical controls. Complete eradication may mean replacing the turf and soil.

**2. DOLLARSPOT
(Sclerotinia homoeocarpa)**
Most grass species are susceptible to this disease, which causes straw-colored spots that range from the size of a silver dollar to 6 inches across. Blades die from the tip down. Dollarspot is most common in late spring to early summer and again in early fall, in dry soil and high humidity. Control it with light, frequent applications of nitrogen fertilizer; water deeply, at most once a week; and use neem, fungicidal soap, or garlic oil.

4. MELTING OUT (Drechslera poae)
This disease may attack Kentucky bluegrass during cool, moist spring and fall weather. Blades first develop tan spots with purplish brown borders. Later, lesions appear water-soaked, and the entire plant rots. Avoid synthetic nitrogen fertilizers, water deeply and infrequently, and mow high. Overseed the lawn with a resistant variety.

**5. NECROTIC RING SPOT
(Leptosphaeria korrae)**
Often found in Kentucky bluegrass, bent grass, and creeping red fescue, necrotic ring spot usually begins during cool, wet weather. The disease strikes plant roots. Circles of dead grass with living plants at the center, often greater than a foot in diameter, may appear; individual plants look purple. Avoid summer fertilizing, mow on schedule at the proper height, and overseed with perennial ryegrass or tall fescue.

To combat a disease, you'll need to assess and repair the cultural and environmental conditions that may be giving it a foothold *(pages 82-84)*. In almost all cases, dethatching and aerating will help, as will watering the lawn deeply and only in the morning. Top-dressing with compost can slow some diseases. You may need to use a light application of a fast-release synthetic fertilizer to quickly get nutrients to ailing grass plants. Also, consider overseeding with one of the newer grass varieties that are resistant to a specific disease.

Descriptions of 10 common lawn diseases and the conditions that trigger them are profiled here. Also, the encyclopedia to be found at the back of this book gives information about other diseases that affect a wide range of plants, including turf grasses.

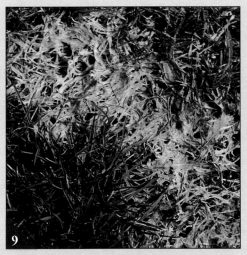

6. PARASITIC NEMATODES
Of the thousands of nematode species, about 50 are turf-grass parasites that feed on roots. Damage—yellowing, wilting, and thinning—is difficult to distinguish from environmental stress. Dig soil samples from several spots on the lawn where the damage borders healthy grass, keep the samples moist, and take them to a Cooperative Extension Service for treatment recommendations based on the species. Mow the grass high, water properly, and fertilize.

7. PYTHIUM BLIGHT
(Pythium species)
High humidity and warm nights, paired with excessive fertilizing and mowing and poor drainage, are ideal conditions for pythium blight. It appears first in shady areas as light brown or reddish brown patches, circles, or streaks. Leaf blades may look watery, and thin, cottony webbing may be evident early in the day. Good preventive maintenance is essential; once it strikes it is impossible to eradicate.

8. RED THREAD
(Laetisaria fuciformis)
This disease most commonly attacks fine fescue, perennial ryegrass, and Kentucky bluegrass during cool, wet, overcast weather. Infected blades in the final stage display reddish threads of cottony webbing; circular patches of infection may measure up to 2 feet across. Apply a synthetic fertilizer lightly and frequently; water deeply and regularly. Check soil pH. Plant a resistant variety.

10. STRIPE SMUT
(Ustilago striiformis)
A foe of Kentucky bluegrass, bent grass, and perennial ryegrass, stripe smut is most noticeable during spring and fall. Plants turn yellow or light green, grayish to black streaks appear on blades, and eventually blades shred and curl. The disease occurs most often when turf is treated with large doses of nitrogen. Mow high during summer, water deeply to avoid drought stress, and in fall apply a balanced fertilizer.

9. SNOW MOLD (Microdochium nivale; Typhula species)
Snow mold can be active at temperatures just above freezing and most often strikes dormant grass. Moist soil, deep snow, and lush grass encourage the disease, which appears as 2- to 3-inch round patches that expand to up to 2 feet. Inside the patch, the grass appears water-soaked; outside, there may be a pink or grayish ring around the patch. Monitor pH, improve drainage, and prune nearby trees and shrubs to increase air circulation.

The Pests and Diseases of 89 Popular Plants

This chart notes the pests (left) and diseases (right) that attack widely grown genera, grouped below by type—trees, shrubs, perennials and bulbs, annuals, and vegetables and fruits. For more information, see the Encyclopedia of Beneficials, Pests, and Diseases that begins on page 94.

PESTS

	Aphids	Bagworms	Beetles	Billbugs	Borers	Caterpillars	Cicadas	Grasshoppers	Lace Bugs	Leafhoppers	Leaf Miners	Mites	Plant Bugs	Planthoppers	Psyllids	Sawflies	Scale Insects	Slugs/Snails	Thrips	Treehoppers	Webworms	Weevils	Whiteflies	Wireworms
TREES																								
ASH (FRAXINUS)			✓		✓	✓	✓	✓				✓	✓	✓			✓		✓			✓	✓	
BEECH (FAGUS)	✓				✓	✓	✓		✓			✓					✓							
CHERRY (PRUNUS)	✓				✓	✓	✓		✓	✓	✓	✓		✓			✓							
CRAB APPLE (MALUS)	✓				✓	✓	✓		✓	✓		✓					✓		✓					
CRAPE MYRTLE (LAGERSTROEMIA)	✓					✓											✓							
DOGWOOD (CORNUS)					✓	✓	✓			✓	✓						✓	✓					✓	
ELM (ULMUS)	✓		✓		✓	✓	✓		✓	✓	✓	✓					✓	✓		✓				
FIR (ABIES)	✓	✓				✓						✓					✓							
HAWTHORN (CRATAEGUS)	✓					✓	✓		✓	✓		✓		✓			✓			✓				
HEMLOCK (TSUGA)		✓										✓			✓	✓	✓					✓		
HONEY LOCUST (GLEDITSIA)	✓				✓	✓				✓	✓								✓	✓				
MAGNOLIA (MAGNOLIA)	✓				✓				✓	✓		✓				✓			✓					
MAPLE (ACER)	✓				✓	✓	✓			✓		✓	✓	✓			✓		✓				✓	
MOUNTAIN ASH (SORBUS)	✓				✓		✓		✓	✓						✓	✓							
OAK (QUERCUS)					✓	✓	✓		✓		✓	✓	✓				✓					✓		
PINE (PINUS)	✓	✓	✓		✓							✓				✓	✓					✓	✓	
POPLAR (POPULUS)			✓		✓	✓	✓			✓		✓					✓	✓			✓	✓		
REDBUD (CERCIS)			✓			✓	✓										✓		✓			✓		
RED CEDAR (JUNIPERUS)	✓	✓										✓					✓				✓			
SPRUCE (PICEA)	✓	✓				✓						✓												
SYCAMORE (PLATANUS)			✓			✓			✓	✓		✓	✓				✓						✓	
WALNUT (JUGLANS)	✓				✓	✓	✓		✓		✓	✓	✓				✓					✓		
WILLOW (SALIX)	✓	✓	✓		✓	✓			✓			✓			✓	✓	✓		✓		✓	✓		
SHRUBS																								
ARBORVITAE (THUJA)	✓	✓			✓				✓		✓	✓					✓							
AZALEA (RHODODENDRON)					✓		✓		✓	✓	✓	✓				✓	✓		✓			✓	✓	
BARBERRY (BERBERIS)	✓					✓						✓					✓			✓				
BOXWOOD (BUXUS)										✓	✓				✓		✓							
CAMELLIA (CAMELLIA)	✓											✓					✓		✓					
COTONEASTER (COTONEASTER)	✓					✓			✓	✓							✓					✓		

DISEASES

Category	Plant	Anthracnose	Aster Yellows	Black Knot	Black Spot	Blight	Canker/Dieback	Damping-Off	Downy Mildew	Gall	Leaf Blister/Curl	Leaf Scorch	Leaf Spot	Mosaic	Needle Cast	Nematodes	Powdery Mildew	Rot	Rust	Scab	Sooty Mold	Wilt
TREES	ASH (FRAXINUS)	✓	✓			✓						✓							✓			✓
	BEECH (FAGUS)					✓					✓	✓					✓					
	CHERRY (PRUNUS)			✓	✓	✓			✓			✓				✓	✓					
	CRAB APPLE (MALUS)				✓	✓											✓		✓	✓	✓	
	CRAPE MYRTLE (LAGERSTROEMIA)											✓					✓					
	DOGWOOD (CORNUS)	✓			✓	✓						✓					✓	✓				
	ELM (ULMUS)	✓				✓				✓	✓	✓	✓				✓					✓
	FIR (ABIES)					✓									✓			✓				
	HAWTHORN (CRATAEGUS)				✓	✓						✓					✓		✓	✓		
	HEMLOCK (TSUGA)				✓	✓												✓				
	HONEY LOCUST (GLEDITSIA)					✓						✓					✓	✓				
	MAGNOLIA (MAGNOLIA)					✓						✓					✓			✓		✓
	MAPLE (ACER)	✓				✓				✓	✓	✓					✓					✓
	MOUNTAIN ASH (SORBUS)				✓	✓						✓							✓	✓		
	OAK (QUERCUS)	✓			✓	✓				✓	✓	✓					✓	✓	✓			✓
	PINE (PINUS)				✓	✓	✓								✓	✓		✓	✓			
	POPLAR (POPULUS)					✓			✓	✓		✓					✓	✓	✓			
	REDBUD (CERCIS)					✓						✓										✓
	RED CEDAR (JUNIPERUS)				✓														✓			
	SPRUCE (PICEA)					✓									✓							
	SYCAMORE (PLATANUS)	✓				✓					✓	✓					✓					
	WALNUT (JUGLANS)	✓			✓	✓						✓										
	WILLOW (SALIX)				✓	✓						✓					✓		✓	✓		
SHRUBS	ARBORVITAE (THUJA)					✓																
	AZALEA (RHODODENDRON)				✓	✓				✓												✓
	BARBERRY (BERBERIS)											✓				✓		✓				
	BOXWOOD (BUXUS)				✓	✓					✓	✓					✓					
	CAMELLIA (CAMELLIA)				✓	✓				✓	✓	✓					✓				✓	
	COTONEASTER (COTONEASTER)				✓	✓						✓								✓		

89

Category	Plant	Aphids	Bagworms	Beetles	Billbugs	Borers	Caterpillars	Cicadas	Grasshoppers	Lace Bugs	Leafhoppers	Leaf Miners	Mites	Plant Bugs	Planthoppers	Psyllids	Sawflies	Scale Insects	Slugs/Snails	Thrips	Treehoppers	Webworms	Weevils	Whiteflies	Wireworms
SHRUBS	EUONYMUS (EUONYMUS)						✔						✔					✔		✔			✔		
	FORSYTHIA (FORSYTHIA)						✔						✔												
	GARDENIA (GARDENIA)	✔											✔					✔		✔					
	HIBISCUS (HIBISCUS)	✔		✔									✔					✔					✔	✔	
	HOLLY (ILEX)	✔										✔	✔										✔		
	JUNIPER (JUNIPERUS)		✔										✔					✔				✔			
	LILAC (SYRINGA)					✔	✔						✔					✔	✔				✔		
	MOUNTAIN LAUREL (KALMIA)					✔				✔													✔	✔	
	PHOTINIA (PHOTINIA)	✔					✔			✔								✔		✔				✔	
	PRIVET (LIGUSTRUM)	✔									✔		✔	✔				✔		✔			✔	✔	
	PYRACANTHA (PYRACANTHA)	✔								✔	✔		✔					✔							
	QUINCE (CHAENOMELES)	✔																							
	RHODODENDRON (RHODODENDRON)					✔				✔	✔	✔	✔					✔					✔	✔	
	ROSE (ROSA)	✔		✔		✔	✔				✔		✔				✔	✔	✔	✔			✔		✔
	VIBURNUM (VIBURNUM)	✔					✔						✔	✔	✔										
	YEW (TAXUS)												✔					✔					✔		
PERENNIALS & BULBS	ANEMONE (ANEMONE)																								
	CARNATION (DIANTHUS)	✔					✔						✔						✔						
	CHRYSANTHEMUM (CHRYSANTHEMUM)	✔		✔			✔			✔	✔	✔	✔	✔				✔	✔						✔
	COLUMBINE (AQUILEGIA)	✔				✔						✔	✔												
	DAFFODIL (NARCISSUS)					✔												✔	✔						
	DAHLIA (DAHLIA)	✔				✔					✔		✔	✔				✔	✔					✔	✔
	DAYLILY (HEMEROCALLIS)	✔							✔									✔	✔						
	GLADIOLUS (GLADIOLUS)	✔				✔							✔					✔	✔						✔
	HOLLYHOCK (ALCEA)			✔		✔				✔			✔					✔							
	HOSTA (HOSTA)																		✔						
	IRIS (IRIS)	✔				✔												✔	✔				✔	✔	✔
	LILY (LILIUM)	✔				✔							✔						✔						
	LUPINE (LUPINUS)	✔													✔										
	PEONY (PAEONIA)																		✔						

90

	Anthracnose	Aster Yellows	Black Knot	Black Spot	Blight	Canker/Dieback	Damping-Off	Downy Mildew	Gall	Leaf Blister/Curl	Leaf Scorch	Leaf Spot	Mosaic	Needle Cast	Nematodes	Powdery Mildew	Rot	Rust	Scab	Sooty Mold	Wilt
SHRUBS																					
EUONYMUS (EUONYMUS)					✔						✔					✔					
FORSYTHIA (FORSYTHIA)					✔											✔					
GARDENIA (GARDENIA)					✔							✔				✔				✔	
HIBISCUS (HIBISCUS)				✔	✔							✔	✔			✔				✔	
HOLLY (ILEX)					✔					✔	✔				✔	✔					
JUNIPER (JUNIPERUS)					✔												✔	✔			
LILAC (SYRINGA)					✔	✔						✔				✔					✔
MOUNTAIN LAUREL (KALMIA)					✔				✔			✔									✔
PHOTINIA (PHOTINIA)					✔							✔				✔			✔		
PRIVET (LIGUSTRUM)	✔											✔				✔					
PYRACANTHA (PYRACANTHA)					✔	✔													✔		
QUINCE (CHAENOMELES)					✔	✔						✔				✔		✔			
RHODODENDRON (RHODODENDRON)					✔	✔			✔	✔						✔					✔
ROSE (ROSA)			✔	✔	✔				✔			✔			✔	✔	✔		✔		
VIBURNUM (VIBURNUM)					✔			✔				✔				✔					
YEW (TAXUS)					✔											✔					✔
PERENNIALS & BULBS																					
ANEMONE (ANEMONE)								✔			✔	✔				✔					
CARNATION (DIANTHUS)					✔		✔				✔	✔			✔	✔	✔	✔			✔
CHRYSANTHEMUM (CHRYSANTHEMUM)		✔			✔						✔	✔			✔	✔		✔			✔
COLUMBINE (AQUILEGIA)											✔	✔				✔	✔				
DAFFODIL (NARCISSUS)					✔							✔					✔				
DAHLIA (DAHLIA)					✔				✔			✔			✔	✔	✔				✔
DAYLILY (HEMEROCALLIS)											✔										
GLADIOLUS (GLADIOLUS)		✔			✔						✔	✔				✔					✔
HOLLYHOCK (ALCEA)	✔										✔	✔				✔	✔	✔			
HOSTA (HOSTA)									✔								✔				
IRIS (IRIS)					✔						✔	✔				✔	✔	✔			
LILY (LILIUM)						✔				✔		✔				✔	✔				✔
LUPINE (LUPINUS)					✔						✔	✔			✔	✔	✔	✔			✔
PEONY (PAEONIA)					✔						✔					✔	✔				

PESTS

		Aphids	Bagworms	Beetles	Billbugs	Borers	Caterpillars	Cicadas	Grasshoppers	Lace Bugs	Leafhoppers	Leaf Miners	Mites	Plant Bugs	Planthoppers	Psyllids	Sawflies	Scale Insects	Slugs/Snails	Thrips	Treehoppers	Webworms	Weevils	Whiteflies	Wireworms
ANNUALS	PHLOX (PHLOX)	✓								✓		✓	✓											✓	
	SALVIA (SALVIA)									✓		✓	✓										✓		
	TULIP (TULIPA)	✓											✓					✓							✓
	TURF GRASSES (GAMINEAE)			✓	✓				✓				✓					✓				✓	✓		✓
	BEGONIA (BEGONIA)	✓																✓		✓					✓
	CALENDULA (CALENDULA)	✓								✓		✓	✓					✓		✓				✓	
	CHINA ASTER (CALLISTEPHUS)	✓	✓							✓		✓	✓							✓					✓
	COSMOS (COSMOS)	✓	✓		✓					✓		✓	✓							✓					
	GERANIUM (PELARGONIUM)	✓				✓						✓	✓					✓		✓				✓	
	MARIGOLD (TAGETES)	✓	✓		✓					✓		✓	✓					✓							
	NASTURTIUM (TROPAEOLUM)	✓								✓			✓							✓					
	PANSY (VIOLA)	✓											✓					✓							
	PETUNIA (PETUNIA)	✓	✓										✓					✓		✓				✓	
	SNAPDRAGON (ANTIRRHINUM)	✓											✓												
	STRAWFLOWER (HELICHRYSUM)	✓											✓												
	ZINNIA (ZINNIA)	✓	✓		✓					✓		✓	✓												
VEGETABLES & FRUITS	APPLE (MALUS)	✓	✓			✓	✓	✓		✓			✓	✓			✓							✓	
	BEAN (PHASEOLUS)	✓	✓			✓	✓		✓	✓		✓	✓					✓	✓					✓	✓
	CABBAGE (BRASSICA)	✓				✓					✓	✓						✓							
	CITRUS (CITRUS)	✓											✓				✓	✓	✓					✓	
	CUCUMBER (CUCUMIS)	✓	✓				✓			✓			✓					✓	✓					✓	
	MELONS (CITRULLUS, CUCUMIS)	✓	✓				✓						✓					✓						✓	
	PEA (PISUM)	✓					✓						✓					✓			✓				
	PEACH (PRUNUS)	✓	✓			✓	✓	✓	✓	✓	✓	✓	✓				✓							✓	
	PEAR (PYRUS)	✓	✓			✓	✓	✓					✓	✓	✓	✓		✓		✓					
	PEPPER (CAPSICUM)	✓	✓			✓	✓	✓	✓	✓			✓											✓	
	PLUM (PRUNUS)	✓	✓			✓	✓	✓				✓	✓	✓				✓			✓				
	POTATO (SOLANUM)	✓	✓			✓	✓	✓	✓	✓			✓					✓							✓
	RASPBERRY (RUBUS)	✓	✓			✓	✓		✓	✓		✓	✓				✓	✓						✓	
	TOMATO (LYCOPERSICON)	✓	✓				✓		✓	✓	✓	✓						✓	✓					✓	

Category	Plant	Anthracnose	Aster Yellows	Black Knot	Black Spot	Blight	Canker/Dieback	Damping-Off	Downy Mildew	Gall	Leaf Blister/Curl	Leaf Scorch	Leaf Spot	Mosaic	Needle Cast	Nematodes	Powdery Mildew	Rot	Rust	Scab	Sooty Mold	Wilt
	PHLOX (PHLOX)		✔		✔								✔			✔	✔	✔	✔			✔
	SALVIA (SALVIA)		✔				✔	✔					✔			✔	✔	✔	✔			✔
	TULIP (TULIPA)				✔									✔		✔		✔				
	TURF GRASSES (GAMINEAE)				✔			✔					✔			✔	✔		✔			
ANNUALS	BEGONIA (BEGONIA)						✔						✔			✔	✔					
ANNUALS	CALENDULA (CALENDULA)		✔		✔							✔	✔			✔	✔	✔		✔		
ANNUALS	CHINA ASTER (CALLISTEPHUS)		✔										✔			✔	✔					✔
ANNUALS	COSMOS (COSMOS)		✔			✔							✔			✔	✔					✔
ANNUALS	GERANIUM (PELARGONIUM)				✔							✔	✔			✔		✔				
ANNUALS	MARIGOLD (TAGETES)		✔		✔							✔	✔			✔						✔
ANNUALS	NASTURTIUM (TROPAEOLUM)												✔						✔			✔
ANNUALS	PANSY (VIOLA)	✔											✔			✔						
ANNUALS	PETUNIA (PETUNIA)													✔		✔						✔
ANNUALS	SNAPDRAGON (ANTIRRHINUM)				✔								✔			✔	✔	✔				✔
ANNUALS	STRAWFLOWER (HELICHRYSUM)		✔														✔					
ANNUALS	ZINNIA (ZINNIA)		✔		✔	✔	✔					✔	✔			✔	✔	✔				✔
VEGETABLES & FRUITS	APPLE (MALUS)					✔	✔										✔	✔	✔	✔		
VEGETABLES & FRUITS	BEAN (PHASEOLUS)	✔				✔	✔	✔					✔			✔	✔	✔				✔
VEGETABLES & FRUITS	CABBAGE (BRASSICA)						✔		✔													
VEGETABLES & FRUITS	CITRUS (CITRUS)						✔										✔			✔		✔
VEGETABLES & FRUITS	CUCUMBER (CUCUMIS)						✔	✔					✔									✔
VEGETABLES & FRUITS	MELONS (CITRULLUS, CUCUMIS)						✔	✔					✔				✔					✔
VEGETABLES & FRUITS	PEA (PISUM)												✔	✔								
VEGETABLES & FRUITS	PEACH (PRUNUS)						✔				✔					✔		✔				
VEGETABLES & FRUITS	PEAR (PYRUS)				✔													✔				
VEGETABLES & FRUITS	PEPPER (CAPSICUM)											✔	✔			✔						✔
VEGETABLES & FRUITS	PLUM (PRUNUS)			✔							✔					✔						
VEGETABLES & FRUITS	POTATO (SOLANUM)					✔						✔	✔			✔				✔		✔
VEGETABLES & FRUITS	RASPBERRY (RUBUS)								✔			✔	✔					✔				
VEGETABLES & FRUITS	TOMATO (LYCOPERSICON)					✔		✔				✔	✔					✔				✔

Encyclopedia of Beneficials, Pests, and Diseases

This encyclopedia will help you recognize the many beneficial insects that inhabit your garden and some of the most common pests and diseases that afflict gardens in the continental United States and southern Canada. Each entry includes a choice of measures designed to prevent problems or to control them if and when they appear in your garden.

The encyclopedia is divided into three sections—Beneficials, Pests, and Diseases. The entries in each section are arranged alphabetically by common name. The first section (right) presents 18 kinds of beneficials—beetles, spiders, and other small creatures that feed on pests and serve as natural controls. Each entry describes the creature's life cycle, so you can recognize it as a welcome ally at different stages of development. Common pests that each beneficial attacks are included, along with suggestions for attracting the beneficial to your garden.

In the section devoted to pests (pages 101-124), some of the 56 entries cover a single species of pest, while others cover several different pests that are either closely related or inflict similar damage. You will find information on the pest's geographical range, the plants it prefers, its life cycle, and descriptions of the damage it inflicts. Recommendations for preventing or eliminating pests include physical controls such as pruning; cultural controls or appropriate gardening techniques; specific beneficials for biological control; and environmentally friendly chemical controls.

The last section (pages 125-140) provides clues for diagnosing 49 infectious and deficiency diseases. You will learn where to look on susceptible plants for typical symptoms and how an infectious disease is transmitted, methods of preventing particular diseases and of controlling them when they appear in your garden, and how to avoid recurrences in the future.

Ambush Bugs

Range: *throughout North America; most prevalent in the West*

Generations per year: *multiple*

Type: *predator*

Ambush bugs are stout bugs that look as if they were wearing armor. They conceal themselves in flowers and wait to attack any unwary insects that come along.

Description and life cycle: Adult ambush bugs have uniquely thickened front legs, equipped for grasping and holding their prey. Most of the several species are small, less than a half-inch long, and are yellowish brown to yellowish green with darker markings. Their coloring provides effective camouflage while they await their prey. The females lay their eggs on plants; nymphs resemble adults but are smaller and wingless.

Beneficial effects: Although small, ambush bugs capture and kill insects considerably bigger than themselves. Both nymphs and adults are predaceous. They prefer to hide in the flowers of goldenrod and boneset. When a bee, wasp, fly, or butterfly visits the flower, the ambush bug uses its strong forelegs to grasp the prey and sucks out the contents of its body. Ambush bugs do not bite humans.

How to attract: Avoid using pesticides. Grow goldenrod and boneset.

Assassin Bugs

Range: *several species found throughout North America*

Generations per year: *usually 1*

Type: *predator*

There are more than 100 native species of assassin bugs in North America. Some attack humans and other animals and can inflict painful bites, but many are voracious predators of insects, and as such they help reduce populations of a wide array of plant pests.

Description and life cycle: Depending on the species, assassin bugs overwinter as larvae, adults, or eggs. Adults are usually flat, brown or black, and a half-inch long. They have long, narrow heads and curved beaks that are folded back under their bodies; many have a hoodlike structure behind their head. Nymphs resemble the adults but are smaller and wingless; some are brightly colored. Eggs are laid in sheltered locations. Once hatched, the nymphs begin feeding on insects and undergo several molts before becoming adults. Most species complete their life cycle in a single year, but some require several years.

Beneficial effects: Adults and nymphs feed on many plant-eating insects, including beetles, caterpillars, aphids, and leafhoppers. They also feed on mosquitoes, bees, and flies.

How to attract: Assassin bugs occur naturally in most gardens. Avoid the use of pesticides.

Big-Eyed Bugs

Range: *throughout western parts of North America*

Generations per year: *2 to 3*

Type: *predator*

Big-eyed bugs resemble tarnished plant bugs and may be mistaken for that pest. However, this small beneficial insect feeds on many troublesome pests, both as a nymph and as an adult.

Description and life cycle: Adult big-eyed bugs overwinter in plant debris or other protected sites. Adults are ⅛ to ¼ inch long, black or yellow-green, with spots on the head and thorax. They emerge in spring, and females lay eggs on plant stems and the undersides of leaves. Nymphs develop for 4 to 6 weeks before molting to become adults and repeat the process. The nymphs look like the adults, but are smaller and wingless. Both adults and nymphs move about very rapidly, and both have large, prominent eyes.

Beneficial effects: Big-eyed bugs prey on aphids, leafhoppers, plant bugs, spider mites, and small caterpillars, and feed on the eggs of mites and insects. When pests are scarce, big-eyed bugs feed on flower nectar.

How to attract: Grow goldenrod and tolerate some pigweed, which big-eyed bugs prefer for egg laying. Avoid pesticide use.

Braconid Wasps

Range: *widespread throughout North America*

Generations per year: *several*

Type: *parasitoid*

More than 2,000 species of braconid wasps are native to North America. Some are raised and sold commercially.

Description and life cycle: Depending on the species, adult braconid wasps are between ¹⁄₁₀ and ½ inch long. Slender, with a distinctly pinched waist, they may be brown, black, yellow, or red. Adults feed on nectar and pollen. Females inject eggs into a susceptible host. The eggs hatch as white, wormlike larvae that parasitize the host by feeding from within, eventually killing it. Some species feed externally as well. The larvae pupate near, on, or in a host, in white or brown cocoons. The life cycle is short and yields several generations per year. Wasps overwinter as larvae or pupae inside their hosts.

Beneficial effects: Braconid wasp larvae help control a wide range of insect pests, including coddling moth, cabbage worms, armyworms, elm bark beetles, hornworms, and aphids.

How to attract: Some species are commercially available, but it is best to encourage native populations. Grow dill, fennel, parsley, and yarrow, to sustain adult wasps. Avoid killing caterpillars bearing brown cocoons. Avoid the use of pesticides.

Chalcid Wasps

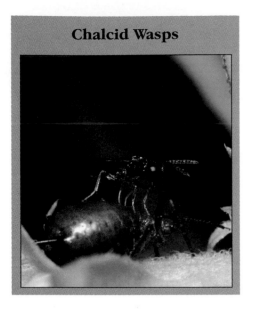

Range: *widespread throughout North America*

Generations per year: *several*

Type: *parasitoid*

Worldwide, there are more than 100,000 species of chalcid wasps. These include both the trichogramma wasp and *Encarsia formosa,* two highly effective parasitoids of plant pests. Chalcid wasps feed on eggs, larvae, and pupae of their prey; species vary in host preference.

Description and life cycle: Adults are tiny, often only 1/100 inch long, and may be black or golden brown. They feed on plant nectar and on honeydew excreted by insect hosts. The females often feed on insect fluids seeping from wounds they make as they lay their eggs. Inserting eggs into a host's body, or under a scale insect's shell-like covering, they often paralyze the host. Larvae develop and feed within the host, eventually killing it; they pupate in or near the host's body. These wasps produce several generations per year; many species overwinter as larvae in hosts.

Beneficial effects: Chalcid wasps are parasitoids of many plant pests, including scale insects, aphids, mealybugs, and tussock moths. One species, *Encarsia formosa,* controls whiteflies.

How to attract: Avoid pesticide use, including sulfur fungicides.

Flower Flies

Range: *many species found throughout North America*

Generations per year: *3 to 7*

Type: *predator*

Flower flies, or syrphid flies, are often called hover flies, for their helicopter-like flying habits. There are more than 800 species native to North America; these differ in both their geographic range and their preferred prey.

Description and life cycle: Adults are 1/3 to 1/2 inch long, black with yellow or white stripes. They resemble honeybees or hornets in appearance and in their attraction to flowers, but unlike bees, they have only a single pair of wings, large eyes, and no stinger. Flower flies overwinter in the soil as pupae; adults emerge in early spring to feed on flower nectar. Females lay small white, pitted eggs singly among colonies of aphids. The hatching larvae are sluglike, and can be mottled in color, or green, brown, or gray. They feed voraciously on aphids for about 2 weeks, then drop to the soil to pupate. Adults emerge in 2 weeks to repeat the cycle.

Beneficial effects: One larva can consume 400 aphids. Larvae may also feed on mealybugs, mites, scale crawlers, and other small insects.

How to attract: Include daisy-flowered plants that provide abundant nectar and pollen, such as Shasta daisy, cosmos, and coreopsis. Stagger plantings so that there is always something in bloom. Avoid the use of pesticides.

Ichneumon Wasps

Range: *widespread throughout North America*

Generations per year: *1 to 10*

Type: *predator, parasitoid*

Both larval and adult ichneumon wasps (sometimes called ichneumon flies) help control insect pests. Some species have a very narrow host range; others attack a wide variety of insects.

Description and life cycle: Adults vary in size from 1/10 to 1 1/2 inches, and are slender and dark colored. They typically are wide ranging and often feed on nectar or pollen. Females have a long, threadlike ovipositor for inserting eggs into the host eggs or larvae. The larvae generally develop and feed within the host, killing it in the process. Larvae are white grubs, tapered at both ends. In some species, adults kill hosts by stinging them and consuming the body fluids. Most species overwinter as mature larvae in cocoons, or as adult females.

Beneficial effects: Larvae feed within host eggs, larvae, or pupae, providing natural control for a wide range of plant pests. Hosts include sawflies, spruce budworms, tent caterpillars, pine tip moths, European corn borers, and woodboring beetles.

How to attract: Include flowers in the garden, to attract and maintain adults. Avoid pesticide use.

Lacewings

Range: *widespread throughout North America*

Generations per year: *3 to 6*

Type: *predator*

Hundreds of species of lacewings are found in North America. Sometimes called aphid lions, and broadly grouped as green or brown lacewings, they are widely distributed and highly beneficial.

Description and life cycle: Lacewings overwinter as adults or pupae. In spring, they emerge as adults, ½ to ¾ inch long with elongated lacy, transparent wings, to feed on pollen and nectar and lay eggs. Green lacewings lay their eggs on the end of a silk thread, while brown lacewings lay eggs directly on leaves. Eggs hatch in less than a week. The larvae are mottled yellow or brown and spindle shaped, with large jaws. They feed for about 3 weeks, pupate for 5 to 7 days, and emerge as adults to repeat the cycle.

Beneficial effects: While lacewing larvae prefer aphids, they also feed on thrips, mealybugs, scale, moth eggs, small caterpillars, other soft-bodied insects, and mites. Adults are not usually predaceous.

How to attract: Grow plants that offer plenty of pollen and nectar, such as dill, fennel, clover, and cosmos. Provide a source of water in dry weather. Buy lacewing eggs from an insectary and distribute them throughout the garden. Avoid use of dormant oil sprays—they may kill overwintering eggs.

Ladybird Beetles

Range: *widespread throughout North America*

Generations per year: *2 to 4*

Type: *predator*

Ladybird beetles, also called lady beetles and ladybugs, are probably the best known of all beneficial insects. Of some 4,000 species worldwide, about 400 are native to North America. Some of the most common and beneficial species include the convergent ladybird beetle, the twice-stabbed ladybird beetle, and the two-spotted ladybird beetle.

Description and life cycle: Adult ladybird beetles are shiny, round, and about ¼ inch long. They may be gray, yellow, or orange-red, with or without black spots; some are solid black, others black with red spots. Larvae are spindle shaped, wrinkled, and up to ⅜ inch long; when young, they are dark and look like tiny alligators. As the larvae mature, they develop conspicuous yellow, red, or white markings. Pupae are reddish black with red markings and are usually attached to the upper leaf surface.

Ladybird beetles overwinter as adults in garden debris. They emerge in spring to feed and lay eggs in clusters among aphids or other potential prey. Once hatched, the larvae feed for about 3 weeks, then pupate, emerging as adults about a week later to repeat the cycle.

The convergent ladybird beetle, the most common species in North America, is red-orange with black spots; it is dis-

tinguished by two converging white lines on its thorax. This species migrates, flying hundreds of miles to overwintering sites and returning in spring. The twice-stabbed ladybird beetle is shiny black with two bright red spots, while the two-spotted ladybird beetle is red with two black spots and a black head.

Beneficial effects: Both larvae and adults feed on many soft-bodied insect pests, including aphids, mealybugs, scales, psyllids, whiteflies, and spider mites; they also eat insect eggs. One larva can eat up to 300 aphids before it molts; then, as an adult beetle, it can eat another 300 to 400 aphids.

Food preferences vary with the species. Convergent ladybird beetles feed mainly on aphids; twice-stabbed ladybird beetles prefer scales; and two-spotted ladybird beetles devour both scales and aphids. A related species known as the

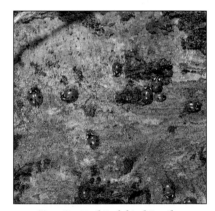

Two-Spotted Ladybird Beetles

mealybug destroyer strongly prefers mealybugs but also eats aphids and scales. The vedalia ladybird beetle, a red-bodied beetle with black marks, prefers soft scales, while the red-mite destroyer feeds on spider mites. Adults also feed on pollen and nectar.

How to attract: Grow dill and tansy to lure adults with pollen and nectar. If you buy convergent ladybird beetles or mealybug destroyers, note that they tend to fly away when released. In a greenhouse, first close all vents; in a garden, first water well, and free the beetles at night, when they are less active.

Pirate Bugs

Range: *widespread throughout North America*

Generations per year: *2 to 4*

Type: *predator*

Also called minute pirate bugs for their tiny size, pirate bugs are voracious predators, attacking most small insects. Not all of their victims are pests, but their overall effect is beneficial.

Description and life cycle: Pirate bugs overwinter as mated adult females, emerging in spring to insert their eggs into plant stems or leaves. Adults are quick fliers, ¼ inch long, and black with white patches on their wings. Eggs hatch in 3 to 5 days; nymphs are oval, ⅛ inch long, and may be yellow, orange, or brown. Nymphs feed for 2 to 3 weeks on the insects they find on leaves and in flowers, then molt to become adults and repeat the cycle.

Beneficial effects: Both nymphs and adults consume large numbers of small insect pests such as thrips, small caterpillars, leafhopper nymphs, spider mites, and insect eggs. They are especially adept at finding prey in flowers and are therefore particularly good at controlling flower thrips.

How to attract: Grow goldenrod, daisies, and yarrow; adults feed on their pollen. In fall, collect pirate bugs on wild goldenrod and release them in your garden. In a greenhouse, release one pirate bug for every five plants.

Praying Mantises

Range: *various species throughout North America*

Generations per year: *usually 1*

Type: *predator*

Of the 20-odd praying mantis species found in North America, several are imports from Europe and China. All are aggressive predators of other insects.

Description and life cycle: Praying mantises overwinter as clusters of 50 to 400 eggs in an egg case of hardened froth stuck to a plant. In early spring, nymphs emerge and begin to feed, taking ever-larger insect prey as they grow—including other praying mantises. After mating, the female often devours the male before laying eggs. Adults are 2 to 4 inches long, green or brown, with large eyes, long hind legs, and powerful front legs adapted for grasping prey. Nymphs resemble adults but are smaller and wingless.

Beneficial effects: Praying mantises feed on both pests and beneficial insects including aphids, beetles, bugs, leafhoppers, caterpillars, butterflies, flies, bees, and wasps. Adults feed on larger insects that usually are not pests.

How to attract: Provide shrubs and other permanent plantings as sites for overwintering eggs. Do not release purchased praying mantises, because they may destroy native populations of bees and butterflies. Instead, protect egg cases found in your yard, keeping them off the ground outdoors, in or near the garden. Avoid pesticide use.

Predatory Mites

Range: *widespread throughout North America*

Generations per year: *multiple*

Type: *predator*

Predatory mites look like plant-feeding mites, but are less hairy and quicker.

Description and life cycle: Adult predatory mites are tiny, about ½₀ inch long. They are usually tan, beige, or red. Nymphs are similar, but even smaller and usually translucent. Females overwinter in soil, crevices in bark, or plant debris. In spring they lay their eggs on leaves near plant-feeding mites. Nymphs hatch in 3 to 4 days and begin to feed. They molt to become adults within 5 to 10 days, and repeat the cycle. There are many overlapping generations each year.

Beneficial effects: Predator mites have varying preferences in their prey. The phytoseiid mite eats several spider-mite species, and controls that pest well by reproducing twice as fast. Other predator-mite species feed on thrips, other mite pests, and pollen.

How to attract: Grow cattails and dandelions, for their pollen. Mist plants to encourage predaceous mites and discourage spider mites. Buy and release commercially available predator mites. Avoid use of pesticides.

Robber Flies

Range: *various species throughout North America*

Generations per year: *1- to 2-year life cycle*

Type: *predator*

Robber flies are fast-flying, loud-buzzing insects that snatch their prey in flight. Once a victim is caught, the robber fly inserts its proboscis into the prey and sucks the juices.

Description and life cycle: Adult robber flies resemble wasps or bees but are usually gray, although some species may be yellow or black. Most are ½ to ¾ inch long and hairy, with a long, narrow abdomen. They are equipped with a long, horny proboscis for piercing prey. Females lay their eggs on the ground, and most species overwinter as larvae in the soil. Larvae are white, slightly flattened, distinctly segmented grubs, and feed on a variety of soil-borne insects. Adults prefer sunny sites such as open fields or woodland edges, where they fly about in search of prey. Many species have a 2-year life cycle.

Beneficial effects: Robber flies are fairly indiscriminate predators, but are on the whole beneficial. Larvae eat a wide variety of white grubs, grasshopper eggs, beetle pupae, and caterpillars. Adults catch and consume many flying insects, including beetles, leafhoppers, butterflies, flies, bugs, and bees.

How to attract: Avoid pesticide use.

Rove Beetles

Range: *widespread throughout North America*

Generations per year: *1*

Type: *predator, parasite, parasitoid*

Of the nearly 30,000 rove beetle species worldwide, about 3,000 occur in North America. They differ in geographic ranges and food preferences. Some are predators of plant pests; some parasitize ants, termites, and fleas; and some feed on decaying organic matter.

Description and life cycle: Rove beetles overwinter as adults, emerging in spring to mate and lay eggs in the soil. Adults are slender, ⅒ to 1 inch long and may be black, brown, or yellow, often with spots. When disturbed, a rove beetle raises the tip of its abdomen in a menacing, combative pose. Most are active at night. The larvae look like wingless adults.

Beneficial effects: Rove beetle species differ in food preferences. Pests they help control include snails, slugs, aphids, springtails, mites, flies, nematodes, and root maggots. They also help decompose organic matter in the soil.

How to attract: Provide permanent beds to help rove beetle populations develop. Provide daytime shelter with organic mulches and living mulches. Avoid the use of pesticides.

Soldier Beetles

Range: *several species throughout most of the United States*

Generations per year: *1 to 2*

Type: *predator*

Soldier beetles, often called leatherwings, resemble lightning bugs without the light. Both larvae and adults are believed to be predaceous, feeding on a wide variety of insects.

Description and life cycle: Soldier beetles overwinter in a late larval stage, in the soil or under tree bark. Larvae are grub-like, hairy or velvety, and may be brown, purple, or black. In spring they pupate and emerge as adult beetles, usually less than ½ inch long, and dark with orange, yellow, or red markings. Beetles are often found on flowering plants such as goldenrod, milkweed, and hydrangea. Many species include pollen and nectar in their diet. Females lay eggs in masses in the soil or other sheltered sites.

Beneficial effects: The Pennsylvania leatherwing, found east of the Rocky Mountains, feeds on locust eggs, cucumber beetles, corn earworms, and European corn borers. The downy leatherwing occurs in most of the United States and eats all kinds of aphids. Other species feed on grasshopper eggs and various caterpillars and grubs.

How to attract: Avoid the use of pesticides. Grow goldenrod, hydrangea, and milkweed.

Spiders

Spined Soldier Bugs

Tachinid Flies

Range: *widespread throughout North America*

Generations per year: *1 to many*

Type: *predator*

All of the 35,000 known species of spiders are natural predators of insects. Spiders themselves are not insects but arachnids, in the same family as mites and scorpions; spiders have four pairs of legs and only two body segments. Species most helpful to gardeners include the crab spider and the wolf spider.

Description and life cycle: Spiders lay their eggs in a silk cocoon. The young resemble adults but undergo several molts before becoming adults. Spiders inject captured victims with paralyzing venom and eat them, or wrap them in silk for a later meal.

Spiders are either hunters or trappers; the wolf spider is a hunter that pounces on its prey. Wolf spiders are ground dwellers, ½ to 1⅜ inches long, and active at night. The crab spider is a trapper, spinning a web and waiting for prey to wander in; it often lies in wait near flowers insects visit.

Beneficial effects: Feeding almost exclusively on the insects they hunt and trap, spiders are highly beneficial in the garden. Most spiders eat a wide variety of insects, but most avoid wasps, hornets, ants, and hard-shelled beetles.

How to attract: Avoid pesticide use. Do not disturb webs.

Range: *widespread throughout North America*

Generations per year: *1 to 2*

Type: *predator*

Spined soldier bugs are common in every part of the United States. The nymphs are voracious predators of some of the most damaging garden and forest pests.

Description and life cycle: Spined soldier bugs overwinter as adults, to emerge in spring and lay eggs on plant leaves. One female may lay up to 1,000 eggs. Adults are about ½ inch long and shield shaped. They are pale brown or yellow with black specks and have spined, or pointed, shoulders. Nymphs resemble adults but have no wings. They feed briefly on plant sap, but after their first molt, they eat only insects for 6 to 8 weeks before becoming adults.

Beneficial effects: Nymphs eat a wide variety of caterpillars, including gypsy moths and tent caterpillars. They also feed on the larval stages of fall armyworms, sawflies, Colorado potato beetles, and Mexican bean beetles.

How to attract: Maintain permanent perennial beds to provide shelter for native populations of spined soldier bugs. Avoid pesticide use. If you buy spined soldier bugs commercially, release them at the rate of two to five nymphs per square yard of garden. Pheromone lures are also available.

Range: *widespread throughout North America*

Generations per year: *1 to 3*

Type: *parasitoid*

There are more than 1,200 native species of tachinid flies. The adult flies live on nectar and honeydew, but the larvae parasitize many serious plant pests.

Description and life cycle: Tachinid fly larvae overwinter inside a host insect. These tiny white maggots feed on the host from the inside out, eventually killing it. The larvae pupate in or near the host's carcass; adult flies emerge and mate. Adults are ⅓ to ½ inch long, gray, brown, or black in color, and look like big, bristly houseflies but have only two wings. Females lay eggs on young host larvae or on leaves where potential hosts are feeding. Eggs or nymphs may be eaten by the host or the nymphs may bore into it, there to feed and develop.

Beneficial effects: Tachinid fly larvae kill the larvae of many harmful species, including armyworms, cutworms, tent caterpillars, cabbage loopers, gypsy moths, hornworms, earworms, and coddling moths. Some species also infest sawflies, squash bugs, and grasshoppers.

How to attract: Grow dill, parsley, and sweet clover; their flowers attract adult tachinid flies. Avoid killing caterpillars with white eggs on their backs. Avoid pesticide use.

Aphids

Range: *most of the United States and southern Canada*

Generations per year: *20 or more*

Host(s): *most ornamentals and vegetables*

More than 4,000 species of aphids are known; most plants are susceptible to at least one.

Description and life cycle: Aphids overwinter as eggs. During the growing season, they feed on soft plant tissues and produce several generations each year. Adult aphids are pear shaped, less than ⅛ inch long, and may be green, yellow, black, brownish, or gray. The nymphs are smaller versions of the adult.

Damage and detection: Feeding in large groups, aphids suck plant sap, leaving leaves wilted and yellow and flowers deformed. They secrete a sticky substance called honeydew, which drops onto plants. Honeydew serves as a growing medium for sooty mold, an unsightly black fungus that further damages plants by blocking light. Aphids also spread certain viral diseases.

Control: PHYSICAL—Knock aphids off affected plants with a jet of water; use reflective mulch and sticky traps; cut off heavily infested leaves. BIOLOGICAL—Convergent ladybird beetle; green lacewing; syrphid fly; aphid midge. CHEMICAL—Horticultural oil; insecticidal soap; pyrethrins; rotenone.

Armyworms

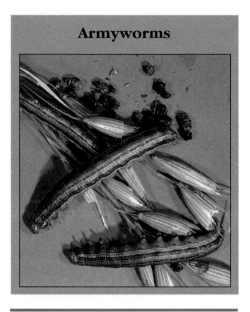

Range: *east of the Rocky Mountains; Arizona, New Mexico, California*

Generations per year: *2 to 6*

Host(s): *turf grasses and vegetables*

The armyworm is a serious pest of grasses and vegetable crops. Its favorite hosts include corn and grasses.

Description and life cycle: Larvae are 1 to 2 inches long, pale green to greenish brown, with yellow or white stripes; they overwinter in plant debris or in soil. Adults are grayish brown moths, with a wingspan of 1 to 2 inches, and are active only at night. Moths lay eggs on the lower leaves of plants and produce as many as six generations per year, depending on the species and the climate.

Damage and detection: Larvae hide during the day in protected areas and feed at night on leaves, stems, and buds. Large numbers can defoliate plants overnight.

Control: PHYSICAL—Handpick worms. CULTURAL—Keep weed growth down; till soil to expose pupae to predators. BIOLOGICAL—Beneficial nematodes; birds; Bt; ground beetles; toads; trichogramma wasps. CHEMICAL—Horticultural oil in July to control second generation; neem.

Bagworms

Range: *east of the Rocky Mountains*

Generations per year: *1*

Host(s): *trees and shrubs*

The bagworm feeds on the leaves of many deciduous and evergreen trees and shrubs, especially juniper and arborvitae.

Description and life cycle: Bagworms overwinter as eggs inside small bags, hatching in late spring or early summer. Each dark brown larva spins a silken bag some 2 inches long around itself and covers it with bits of plant debris. In late summer, the larva attaches its bag to a twig and pupates. In a few days adult males emerge from their bags as black, clearwinged moths and fly off in search of adult females, which remain inside their bags. Females lay 500 to 1,000 eggs after mating, and then both sexes die.

Damage and detection: Larvae feed on a host's leaves, often stripping twigs bare and giving the plant a ragged look. Heavy infestations may defoliate entire trees. The bags are very easy to spot.

Control: PHYSICAL—Handpick and destroy bags in winter or early spring, before eggs hatch; set pheromone traps. BIOLOGICAL—Bt when larvae begin to feed; parasitic wasps. CHEMICAL—Rotenone applied when bags are small, usually in June.

Bark Beetles

Range: *most of the United States and southern Canada*

Generations per year: *1 to 3*

Host(s): *deciduous and coniferous trees*

Bark beetles include many species of minute or small beetles that are typically stout and cylindrical in shape; the scientific name of the family to which all the species belong means "cut short" in Greek. These pests tunnel into tree bark to lay their eggs. They attack various hosts, but most evergreen and many deciduous trees are susceptible to one or more species. Some of the most destructive bark beetles include the ambrosia beetle *(Corthylus punctatissimus),* the elm bark beetles *(Scolytus multistriatus* and *Hylurgopinus rufipes),* the pine engraver *(Ips pini),* the shothole borer *(Scolytus rugulosus),* and the Southern pine beetle *(Dendroctonus frontalis).*

Description and life cycle: Adults are commonly black or brown and less than ¼ inch long; they have short snouts and are covered with fine hairs or bristles. The adult beetle—in some species the male and in others the female—bores into the bark of a living or rotting tree to make a tunnel in which the female deposits her eggs. When the eggs hatch, the larvae begin to feed on the wood, creating tunnels, or galleries, beneath the bark, usually at right angles to the original tunnel bored by the male. The adult male ambrosia beetle carries fruiting bodies of a fungus into the tunnels to serve as food for the larvae. At the ends of the galleries, the larvae pupate, then emerge as adults to mate and repeat the process for a total of two or three generations a year, depending on species and location. Beetles overwinter in a dormant state in the galleries.

Damage and detection: Evidence of bark beetle infestation includes holes in the bark that frequently ooze sap. Sawdust from the hole may be found at the base of the tree. Shothole borer holes are numerous and small, giving the tree the appearance of having been hit with buckshot. Tunneling by feeding larvae destroys tissue in the cambium, the layer that produces new growth—and can eventually kill the infested tree. Those not killed by beetle damage are susceptible to invasion by pathogens. In the case of the elm bark beetle, it spreads the fungus responsible for Dutch elm disease. The adult elm bark beetle tunnels and lays eggs in weakened or diseased elm wood, which is often infected with Dutch elm disease. When the new generation of adults emerges, they fly to healthy leaves of nearby elms and spread the disease as they feed.

Control: PHYSICAL—Remove and destroy infested trees; prune and destroy infested branches; set pheromone traps. CULTURAL—Plant species that are resistant to Dutch elm disease. BIOLOGICAL—Beneficial nematodes; braconid wasps.

Billbugs

Range: *United States and southern Canada in grassland regions and lawns*

Generations per year: *1*

Host(s): *grasses*

Billbugs are named for the adult's peculiar bill-like elongated snout. The larvae do most of the damage to lawns.

Description and life cycle: Billbugs overwinter as adults in the soil. They are ¼ to ½ inch long and may be gray, brown, or black. They emerge in spring to feed and lay their eggs on the leaf sheaths of grass. The hatching larvae, white, legless, and very small, begin feeding on stems but move into the soil to continue feeding on grass roots.

Damage and detection: Symptoms of billbug damage include brown or yellow patches in the lawn, showing up first during periods of drought, especially near driveways or sidewalks, where soil tends to be driest. Sawdustlike material around grass stems may also indicate billbug feeding. Infested areas of turf are easy to pull up because the roots have been eaten.

Control: CULTURAL—Plant grass varieties that are resistant to billbugs. PHYSICAL—Dethatch lawn if thatch layer is more than ¾ inch thick. BIOLOGICAL—Beneficial nematodes. CHEMICAL—Neem.

Blister Beetles

Range: *most of the United States and southern Canada*

Generations per year: *1*

Host(s): *most ornamentals and vegetables*

Most common east of the Rocky Mountains, blister beetles feed on the flowers and foliage of many ornamentals, vegetables, and fruits; members of the tomato family are favorite hosts. When crushed, these beetles emit a liquid that causes blisters on the skin; hence their common name.

Description and life cycle: Larvae of the blister beetle overwinter in the soil. They pupate and emerge as adults in midsummer. The adults have an elongated body, less than ¾ inch long, and may be black, brown, gray, blue, or striped. Females lay their eggs in grasshopper burrows, and when the larvae hatch, they feed on grasshopper egg masses.

Damage and detection: Large numbers of beetles can defoliate plants very rapidly. Only the adult is damaging; the larva is considered beneficial because it serves to control grasshoppers.

Control: PHYSICAL—Wearing gloves to protect skin, handpick beetles; cover valuable plants with cheesecloth. BIOLOGICAL—Beneficial nematodes. CHEMICAL—Pyrethrins; rotenone.

Borers/Clearwing Moths

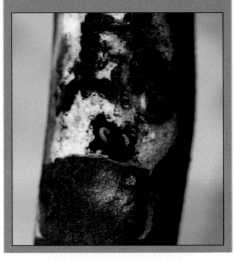

Range: *throughout the United States and southern Canada*

Generations per year: *1*

Host(s): *many ornamentals and vegetables*

There are many species of clearwing moths. The larvae, or caterpillars, cause serious injury to a wide variety of woody and herbaceous plants by boring into stems, twigs, or trunks and feeding on interior plant tissues. Some of the most destructive are the dogwood borer, greater peach tree borer, lilac borer, and rhododendron borer.

Description and life cycle: Most clearwing moths overwinter as larvae in host tissue. They are ⅛ to 1 inch long, yellow or white with dark heads. In spring the larvae pupate and emerge as adult moths, swift fliers that resemble wasps. The wings are at least somewhat transparent, and the bodies are often striped with yellow, brown, or orange bands. Females lay eggs on bark or stems of susceptible host plants, especially near wounds.

After hatching, the larvae enter their host through wounds, scars, or twig crotches. The dogwood borer (known in the South as the pecan borer) infests many hardwood trees, including cherry, apple, hickory, willow, birch, and oak. It afflicts cultivated dogwoods more often than those growing in the wild. The greater peach tree borer infests stone fruits, birch trees, and several species of ornamental shrubs. It enters plants near the base of the trunk and some-times invades surface roots. The lilac borer attacks not only lilac but also privet and ash trees. It generally enters a host within 3 feet of the soil line. The rhododendron borer, the smallest of the clearwing moths, is most serious in the mid-Atlantic region. It attacks mountain laurel as well as azaleas and rhododendrons.

Damage and detection: Symptoms of borer infestation include wilted leaves; loose, sloughing, or cracking bark; and dieback of branches. Any evident holes are usually the exit holes, since entry holes are so tiny they go undetected. The borer feeds on and destroys the cambium a layer of tissue that produces girth-increasing growth, and often girdles the plant. Branches above the site of infection usually die. If the borers

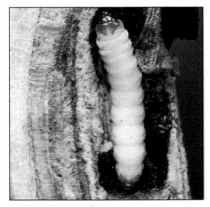

Lilac Borer

invade the host near the soil line, the entire plant dies.

Control: PHYSICAL—Remove infested branches and badly infested plants; encircle peach trees with a 4- to 6-inch ring of tobacco dust in spring; set pheromone traps. CULTURAL—Keep trees and shrubs healthy and vigorous and avoid mechanical injuries, since borers generally enter through wounds or scars. BIOLOGICAL—Bt; parasitic wasps. CHEMICAL—Horticultural oil.

Cabbage Loopers

Range: *throughout the United States and southern Canada*

Generations per year: *2 to 7*

Host(s): *many ornamentals and vegetables*

Cabbage loopers feed on members of the cabbage family and other vegetables, as well as many herbaceous ornamentals including carnations, chrysanthemums, nasturtiums, and geraniums. Cabbage loopers closely resemble the imported cabbage worm in appearance and in the damage they cause.

Description and life cycle: Cabbage loopers overwinter as pupae on plant leaves or stems. Adults emerge in spring as brown moths with a silver spot on each forewing, and a wingspan of 1½ to 2 inches. Eggs are laid on host plants, where they hatch in about a week. The caterpillars are green, with white stripes down their back. They feed for 2 to 4 weeks before pupating.

Damage and detection: The larvae chew large, irregular holes in leaves. While their color provides an effective camouflage, their damage is easily spotted.

Control: PHYSICAL—Handpick larvae and destroy greenish white eggs; use row covers. BIOLOGICAL—Apply Bt at 2-week intervals; lacewings; trichogramma wasps; birds. CHEMICAL—Pyrethrins; rotenone; sabadilla.

Cankerworms

Range: *Maine to North Carolina, west to Missouri; Colorado, Utah, California*

Generations per year: *1*

Host(s): *deciduous trees and shrubs*

Cankerworms are often referred to as inchworms or measuring worms because of the way they arch their backs as they move. They feed on the leaves and buds of many deciduous plants; beech, cherry, elm, maple, and oak are favorite hosts.

Description and life cycle: Fall cankerworms overwinter as eggs, hatching in spring when trees and shrubs are putting out new leaves. The slender caterpillars may be green, brown, or black, with white stripes; they grow to 1 inch in length. They feed for 3 or 4 weeks, then crawl into the soil to pupate. Adults emerge in late fall to lay their eggs on the bark of trees. Spring cankerworms are similar but overwinter as moths that emerge in spring.

Damage and detection: The leaves are chewed to the midrib. Heavily infested plants are defoliated.

Control: PHYSICAL—Wrap sticky bands around trunks of susceptible trees before egg laying occurs; destroy egg masses. CULTURAL—Till the soil to expose pupae. BIOLOGICAL—Bt; spined soldier bugs; trichogramma wasps. CHEMICAL—Horticultural oil; neem.

Chinch Bugs

Range: *throughout the United States, southern Canada, and Mexico*

Generations per year: *2 to 3*

Host(s): *grasses*

Chinch bugs are found throughout North America but are most prevalent in the Mississippi, Ohio, and Missouri river valleys, as well as Texas and Oklahoma.

Description and life cycle: Chinch bugs overwinter under plant debris as adults, which are about ⅕ inch long and have a black body and white wings. In spring the females lay eggs over a period of 3 weeks. Young nymphs are bright red with a white band across the back; older nymphs are black with white spots.

Damage and detection: The nymphs are the most damaging stage. They feed on both the roots and stems of grasses, sucking juices and secreting toxic salivary fluids. Infested turf turns yellow and often dies in patches. Injury resembles that of Japanese beetle grubs and is most serious during hot, dry periods.

Control: PHYSICAL—Dethatch heavily thatched lawn. CULTURAL—Plant resistant varieties; reduce nitrogen fertilizer. BIOLOGICAL—Big-eyed bugs; lacewings; ladybird beetles; pirate bugs. CHEMICAL—Flood an infested area with soapy water and cover with a light-colored flannel sheet; the bugs will crawl onto the underside of the sheet to escape the soap. Kill them by dipping the sheet in a large container filled with hot soapy water; neem; pyrethrins; sabadilla; soap sprays.

Cicadas

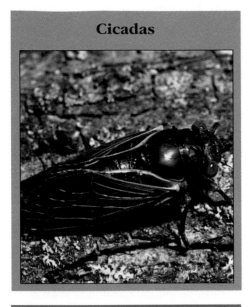

Range: *eastern United States, west to Texas and Oklahoma*

Generations per year: *variable*

Host(s): *deciduous trees and shrubs*

Periodical cicadas live either 13 or 17 years, but because generations overlap, almost every year brings at least a few periodical cicadas. The dog-day cicada is also known as the annual cicada—erroneously, since it has a 2- to 4-year cycle. Its generations also overlap, with some of the pests appearing every year

Description and life cycle: Cicadas spend most of their lives as nymphs below ground, feeding on plant roots. They emerge and climb into trees for their last molt. The adults are 1 to 2 inches long. Within weeks they mate, lay eggs, and die. Eggs hatch in about 2 months; the new nymphs burrow into the soil.

Damage and detection: Although adult cicadas suck sap from young twigs, they do their greatest harm in laying eggs. The female cuts into the bark of twigs and splinters the sapwood as she deposits her eggs. One female may make 20 separate egg pockets, each of which can cause twig dieback and make the host vulnerable to infection.

Control: PHYSICAL—Apply sticky bands to tree trunks; remove injured twigs before eggs hatch; cover shrubs with netting. CULTURAL—Avoid planting young trees when major outbreaks are expected. BIOLOGICAL—Beneficial nematodes.

Colorado Potato Beetles

Range: *throughout the United States except the South and the Pacific Northwest*

Generations per year: *1 to 3*

Host(s): *many solanum family members*

The Colorado potato beetle is a serious garden pest in most parts of the country. In addition to potato plants, eggplants, peppers, tomatoes, and petunias are often attacked.

Description and life cycle: The Colorado potato beetle overwinters as an adult. It is oval, ⅓ inch long, with yellow-and-black striped wing covers. Beetles emerge in spring, feed, and lay eggs that hatch in about a week. The plump larvae are orange-red with black spots. They feed, reenter the soil to pupate, and emerge as adults in 1 to 2 weeks.

Damage and detection: Adults and larvae alike decimate the foliage and stems of potatoes, tomatoes, and related plants, reducing yields in both quantity and quality. Heavy infestations can be fatal, especially to young plants. While feeding, beetles leave highly visible black excrement on leaves and stems.

Control: PHYSICAL—Use a thick organic mulch to inhibit migrating larvae; handpick beetles, larvae, and eggs. CULTURAL—Rotate crops; plant resistant varieties. BIOLOGICAL—Bt San Diego strain; ladybird beetles; spined soldier bugs. CHEMICAL—Neem; pyrethrins; rotenone.

Conifer Sawflies

Range: *eastern United States to the Mississippi River, southeastern Canada*

Generations per year: *1 to 5*

Host(s): *coniferous trees and shrubs*

Conifer sawflies are among the most damaging insect pests of pine, spruce, and hemlock. There are several species, each with its own range of host plants.

Description and life cycle: With sawlike egg-laying organs, females slit needles and deposit eggs in the slits. Depending on the species, sawflies overwinter as eggs or as cocooned pupae in soil or on lower tree bark. Larvae are as much as 1 inch long, gray, green, yellow, or tan, with dark brown or red heads and black dots along their bodies. Adults are less than ½ inch long and stout, with translucent wings.

Damage and detection: Hundreds of larvae feed together on the current season's needles, devouring an entire shoot before moving on to the next. Their color blends with the foliage, so they often do serious damage before being seen. Left untreated, they can defoliate and even kill the host.

Control: PHYSICAL—Spread flannel dropcloths under trees, shake limbs to dislodge larvae, and destroy them in a soap solution. CULTURAL—Keep trees healthy and vigorous. BIOLOGICAL—Parasitic wasps; predaceous beetles; shrews; tachinid flies. CHEMICAL—Horticultural oil; soap sprays.

Corn Ear Worms

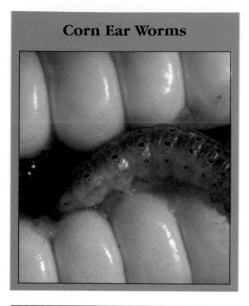

Range: *throughout the United States, especially southern and central states*

Generations per year: *2 to 7*

Host(s): *corn and tomato*

The corn ear worm is also known as the tomato fruit worm, depending on the host it infests. It may also attack potatoes, beans, peas, peppers and squash.

Description and life cycle: Corn ear worms overwinter as pupae in the soil. In spring the gray-green or brown moths emerge and lay eggs on corn silk or the undersides of leaves; the eggs hatch in a few days. The larvae, ½ inch long, are green, yellow, or white caterpillars with black longitudinal stripes. They feed for 3 to 4 weeks, then return to the soil to pupate. In the North, they usually produce two generations each year; in the South, as many as seven.

Damage and detection: Larvae feed on corn silk, leaves, and fruit, inhibiting pollination, disfiguring ears and opening them to invasion by other insects or pathogens. Similar damage occurs with other hosts.

Control: CULTURAL—Till vegetable garden in fall to expose pupae. PHYSICAL—Handpick worms. BIOLOGICAL—Larvae are cannibalistic and help control their own numbers; Bt; tachinid flies; trichogramma wasps. CHEMICAL—Neem; ryania.

Crickets and Grasshoppers

Range: *widespread throughout North America*

Generations per year: *1 to 3*

Host(s): *most ornamentals and vegetables*

Crickets and grasshoppers are common pests that attack almost all cultivated plants. Although they usually cause only minor damage to crops, populations may build up, and migrating swarms devour nearly all vegetation in their path. Such attacks are infrequent in North America, but the common name of one species, the Mormon cricket, is a reminder of the swarm that attacked the crops of Mormon settlers in Utah in 1848. This pest, which is actually a grasshopper and not a true cricket, ranges from California to Minnesota and Kansas. Including the Mormon cricket, there are only five North American grasshopper species that become numerous enough to damage crops significantly. Weather conditions play an important role in determining the size of grasshopper populations in a given year. They are smaller in years with a cool, wet spring and summer, but a long, hot dry season can see the populations rise dramatically. True crickets are less destructive than grasshoppers. They damage seedlings in gardens and are also household pests, feeding on clothing, paper, and foods such as fruit and potatoes.

Description and life cycle: The many species of grasshoppers differ in appearance, range, and preferred host. Most species produce one generation per year, although in the South, a few produce two. Like other grasshoppers, the Mormon cricket overwinters in soil as eggs that hatch the following spring. The nymphs go through seven molts before taking on their final adult form, some 2 to 3 months after hatching. The nymphs feed on any available plant material, ex-

Mormon Cricket

hausting one food source completely before moving on to another. In late summer adult females, which are about 1 inch in length, deposit tiny sacs or packets holding up to 100 or so eggs in soil. Female and male adults continue to feed until they are killed by cold weather.

Crickets have one to three generations per year, overwintering in the South as nymphs or adults and in cooler climates as eggs. After hatching, nymphs go through 8 to 12 molts before emerging as full-size adults that are ¾ to 1 inch long and dark brown or black, with wiry antennae. They often have large hind legs and flat, folded wings, although some species are wingless. Males of species common to the United States make a loud, chirping noise by rubbing together parts of their forewings. Most crickets are nocturnal and seek shelter during the day, some in vegetation and others in the ground. Females lay their eggs in soil or in plant stems in late summer or early fall. In winter, adult crickets frequently seek shelter indoors.

Damage and detection: Among the most damaging of grasshopper species is the migratory grasshopper, which causes significant crop losses in the western United States and southwestern Canada. They feed in swarms, stripping away the leaves and stems of nearly all vegetation in areas of up to several square miles; they prefer grasses but in its absence will feed on virtually any other kind of plants. The swarm then migrates to another feeding ground. Other species feed in a similar manner but may have a narrower range of hosts.

Crickets, like grasshoppers, are not a serious problem until they are present in large numbers. Masses of field crickets damage plantings of tomatoes, peas, beans, cucumbers, and squash by consuming seeds or seedlings. Further damage occurs when adults and nymphs chew on the foliage and flowers of vegetable crops. Tree crickets injure stems of trees or shrubs by inserting their eggs into the plant tissue.

Control: CULTURAL—Cultivate soil in fall to expose overwintering eggs. PHYSICAL—Use row covers; trap in jars buried to the brim and containing a mixture of one part molasses to nine parts water. BIOLOGICAL—The pathogen *Nosema locustae* is effective for long-term control over large areas; beneficial nematodes; blister beetle larvae; praying mantises; predatory flies. CHEMICAL—Insecticidal soap.

Cucumber Beetles

Range: *United States and Canada, east of the Rocky Mountains*

Generations per year: *1 to 4*

Host(s): *many vegetables and ornamentals*

Widespread east of the Rockies, cucumber beetles are most damaging in the South, where they often produce four generations a year. They attack cucumbers, melons, squash, and other members of the cucumber family. Ornamentals commonly infested include chrysanthemums, cosmos, dahlias, roses, zinnias, and grasses.

Description and life cycle: Adults are ¼ inch long, yellowish green with black spots or stripes. They overwinter in garden debris, emerging in spring to lay eggs at the base of host plants. The eggs hatch in about 10 days, and slender, white larvae, which reach ½ inch in length, burrow into the soil to feed on plant roots and pupate. Emerging as adults, they feed on leaves, flowers, and fruit, and repeat the cycle.

Damage and detection: Larvae feeding on roots stunt and may kill plants. Adults chew holes in leaves and flowers; some species also eat fruit. Adults and larvae can carry cucumber mosaic virus and cucumber wilt, diseases that can kill plants.

Control: PHYSICAL—Handpick beetles; use row covers. CULTURAL—Plant varieties resistant to the diseases carried by cucumber beetles. BIOLOGICAL—Beneficial nematodes; braconid wasps; tachinid flies. CHEMICAL—Rotenone; sabadilla.

Cutworms

Range: *various species throughout North America*

Generations per year: *1 to 5*

Host(s): *most herbaceous plants*

The roughly 3,000 species of cutworms in North America can be grouped according to their feeding habits as tunnelers, climbers, and subterraneans.

Description and life cycle: Most cutworms overwinter as larvae or pupae. The soft, gray-brown larvae, 1 to 2 inches long, feed at night, burrow into the soil during the day, and curl into a C-shape when disturbed. They pupate in the soil and emerge as night-flying adult moths, brown or gray, with a 1½ inch wingspan. Females lay their eggs on leaves and stems; eggs hatch in 2 to 10 days.

Damage and detection: Tunneling cutworms chew on seedlings near the soil surface, making them topple and die. Climbing cutworms feed on leaves and flowers of vegetables and herbaceous ornamental plants. Subterranean cutworms feed on roots and underground stems, causing wilting and stunting.

Control: PHYSICAL—Use plant collars around seedlings. CULTURAL—Till soil in fall to expose the larvae or pupae; till again in early spring and wait 2 weeks before planting. BIOLOGICAL—Beneficial nematodes; braconid wasps; Bt; tachinid flies; trichogramma wasps.

Elm Leaf Beetles

Range: *throughout North America wherever elms grow*

Generations per year: *1 to 4*

Host(s): *elm, zelkova*

Both adults and larvae of the elm leaf beetle cause serious damage to elms, especially in California, where there are three or four generations each year.

Description and life cycle: Adult elm leaf beetles overwinter in protected places such as the crevices in tree bark, garages, or sheds. The beetle is yellow or dull green and ¼ inch long. In spring, as tree leaves unfurl, beetles fly to elms to feed and mate. Females lay eggs in clusters on the leaves. Larvae are up to ½ inch long, yellow-green with black stripes and head. They feed on the undersides of leaves for several weeks, then move down the tree to pupate on the trunk or on the ground. In about 2 weeks adults emerge to repeat the cycle.

Damage and detection: Adults chew roughly round holes in leaves; larvae skeletonize foliage, leaving only veins. Leaves turn brown and drop prematurely, often to be replaced by a new flush of foliage just in time for the next generation of beetles. Repeated defoliations can weaken a tree, making it vulnerable to Dutch elm disease, borne by elm bark beetles *(pages 102 and 139)*.

Control: PHYSICAL—Handpick adults; apply sticky bands. BIOLOGICAL—Bt San Diego strain; chalcid wasps; tachinid flies.

European Corn Borers

Range: *north and central United States and southern Canada*

Generations per year: *1 to 3*

Host(s): *many herbaceous plants*

Although the European corn borer, as its name suggests, is primarily a pest of corn, it also attacks many other plants, including tomato, celosia, sunflowers, cosmos, hollyhocks, chrysanthemums, asters, and dahlias.

Description and life cycle: The European corn borer overwinters as larvae in plant debris and pupates in early spring. Adult moths are pale brown, with dark markings on their wings and a 1-inch wingspan. Females lay masses of eggs on the undersides of leaves. Eggs hatch in about a week and the larvae begin to feed. Larvae are 1 inch long when fully grown, beige with brown spots and dark heads. They feed for 3 to 4 weeks, pupate, and repeat the cycle.

Damage and detection: Larvae bore into corn ears at either end to feed on kernels. They also feed on tassels and leaves. On other plants, the larvae tunnel into stems and fruits.

Control: PHYSICAL—Remove and destroy plant debris. CULTURAL—Plant varieties resistant to borers; time plantings to avoid peak periods of borer infestation. BIOLOGICAL—Bt, applied before larvae enter stems or ears; braconid wasps; ladybird beetles; tachinid flies. CHEMICAL—Pyrethrins, ryania, sabadilla.

Flea Beetles

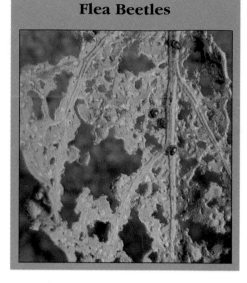

Range: *several species throughout North America*

Generations per year: *2 to 4*

Host(s): *most herbaceous plants*

Flea beetles, common garden pests, attack most herbaceous ornamentals and vegetables. They are especially troublesome on members of the cabbage family and the solanum family, which includes eggplant, peppers, potatoes, and tomatoes. The beetles get their name from the way they jump when disturbed.

Description and life cycle: Flea beetles overwinter as adults near the soil surface, emerging in spring to feed and mate. Beetles are small—¹⁄₁₀ inch long—black, brown, or bronze; they lay eggs in the soil near hosts. The larvae, ¾-inch, legless white grubs with brown heads, eat plant roots, pupate, and emerge as adults to repeat the cycle.

Damage and detection: Adults chew tiny round holes in leaves, making the plant look as if it's been peppered with shot. Seedlings are seriously weakened or may be killed by a heavy infestation. Larvae weaken plants with their root feeding. Flea beetles carry several viral diseases.

Control: PHYSICAL—Use row covers; spray with jets of water; ring plants with diatomaceous earth or wood ashes. CULTURAL—Cultivate soil often to expose eggs and larvae. BIOLOGICAL—Beneficial nematodes; braconid wasps; tachinid flies. CHEMICAL—Pyrethrins; rotenone; sabadilla.

Gall Mites

Range: *various species throughout North America*

Generations per year: *many*

Host(s): *many trees and shrubs*

Mites are not insects; they belong to the arachnid class, which includes spiders. There are many species of mites, each with its own range of host plants. Some of the most common mites are the maple bladder gall mite, the maple spindle gall mite, and the hickory bladder gall mite. Other mite species cause galls on beech, cherry, elm, linden, and poplar.

Description and life cycle: Most mites are too small for the unaided eye to see, and their life cycles are poorly understood. Maple gall mites overwinter as adults in maple bark. In early spring, the mites singly enter leaves, injecting a toxin that stimulates the leaf to grow a gall. Each mite feeds inside its gall, and the females lay eggs in their galls; when the eggs hatch, the resident adults move to new leaves. Mites often produce a new generation every 2 or 3 weeks.

Damage and detection: The maple bladder gall mite causes wartlike growths on the upper sides of maple leaves; these galls gradually turn from green to brilliant red. The maple spindle gall mite causes narrow, spindlelike projections; another mite causes colorful, feltlike patches. A large number of galls may distort leaves, but the damage is rarely serious.

Control: BIOLOGICAL—Predatory mites. CHEMICAL—Dormant lime-sulfur spray.

Gall Wasps

Range: *various species throughout the United States and Canada*

Generations per year: *2*

Host(s): *oak, rose, and thistle families*

Gall wasps stimulate host plants to form enlarged growths called galls on leaves, twigs, or stems. There are hundreds of species of gall wasps, which have specific host ranges and produce characteristic galls. Most of these galls, while unsightly, do little to harm the host.

Description and life cycle: Adult gall wasps overwinter in the gall and emerge in spring. Females lay eggs on the host; after hatching, the larvae begin to feed. Where each one feeds, it stimulates the host to form a new gall, then uses this mass of plant tissue as food and as shelter during pupation. Adults emerge in summer to produce a second brood; this generation overwinters as adults in new galls.

Damage and detection: Galls may form on leaves or stems of host plants. They are often high in tannins and have been used in the past to make ink. While the galls may be somewhat unsightly, they rarely injure or even weaken a plant.

Control: PHYSICAL—Prune and destroy overwintering galls to reduce gall wasp population.

Gypsy Moths

Range: *eastern and central United States; sometimes the Pacific Northwest*

Generations per year: *1*

Host(s): *many trees and shrubs*

The gypsy moth was introduced to Massachusetts from Europe in 1869, in an effort to improve American silk production. Accidentally released, it spread rapidly throughout New England, feeding on a wide variety of deciduous and evergreen trees and shrubs. Among its preferred hosts are oak, apple, alder, hawthorn, poplar, and willow. Its spread has continued throughout the eastern and central United States and southeastern Canada. In the West, there are occasional outbreaks in Washington, Oregon, and California. A closely related Asian species has appeared on the West Coast, where it is attacking an even wider range of plants than the gypsy moth.

Description and life cycle: Gypsy moths overwinter as eggs, which hatch in April or early May. The larvae are gray caterpillars that grow up to 2 inches in length and have tufts of brown hairs on the sides of their bodies. They are easy to identify because of the distinctive markings on their backs—five pairs of blue tubercles, or dots followed by six pairs of red dots. At first, larvae feed at night on leaves of trees and shrubs and take shelter under fallen leaves, in woodpiles, or other dark or shady places during the day. As the larvae grow larger, they begin to feed during the day as well as at night.

When a tree suffers an unusually heavy infestation, the larvae are so numerous that their excrement rustles like a gentle, constant rain as it falls through the leaves, to accumulate in a visible layer of tiny tan pellets on the ground. After approximately 7 weeks of feeding, each caterpillar finds a protected spot, such as a crevice in the bark or the crotch of a branch, in which to pupate. Adult moths emerge from mid- to late summer.

The moths are an inch long, with a 2-inch wing span. Wings are gray-brown in the male, off-white in the female, with dark wavy markings in both. The males fly freely, but the females do not fly until after mating. The females lay their eggs in fuzzy, chamois-colored masses of 100 to 1,000, on any hard surface. Gypsy moth

Gypsy Moth Caterpillar

egg masses are often found attached to vehicles or camping gear and may be inadvertently transported over many miles by such means. Checking infested trees and nearby buildings for these egg masses and eliminating them when found is one way to reduce future infestations.

Damage and detection: Gypsy moths defoliate plants, leaving only the midrib of each leaf. Infested plants are left weakened and susceptible to disease. Deciduous trees often die if defoliated two or three consecutive seasons, and evergreens may die after a single defoliation.

Control: PHYSICAL—Handpick egg masses; paint egg cases with creosote; apply tree bands and sticky bands around trees; set pheromone traps. CULTURAL—Plant resistant varieties. BIOLOGICAL—Bt; chalcid wasps; ground beetles; tachinid flies; trichogramma wasps. CHEMICAL—Neem; pyrethrins; ryania.

Hemlock Woolly Adelgids

Range: *eastern United States from North Carolina to Connecticut*

Generations per year: *2 to 3*

Host(s): *eastern hemlock, spruce*

The hemlock woolly adelgid is an extremely destructive pest of eastern hemlock *(Tsuga canadensis)*. It also occurs in the Pacific Northwest but is not so serious a problem there because western hemlocks are somewhat resistant.

Description and life cycle: The hemlock woolly adelgid overwinters as a tiny adult covered with a protective white, cottony sac about ¼ inch long. From February to June, the female lays 50 to 300 eggs inside her sac. Chocolate-colored, oval nymphs hatch in spring and early summer, after which they crawl away from the egg sac and settle into their own feeding sites. Some of the nymphs mature into wingless females and stay on the same hemlock, where they produce another generation. Other nymphs mature into winged adults that spend part of their life cycle on spruce trees.

Damage and detection: The woolly egg sacs are easy to see at the base of needles. Needles turn yellow, then brown, and drop off. The adelgids suck sap and weaken trees. If left untreated, an infested tree generally dies in 4 years. In cases of severe infestation, it may die within as little as 1 year.

Control: CHEMICAL—Horticultural oil or insecticidal soap, applied as soon as infestation is detected.

Hornworms

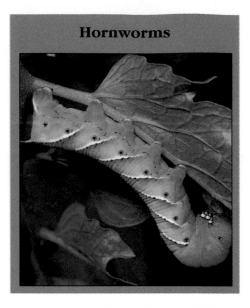

Range: *widespread throughout North America*

Generations per year: *1 to 4*

Host(s): *tomato, pepper, eggplant*

The hornworm, which is the larva of the sphinx moth, is large and eats voraciously; even a single hornworm feeding on a plant can cause significant damage.

Description and life cycle: Hornworms overwinter in the soil as brown, 2-inch pupae. These emerge in summer as mottled gray moths with yellow-spotted abdomens and a 4- to 5-inch wingspan, and lay eggs on the undersides of leaves. When the eggs hatch, the emerging larvae are bright green caterpillars 3 to 4 inches long with diagonal white side bars and a black, green, or red horn at the tail end. The caterpillars eat leaves for 3 to 4 weeks before entering the soil to pupate.

Damage and detection: Hornworms eat large holes in leaves and fruit. Their color camouflages them well in foliage, but the sudden appearance of leafless stems gives away their presence, as do greenish black droppings on the leaves.

Control: CULTURAL—Cultivate soil in fall. PHYSICAL—Handpick caterpillars, unless their backs bear the white cocoons of braconid wasps, a natural predator. BIOLOGICAL—Braconid wasps; lacewings; ladybird beetles; trichogramma wasps. CHEMICAL—Bt; pyrethrins; rotenone.

Imported Cabbage Worms

Range: *widespread throughout North America*

Generations per year: *3 to 6*

Host(s): *members of the cabbage family*

Brought from Europe in the late 19th century, the cabbage worm is now a common pest in gardens throughout the United States. The larva of the cabbage butterfly, it attacks ornamental kale along with its edible relatives.

Description and life cycle: Cabbage worms overwinter as pupae in garden debris. Adults emerge in early spring as day-flying white or pale yellow butterflies, with dark gray or black wing tips and a 1½-inch wingspan. Eggs are laid on the underside of hosts' leaves, and hatch in 4 to 8 days. Each larva—1¼ inches long, velvety green, with one yellow stripe along its back—feeds for 2 to 3 weeks, then pupates on or near its host. A new generation of adults emerges in 2 to 3 weeks. Generations overlap, so infestations may appear continuous.

Damage and detection: Larvae chew large, ragged holes in leaves, tunnel into heads of cabbage, kale, and cauliflower, and eat broccoli florets. They leave large amounts of green-black droppings.

Control: PHYSICAL—Handpick larvae; use row covers. BIOLOGICAL—Bt at 1- to 2-week intervals; green lacewings; spined soldier bugs; trichogramma wasps. CHEMICAL—Neem; rotenone; sabadilla.

Iris Borers

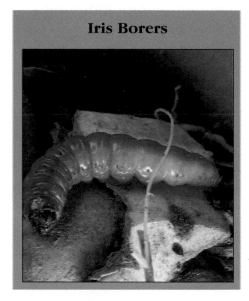

Range: *eastern North America, west to Iowa and Ontario and south to Georgia*

Generations per year: *1*

Host(s): *iris*

In its geographic range, this larva is the most serious insect pest of the iris. The night-flying miller moth is the adult stage.

Description and life cycle: Iris borers overwinter as eggs on old leaves. They hatch in midspring as green larvae that mature to dusky pink with brown heads; the backs bear a light stripe and rows of black dots. Fat and up to 2 inches long, the larvae tunnel into iris foliage to feed for several weeks, then pupate in the soil near the iris rhizomes. The adult miller moths emerge in late summer; they have brown forewings, yellow hind wings, and a 2-inch wingspan. They lay eggs on leaves and flower stalks.

Damage and detection: Larvae tunnel through leaves and crowns and into rhizomes as they feed; infested leaves develop ragged edges and areas that appear water soaked. Infested rhizomes are extremely vulnerable to bacterial soft rots.

Control: PHYSICAL—Remove and destroy leaves and stems in late fall to eliminate eggs; dig infested rhizomes and either discard them or poke a wire into visible borer holes to kill pests; dust with sulfur before planting.

Japanese Beetles

Range: *eastern United States, southeastern Canada, occasionally California*

Generations per year: *1*

Host(s): *more than 275 species of plants*

Native to the Far East, Japanese beetles were introduced to the United States around 1916. They first appeared in New Jersey but have gradually spread north to Nova Scotia and Ontario, west to the Mississippi River, and south to the Gulf of Mexico, and are occasionally found in California. They cause serious damage to a wide variety of plants in both the larval (grub) stage and the adult (beetle) stage. Among their preferred hosts are rose, grape, willow, hibiscus, apple, hydrangea, linden, raspberry, and grasses. They are particularly destructive in nurseries, orchards, and on turfs of golf courses.

Description and life cycle: Japanese beetles overwinter as partially grown grubs in the soil below the frostline. Grayish white with dark heads, grubs are fat and up to ¾ inch long; they are usually found curled in a C-shape. They feed on the roots of grasses before pupating in late spring or early summer, and emerge as adults in May, June, and July.

Beetles are ½ inch long, with shiny, metallic blue or green bodies and copper-colored wings. Their bodies are covered with grayish hairs, with tufts of white hairs on the abdomen. Beetles fly only during the day and prefer feeding in sunny locations. When they find a suitable host plant, they release feeding and sex pheromones that attract many other Japanese beetles. They feed for 30 to 45 days, then the females lay as many as 60 eggs each, in clusters of one to four, several inches deep in the soil. Females prefer to lay eggs in loose, acid soils in sunny sites; the heaviest infestations usually occur in soils with a pH of 5.3 or lower. Grubs hatch in about 2 weeks and feed on grass roots until cold weather forces them to burrow below the frostline. In spring, grubs migrate back to the soil surface and resume feeding on roots.

Damage and detection: Grub damage begins as patches of turf that grows poorly and starts to turn yellow. These patches get larger and gradually turn brown. To check such a patch for Japanese beetle grubs, peel back the turf and examine the root zone. Severely damaged turf has lost most of its roots and can be rolled up like carpet to reveal the grubs. Unnoticed and untreated, an infestation of grubs can do irreversible damage, even kill an entire lawn. Adult beetles ignore grasses, preferring to attack woody and herbaceous ornamentals as well as vegetables and fruits. Feeding in groups in daytime, they chew away leaf tissue between the veins, skeletonizing foliage; they may cause defoliation. They also feed on buds and flowers, causing disfiguration.

Control for adults: PHYSICAL—Handpick beetles in the early morning while they are sluggish; knock beetles off foliage onto a sheet spread under infested plants; collect beetles with hand-held vacuum, then immerse them in soapy water. CHEMICAL—Neem as a repellent; pyrethrins; rotenone.

Control for grubs: CULTURAL—Check lawn for grubs in early spring or fall by selecting four or five different areas, marking off a square foot, and peeling back the sod. Control is warranted if you find more than 10 grubs per square foot. BIOLOGICAL—Beneficial nematodes; milky spore; parasitic wasps; tachinid flies. CHEMICAL—Neem.

Lace Bugs

Range: *various species throughout North America*

Generations per year: *2 to 5*

Host(s): *many woody and herbaceous plants*

Lace bugs are sucking insects that feed primarily on woody ornamentals such as rhododendron, hawthorn, pyracantha, and azalea. One species infests chrysanthemums and asters. Species vary in both geographic range and host preference.

Description and life cycle: Lace bugs overwinter as eggs or adults in garden debris. Nymphs undergo five molts in as little as 2 to 3 weeks to become adults. They are tiny and dark; many are covered with spines. Adults are ⅛ inch long, with lacy, nearly transparent wings. Adults lay black eggs on the undersides of leaves, along the midrib, usually near the tops of plants.

Damage and detection: Both nymphs and adults feed in clusters and suck the plant's juices, giving leaves a stippled or blanched upper side. Plants lose color, become unsightly, and bloom poorly. Nymphs feeding on the undersides of leaves excrete distinctive brown, sticky droppings. Repeated infestations can weaken and kill plants.

Control: PHYSICAL—Spray with water. CULTURAL—Maintain vigor and health of plants. CHEMICAL—Horticultural oil; insecticidal soap; neem; pyrethrins; rotenone; sabadilla.

Leafhoppers

Range: *widespread throughout North America*

Generations per year: *2 to 5*

Hosts(s): *most ornamentals and vegetables*

North America has more than 2,700 leafhopper species. They especially favor calendula, marigold, and other members of the composite family but also attack other herbaceous and woody ornamentals, vegetables, and fruits.

Description and life cycle: Adult leafhoppers overwinter on host plants. In spring the females insert eggs into leaf or stem tissue. Adults are wedge shaped, ⅒ to ½ inch long; most are green, brown, or yellow, with colorful spots or bands. Nymphs are smaller, often wingless versions of adults. Each generation lives only a few weeks.

Damage and detection: Nymphs and adults feed on the undersides of leaves, sucking sap and injecting their toxic saliva into the plant. Heavy infestations can stunt, bleach, or mottle leaves; leaves may brown at the margins and drop prematurely. Leafhoppers also carry serious plant diseases such as aster yellows and curly top virus.

Control: PHYSICAL—Use row covers; strong streams of water. CULTURAL—Till in fall. BIOLOGICAL—Big-eyed bugs; lacewing larvae. CHEMICAL—Horticultural oil; insecticidal soap; rotenone; sabadilla; systemic pesticide.

Leaf Miners

Range: *throughout North America*

Generations per year: *variable*

Host(s): *many ornamentals and vegetables*

Leaf miners are the larvae of different species of beetles, flies, sawflies, and moths and feed between the upper and lower surfaces of leaves. Among the plants often disfigured by leaf miners are azalea, birch, boxwood, chrysanthemum, columbine, holly, and delphinium.

Description and life cycle: Birch leaf miners, which also infest elms, overwinter as larvae in cocoons in the soil and pupate in spring. The adults, which are black with transparent wings, emerge in spring, mate, and lay eggs in leaves. The hatching larvae feed inside the leaves, then pupate. This species has up to four generations a year. The boxwood miner has only one generation per year. Eggs are laid in leaves in midspring; the larvae overwinter in leaves and pupate the following year. Adults are very small, gnat-like flies. They emerge in midspring and mate, lay eggs, and die in a few days.

Damage and detection: Larvae feeding inside leaves make blotches, blisters, or winding tunnels. These mines weaken plants and are very unsightly.

Control: PHYSICAL—Use row covers; destroy damaged leaves; remove such weed hosts as lamb's-quarters and dock. CULTURAL—Rotate crops. BIOLOGICAL—Lacewings; birds. CHEMICAL—Horticultural oil; neem.

Locust Leaf Miner Beetles

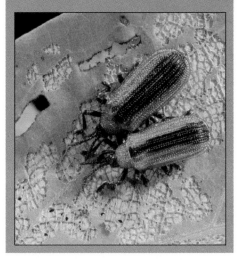

Range: *eastern United States, west to the Mississippi River*

Generations per year: *1 to 2*

Host(s): *primarily black locust*

The locust leaf miner beetle feeds on black locust trees, making them extremely unsightly. It also feeds on a number of other hosts in the legume family, such as sophora and American yellowwood, but rarely does much damage.

Description and life cycle: The adult beetle overwinters in a sheltered site, then emerges in spring to feed on the margins of growing leaves of black locust. The ¼-inch adult is orange-yellow, with a wide black stripe along the back. Females lay eggs in clusters of three to five on the undersides of leaves. Larvae are flattened, yellow-white with dark heads; on hatching, they tunnel into leaves, feed for a month, and pupate. There is often a second generation.

Damage and detection: Feeding at the margins of leaves, adults cause little damage, but larvae tunnel into leaves to form mines that create irregular blotches, spreading back from the leaf tip. Leaves turn brown and drop prematurely. Sometimes trees produce a second set of leaves, which is often infested with the second generation of leaf miner beetles. Repeated infestations can weaken trees.

Control: BIOLOGICAL—Wheel bugs; trichogramma wasps.

May/June Beetles

Range: *throughout the United States; most troublesome in the South and Midwest*

Generations per year: *1- to 4-year life cycles*

Host(s): *many ornamentals; lawn grasses*

The adult stage of this pest is known as the May beetle, June beetle, or daw bug; the larva is often called a white grub. Both the adults and the larvae cause plant damage.

Description and life cycle: May beetles overwinter as larvae in the soil, feeding on roots, especially those of lawn grasses. The grubs are ½ to 1½ inches long, white with dark heads. Depending on the species, they stay in the larval stage 1 to 3 years. Then they pupate, emerging in late spring as 1-inch black, brown, or green beetles. Active at night, beetles feed on the foliage of a wide range of trees and shrubs, vegetables, and flowers. By day, they hide in debris or foliage. Eggs are laid in the soil and hatch in about 3 weeks.

Damage and detection: Grubs eat roots of grasses and other plants such as potato and strawberry, giving them a wilted, stunted look. Where grubs dig out dime-size holes in turf, grass turns brown. Adults chew ragged holes in leaves.

Control: PHYSICAL—Handpick beetles. CULTURAL—Cultivate soil in fall to kill larvae. BIOLOGICAL—Beneficial nematodes; milky spore; vertebrate predators of grubs including birds, skunks, and moles. CHEMICAL—Neem; pyrethrins.

Mites

Range: *widespread throughout North America*

Generations per year: *many*

Host(s): *many ornamentals and vegetables*

Mites are not insects but belong to the class of animals called arachnids, which includes ticks and spiders. Of the hundreds of mite species, most benefit gardeners by feeding on pests. Other species, however, are parasites of plants or animals. Among the most damaging to plants are the two-spotted spider mites, cyclamen mites, and rust mites.

Description and life cycle: Mites have short life cycles; in warm climates, homes, and greenhouses, reproduction is continuous. Uncontrolled populations of mites can build rapidly, resulting in serious plant infestations and losses.

Outdoors, most plant-feeding mites overwinter as adults or eggs, in garden debris or on the bark of trees or shrubs. Mites are barely visible to the naked eye; a spider mite is about the size of a grain of salt, less than $\frac{1}{20}$ inch long. Magnification through a hand lens shows that the adult spider mites have 8 legs and hairy, oval-shaped bodies. They may be brown, green, red, or yellow; their color varies, to a large degree, according to their diet. Nymphs are similar to adults but smaller, and early stages have only 6 legs.

Cyclamen or rust mites, about a fourth the size of adult spider mites, are hardly visible without a hand lens that magnifies at least 15x. Adult cyclamen mites are pinkish orange; nymphs are translucent. Rust mites have only 4 legs, are wedge shaped, and are usually pinkish white or yellow.

Mites emerge in spring to feed and mate. Eggs are laid on the host plant and usually hatch in less than a week. The new generation reaches maturity in 5 to 10 days. New broods are produced continuously until cold weather sets in.

Damage and detection: In both nymph and adult forms, mites feed on plants by sucking the cell sap, generally feeding in large colonies. Because of their minute size, however, their damage tends to go unnoticed until long after mites have become established in a planting.

Spider mites cause leaves to become stippled, bleached, yellow, or brown. Leaves often drop prematurely, weakening plants and stunting fruit. A heavy spider mite infestation may cover affected plant parts with a fine webbing, spun by the mites as they feed. Spider mite damage is most severe in the hot, dry, and dusty conditions that accelerate their reproduction rate.

Cyclamen mites generally infest new, unfolding leaves. As the leaves continue to develop, they appear crinkled and deformed; stems may fail to elongate normally. Cyclamen mites also attack young flowers, causing growth distortions. On strawberry, they feed on the fruit, stunting its development and making it look dry and shriveled. Rust mites damage the surfaces of the leaves on which they feed, disrupting the chlorophyll and turning leaves brown or rust colored.

Control: PHYSICAL—Remove and destroy heavily infested leaves, branches, or entire plants; spray with water. BIOLOGICAL—Lacewings; ladybird beetles; predatory mites. CHEMICAL—Use insecticides only as a last resort, as they may harm predators and result in a greater mite problem; horticultural oil; insecticidal soap; neem; pyrethrins.

Pine Tip Moths

Range: *various species throughout North America*

Generations per year: *1 to 5*

Host(s): *pine trees*

Seven species of pine tip or pine shoot moths occur in different parts of the United States. Although they have different hosts among the many species of pine, the damage they do is similar.

Description and life cycle: Pine tip moths hibernate as larvae or pupae in the tips of shoots or in buds. Adults are night-flying moths, reddish brown to gray, with a wingspan up to ¾ inch. Females lay their eggs at the tips of host branches. Larvae are about ½ inch long, and may be brown, reddish brown, or yellow; they tunnel into the bases of needles and buds to feed. They pupate in these hollows or near the base of the tree. Most species produce one generation each year. The Nantucket pine tip moth, however, may produce as many as five.

Damage and detection: Larvae kill the host's shoot tips, turning them brown and dry. Pine resin and insect excrement accumulate near the feeding site. Buds are blasted, and growth is stunted or produces a tuft of thin, weak twigs. Heavy infestations can kill young trees.

Control: PHYSICAL—Prune and destroy infested branches in early spring to remove overwintering larvae or pupae. BIOLOGICAL—Braconid wasps; predatory spiders. CHEMICAL—Systemic pesticide.

Plant Bugs

Range: *widespread throughout North America*

Generations per year: *3 to 5*

Host(s): *many ornamentals and vegetables*

The plant bugs are a large family of insects that includes predaceous and beneficial species as well as several serious pests. Among the most common pests are the four-lined plant bug and the tarnished plant bug, or lygus bug. The four-lined plant bug feeds on more than 250 plant species. Its geographic range is east of the Rocky Mountains. Most of its hosts are herbaceous ornamentals, such as aster, chrysanthemum, dahlia, phlox, and zinnia. It also infests such ornamental trees and shrubs as azalea, dogwood, forsythia, rose, and viburnum.

The more common tarnished plant bug, found throughout North America, is probably the most damaging member of this family. It attacks over 385 plant species including most vegetables and fruits as well as numerous woody and herbaceous ornamentals.

Description and life cycle: Four-lined plant bugs overwinter as eggs in young plant shoots. The egg clusters, protruding from slits across the stem, are easy to see in fall after the leaves have dropped. They hatch in spring, and the nymphs feed for about a month before their final molt to become adults. Nymphs are bright red, yellow, or orange with black spots. Adults are ¼ to ⅓ inch long, greenish yellow, with 4 black stripes and yellow or bright green forewings. There is one generation per year.

Tarnished plant bugs overwinter as adults under bark or in garden debris, emerging in early spring to attack opening buds. Females lay eggs in the stems and flowers of herbaceous host plants. Adults are ¼ inch long, oval, and mottled brown and tan; each forewing has a black-tipped yellow triangle. Eggs hatch in about 10 days. The yellow-green nymphs resemble the adults but are wingless. They feed for 3 or 4 weeks, then molt to become adults, and repeat the cycle. There are as many as five generations per year.

Damage and detection: Plant bugs injure their host by sucking plant sap in both nymph and adult stages. Four-lined plant bugs feed on leaves, removing the chlorophyll and causing spots that lose color or turn brown or black. The injured

Tarnished Plant Bug

area may fall out, or the entire leaf may fall prematurely. The tarnished plant bug feeds on leaves, stems, buds, fruit, and flowers. Adults feeding on buds in spring often kill the growing tip of a twig. As a consequence lateral shoots develop, giving the plant a bushy, often stunted appearance. Besides sucking sap, the tarnished plant bug injects a toxin that disrupts plant growth.

Control: PHYSICAL—Use row covers; remove plant debris where eggs or adults may be overwintering; set white sticky traps. BIOLOGICAL—Big-eyed bugs; braconid wasps; chalcid wasps; damsel bugs; pirate bugs. CHEMICAL—Insecticidal soap; rotenone; sabadilla; apply sprays in the early morning when bugs are sluggish.

Planthoppers

Range: *throughout the United States and southern Canada*

Generations per year: *1*

Host(s): *ornamentals, vegetables, and fruits*

Planthoppers infest a broad range of trees, shrubs, and woody vines, and a few herbaceous ornamentals, as well as vegetables and fruits. Some of the more common plants attacked include boxwood, viburnum, magnolia, maple, oak, and many fruit trees. Although various species are found throughout the United States, they are most troublesome in the South.

Description and life cycle: Planthoppers overwinter as eggs in the twigs of host plants. Hatching in late spring, the nymphs are white or yellow-green. They cover themselves with a white, cottony material and suck plant sap from leaves or shoots. In about 9 weeks, nymphs molt to become adults up to ⅓ inch long that are brown, gray, green, white, or yellow. Females slit the bark of twigs and lay eggs in the slits.

Damage and detection: The white cottony covering of planthoppers detracts from the appearance of ornamentals. Egg laying may cause some dieback in twigs, but planthoppers seldom do other harm. In fruit trees, however, the loss of sap injures fruit and foliage.

Control: PHYSICAL—Spray with water. CHEMICAL—Pyrethrins.

Psyllids

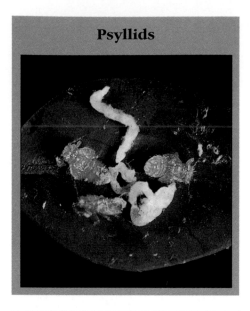

Range: *widespread throughout North America*

Generations per year: *1 to 5*

Host(s): *many ornamentals and vegetables*

Each of the many psyllid species has its own preferred host. The boxwood psyllid and the pear psyllid are two of the most damaging species.

Description and life cycle: Boxwood psyllids overwinter as eggs that hatch in spring. The nymphs feed on new leaves, secreting a waxy material for their own protection. After several weeks, the nymphs become gray-green adults, with transparent wings ⅛ inch across. Females insert eggs in the bases of buds; there is one generation per year. Pear psyllids hibernate in bark crevices or plant debris as tiny brown adults with transparent wings. In early spring they fly to pear trees, mate, and lay eggs; nymphs suck sap from leaves. There are three to five generations per year.

Damage and detection: Nymphs harm plants by sucking sap; some cause gall formation, others spread serious plant diseases. Boxwood psyllids distort new leaves and stunt twig growth. Pear psyllid nymphs turn leaves yellow, carry the pear-decline virus, and secrete honeydew, which supports sooty mold fungus.

Control: PHYSICAL—Remove any water sprouts to discourage feeding. BIOLOGICAL—Chalcid wasps; lacewings; pirate bugs. CHEMICAL—Horticultural oil; rotenone.

Rose Chafers

Range: *widespread throughout North America*

Generations per year: *1*

Host(s): *many*

The rose chafer prefers a light, sandy soil, and this factor somewhat limits its range. Where it is found, it feeds on bramble fruit, grape, peony, hollyhock, rose, strawberry, and many other fruit, vegetable, and ornamental plants.

Description and life cycle: Larvae, or grubs, overwinter in the soil, pupating and emerging as adults in spring. They often appear suddenly in swarms to feed on leaves, flowers, and fruit. Adults are ½-inch reddish brown beetles with spiny legs. They feed for 4 to 6 weeks, then females lay eggs in clusters in the soil. Eggs hatch in about 2 weeks. The larvae are ¾-inch white grubs with brown heads; they feed on the roots of grasses.

Damage and detection: Adults eat flowers and fruit, skeletonize leaves, and soil other plant parts with black excrement. The larvae do minor root damage. Rose chafers are poisonous to many birds.

Control: PHYSICAL—Handpick beetles; row covers; white sticky traps. CULTURAL—Cultivate to destroy larvae and pupae in soil. BIOLOGICAL—Beneficial nematodes for grubs. CHEMICAL—Pyrethrins; rotenone.

Sawflies

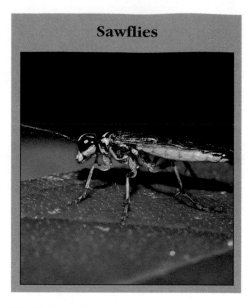

Range: *various species throughout North America*

Generations per year: *1 to 6*

Host(s): *many trees and shrubs*

Although the hundreds of species of sawflies look similar and cause similar damage, each has particular host preferences. Sawflies are common pests of azaleas, birches, dogwoods, roses, and many other deciduous and evergreen trees and shrubs.

Description and life cycle: Most sawflies hibernate as larvae or pupae in cocoons in the soil. Some species may remain in this state for two or more seasons. Emerging in spring and summer, adults resemble clearwing wasps, which belong to the same family. Instead of a stinger, however, females have a sawlike organ for inserting eggs into leaves or needles. Newly hatched larvae are wormlike and are usually green, yellow, or brown. They feed in colonies until mature, then drop to the ground to pupate.

Damage and detection: Larvae eat their host's leaves, beginning with the outermost portions. They feed in masses, completely defoliating one branch before moving to the next, and sometimes stripping an entire tree. Some sawfly species mine leaves, bore into fruit, or stimulate galls.

Control: CULTURAL—Remove garden debris. PHYSICAL—Spray plants with water. BIOLOGICAL—Parasitic wasps. CHEMICAL—Horticultural oil; ryania.

Scale Insects

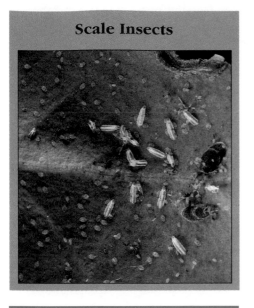

Range: *widespread throughout North America*

Generations per year: *1 to 6*

Host(s): *many*

The roughly 200 species of these piercing-sucking insects can be divided into two major groups, armored scales and soft scales. The armored scales bear a hard, scalelike shell that entirely covers the insect's body and can be separated from it. The soft scales have a waxy covering that does not quite enclose the body and cannot be separated from it. Scales attack many trees and shrubs and can be troublesome indoors on houseplants and in greenhouses, where their reproduction is continuous. Scale species differ in both geographic ranges and hosts.

Description and life cycle: Scales may overwinter as eggs, as nymphs, or as adults. In many species, female adults look significantly different from males; they may lay eggs or give birth to live nymphs. Called crawlers, young nymphs are soft bodied and about ¹⁄₁₀ to ¹⁄₁₆ inch long. They crawl out of the shell to feed, sucking plant sap. They may remain on the same plant or be carried by wind to infest a new plant. The crawler stage may last for a few hours or a few days. The female nymph then settles onto one spot and secretes her protective shell. She pupates within the shell, matures, and lays her eggs there. Male crawlers pupate to become winged adults.

Common armored species include:

- euonymus scale, which attacks many species of bittersweet, citrus, euonymus, lilac, and pachysandra. Mature females overwinter on branches under their protective brown, shell-like scales; males overwinter under narrow, white scales. The pale yellow crawlers begin to appear in late spring. There are one to three generations per year.
- juniper scale, which infests arborvitae, cypress, incense cedar, and juniper. The insects overwinter as fertilized females under round white scales with yellow centers. Crawlers appear in early summer. Males have slender white bodies. There is one generation per year.
- obscure scale, most troublesome in the South. It infests shade trees and is a serious pest of pecan. The insects overwinter as fertilized females, and

Wax Scale

crawlers are present throughout the summer. The shell is gray and roughly circular. One generation is produced each year.

- oystershell scale, which is very widespread in its geographic range but most common in the northern parts of the United States. This pest can occur in such large numbers that the shells cover all of the bark of a host plant. While oystershell scale attacks many deciduous trees and shrubs, it is most troublesome on apple, ash, lilac, pear, poplar, and willow. The insects overwinter as eggs under the female's grayish brown, oyster-shaped shell. The male shell is smaller and oval. These scales infest only the bark

of their host, and do not feed on leaves. Nymphs appear in late spring and move about as crawlers only a few hours before settling permanently to feed and produce their shells. There are one to two generations per year.

- San Jose scale, which is found throughout the United States and southern Canada. It infests many or-

Oystershell Scale

namental trees and shrubs but is most serious on deciduous fruit trees. Partially grown nymphs overwinter under their scale coverings and resume their feeding and development in late spring. Young scales are light in color but become gray-black and crusty at maturity. Nymphs are yellow. San Jose scale usually occurs in large numbers, making fruit and bark look as if covered with ashes. Female scales are round; males are smaller and oval. Generations overlap, and there are as many as five per year.

Common soft species include:

- hemispherical scales, a tropical pest common in southern California and Florida, where they infest a number of ornamental plants and citrus trees. Hemispherical scales are also a common greenhouse and houseplant pest nearly everywhere, favoring ferns as a host. Young hemispherical scales are oval in shape. The shell of mature females is a nearly perfect hemisphere, shiny and brown. There are one or two generations per year, but they overlap, so all stages may be present at any time.
- wax scales, which are distinguished from other species of scale by their

waxy white covering. Most common in the South, they feed on many hosts, including barberry, boxwood, camellia, euonymus, flowering quince, hemlock, holly, pyracantha, and spiraea. Wax scales also attack plants in greenhouses. Most overwintering individuals are adult females, which begin egg laying in midspring. The eggs hatch in late spring or summer, and after a short period of mobility, the crawlers settle to feed and secrete their waxy covering. Some wax scale species settle on leaves, others on stems. There are one or two generations per year.

Damage and detection: Because of their generally dull color and limited mobility, scales often remain unnoticed until dam-

Euonymus Scale

age to the host has occurred. As piercing-sucking insects that feed on plant sap, many scales settle on stems, others on foliage, often on the undersides of leaves, along the major veins. Leaves of infested plants turn yellow and may drop prematurely. Plants lose vigor. Many scales, especially soft scales, secrete honeydew, a sugary, sticky substance that serves as a growing medium for sooty mold. This dark fungus blocks light from the leaf surface, reducing photosynthesis, causing further yellowing, and seriously reducing a plant's ornamental value.

Control: PHYSICAL—Remove scales with a cotton-tipped swab or soft toothbrush dipped in soapy water or solution of rubbing alcohol and water; prune and destroy infested branches. BIOLOGICAL—Ladybird beetles; parasitic wasps; soldier beetles. CHEMICAL—Horticultural oil.

Slugs and Snails

Range: *widespread throughout North America*

Generations per year: *may live for years*

Host(s): *most ornamentals and vegetables*

Among the hundreds of species of slugs and snails, only a few are significant pests of plants. The difference between a slug and a snail is a shell: a snail has one, a slug does not. Both are mollusks, related to clams and oysters. They need moist conditions and prefer cool, dark places because they dry out easily. For this reason, they are primarily night feeders, although they may come out of their dark hiding places on cloudy or rainy days. Both secrete slimy mucus as they slither along, leaving a narrow, shiny trail in their wake. They are common pests, infesting nearly every garden moist enough to support them.

Description and life cycle: Slugs and snails pass the winter in sheltered locations—often in garden debris, under boards, or in soil. Some species overwinter only as eggs, although most will survive at any stage. In warmer regions and in greenhouses, their activity is continuous, year round.

Each slug and snail is hermaphroditic, having both male and female sex organs. They breed throughout the warm parts of the year. Adults lay eggs in clusters of 25 or more in moist soil or garden debris. Clear to white and up to ⅛ inch across, eggs hatch in about a month. Slugs can be gray, black, brown, pink, or

beige, and some have spots. Snails are usually brown or gray. Both have eyes at the tips of protruding tentacles; two other tentacles bear smelling organs.

Slugs range from ½ to 8 inches long; a snail's body is rarely larger than 3 inches. Snail shells are spiral shaped and usually between ½ and 1½ inches across. Given their shells, snails are more protected than slugs, and if conditions become too dry, snails can retreat to their shells and live in dormancy for up to 4 years. Young slugs and snails look like adults but are smaller. Depending on conditions, they take several months or several years to mature.

Damage and detection: Slugs and snails have rasping file-like mouth parts, with which they tear fleshy leaves, especially those near the ground. Because they feed at night, they are rarely seen, but their damage is plain. They make tender

Snail

seedlings disappear overnight. They eat large ragged holes in the middles and edges of leaves on mature plants, and defoliate favorite hosts. They feed on fleshy fruit and vegetables. The slimy trails they leave behind are a telltale sign of a slug or snail infestation.

Control: CULTURAL—Cultivate soil in early spring to expose eggs, juveniles, and adults. PHYSICAL—Handpick at night by flashlight until damage ceases; use copper barriers; set board traps, checking them each morning and destroying pests; bury a shallow pan filled with beer, for slugs and snails to climb into and drown; spread sand or cinders around plants. BIOLOGICAL—Decollate snails. CHEMICAL—Spread diatomaceous earth around plants.

Sod Webworms

Range: *widespread throughout the United States and southern Canada*

Generations per year: *2 to 3*

Host(s): *turf grasses*

The sod webworm feeds on lawn turf grasses including bent grass, fescues, Kentucky bluegrass, perennial ryegrass, and zoysia. It also attacks corn.

Description and life cycle: Sod webworms hibernate as larvae in tunnels near the soil surface. The ¾-inch larvae are light brown with dark spots. In spring they feed briefly, pupate, and emerge as adults, which are 1 inch long, dull gray or brown moths with spotted wings. They fly evening and night in a zigzag fashion, laying eggs near the bases of grass stems. Upon hatching, the larvae feed on grass blades and form tunnels near the soil surface. Pupation occurs in the tunnel. There are usually two to three generations per year, although in warm areas reproduction is continuous.

Damage and detection: A lawn develops small brown patches in which blades are chewed off at the base. To test for sod webworms, soak damaged lawn areas with a mild detergent solution; if there are more than two webworms per square foot, treatment is recommended.

Control: CULTURAL—Plant turf grass containing endophytic fungi; dethatch in fall. BIOLOGICAL—Beneficial nematodes; birds; Bt; parasitic wasps. CHEMICAL—Insecticidal soap; pyrethrins.

Spittlebugs

Range: *widely distributed throughout North America*

Generations per year: *1 to 2*

Host(s): *many ornamentals and vegetables*

Although spittlebugs have inhabited most of North America for a long time, only in the past two or three decades have their populations increased enough to make them significant plant pests. Sometimes called froghoppers, spittlebugs are related to cicadas and aphids. The several spittlebug species have different hosts and geographic ranges. One of the most destructive species is the Saratoga spittlebug, which infests pines throughout the United States. The most abundant and widely distributed species, the meadow spittlebug, feeds on a broad range of herbaceous plants.

Some spittlebugs complete their entire life cycle on one plant, feeding on the same plant on which the egg was laid. Others feed first on low-growing, herbaceous plants, then migrate to taller, woody plants. Many spittlebugs are most troublesome in high-humidity areas like the Northeast and the Pacific Northwest. Commonly infested hosts include strawberry, legumes, corn, clover, and pines.

Description and life cycle: Spittlebugs overwinter as eggs in grasses or weeds, or on host plants, and hatch in midspring. The nymphs are tiny, wingless, and yellow or green. They produce drops of clear liquid that they mix with air to form a froth that surrounds their bodies, pro-

tecting them from sun and predators. The nymphs keep hidden under this mass of bubbles, usually in groups of three or four, and feed for 6 or 7 weeks. When adults emerge, they continue to feed, but since they do not create spittle, they can walk, hop, or fly. They move quickly when disturbed and may migrate to other hosts. Adults are usually tan, mottled brown or black, often with stripes or bands on their wings. Bluntly wedge shaped, with sharp spines studding their hind legs, they resemble leafhoppers but are somewhat stouter and ¼ to ⅓ inch long, depending on the species. Females lay rows of white or beige eggs on or near hosts.

Damage and detection: The bubbly froth formed by feeding nymphs is the best evidence of spittlebugs' presence. Both nymph and adult spittlebugs feed on tender stems and leaves, by sucking plant sap. A few spittlebugs on a plant rarely cause significant damage, but when their populations are great, they can cause stunting, loss of vigor, and reduced yields. Heavy infestations of pine and Saratoga spittlebugs can reduce growth of the trees' twigs, and make needles lose color and die. Twigs die back from their tips, diminishing the plant's ornamental value.

Control (for use only when significant numbers are present): CULTURAL—In fall, remove and destroy plant debris that can harbor overwintering eggs. PHYSICAL—Spray with water; prune and destroy parts of plants where spittle is present; row covers. CHEMICAL—Insecticidal soap.

Spruce Budworms

Range: *northern half of the United States and most of Canada*

Generations per year: *1*

Host(s): *conifers*

Spruce budworms are the most serious defoliators of coniferous plants in the United States. They prefer to feed on spruce and balsam fir, but they also attack larch, pine, and hemlock.

Description and life cycle: Spruce budworms overwinter as larvae in cocoon-like shelters on twigs of the host tree. In spring they emerge to feed on buds, flowers, and new needles for three or four weeks. When mature, each of the thick, dark brown 1-inch larvae ties young shoots together with silk threads, forming a shelter in which to pupate. The adult moths that emerge less than 2 weeks later are capable of migrating long distances. Females lay their eggs on hosts in a series of elongated overlapping clusters, each of which contain as many as 60 eggs. Larvae hatch in about 10 days and feed until they prepare their winter cocoons.

Damage and detection: Spruce budworms mine needles and buds, and defoliate trees. Heavy infestations often kill hosts in 3 to 5 years. Surviving trees are weakened and susceptible to further insect or disease damage.

Control: BIOLOGICAL—Bt; parasitic wasps.

Tent Caterpillars

Range: *two species, one in eastern and the other in western North America*

Generations per year: *1*

Host(s): *most deciduous trees and shrubs*

Tent caterpillars spin silk tents in the crotches of trees or shrubs. Plants commonly infested are apple, aspen, crab apple, and wild cherry.

Description and life cycle: Tent caterpillars overwinter as eggs on host twigs. Eggs hatch in early spring, and the larvae move to the nearest crotch and spin a silk tent. They feed at night and return to the protection afforded by the tent by day. The 2- to 2½-inch caterpillars are hairy and black with white stripes and blue or red side markings. After 5 to 8 weeks, they pupate, emerging about 10 days later as adult moths, tan or brown with striped forewings and a 1- to 1½-inch wingspan. Females lay a black, lumpy ring of eggs around host twigs.

Damage and detection: This pest's large tent is easy to spot. Larvae eat leaves and can cause total defoliation. Trees may produce a second flush of leaves but are weakened and stunted.

Control: PHYSICAL—Handpick; prune and destroy infested branches; sticky bands on trees; remove egg masses in winter. BIOLOGICAL—Bt; parasitic flies; parasitic wasps; spined soldier bugs. CHEMICAL—Insecticidal soap.

Thrips

Range: *widespread throughout North America*

Generations per year: *5 to 15*

Host(s): *most ornamentals and vegetables*

Thrips are tiny insects that feed on a wide range of plants. Some of their favorite hosts are roses, peonies, gladiolus, daylilies, and onions.

Description and life cycle: With a life cycle of about 3 weeks, thrips produce many generations per year, especially in warm climates. They overwinter as adults or eggs. Adults have bristly wings, are yellow, brown, or black and are only ⅟₅₀ to ⅕ inch long. Nymphs are even smaller, and light green or yellow.

Damage and detection: Thrips usually feed in groups, scraping host tissue with their specialized mouthparts and sucking the released sap. They cause silvery speckling on leaves; infested plants may be deformed or stunted, with buds that turn brown without opening. Some thrips also spread viral diseases.

Control: PHYSICAL—Remove infested buds and flowers; spray with water; sticky yellow traps. CULTURAL—Remove garden debris to eliminate overwintering adults or eggs; rotate crops. BIOLOGICAL—Green lacewings; ladybird beetles; pirate bugs; predatory mites. CHEMICAL—Horticultural oil; insecticidal soap; rotenone.

Treehoppers

Range: *widespread throughout North America*

Generations per year: *1*

Host(s): *many woody and herbaceous plants*

Treehoppers are unusual-looking insects that injure plants both as nymphs and as adults. They infest herbaceous plants as nymphs and trees as adults.

Description and life cycle: Treehoppers overwinter as eggs on bark. In spring the hatching nymphs, green with a humped back, drop to the ground and feed on low-growing herbaceous plants for about 6 weeks. After molting to become adults, they return to trees to continue feeding and to lay eggs.

Damage and detection: In both nymph and adult stages, treehoppers pierce stems and leaves with their mouthparts and suck the sap. The worst damage is done when females slit the bark of twigs and deposit their eggs in the slits. Twigs may dry out and die above the point where the eggs are laid, and they may also be invaded by fungi or bacteria.

Control: CULTURAL—Cultivate soil under fruit trees to eliminate nymph feeding sites, especially around young trees. CHEMICAL—Dust plants with diatomaceous earth; horticultural oil.

Webworms

Range: *throughout the United States and southern Canada*

Generations per year: *1 to 4*

Host(s): *many ornamentals and vegetables*

The several species of webworm differ mainly in their preferred hosts. Fall webworms feed on a wide range of deciduous trees and shrubs. Garden webworms feed on many vegetables and strawberries. Juniper webworms attack juniper.

Description and life cycle: Fall webworms overwinter as pupae on tree bark or in plant debris. In spring the adults, 2-inch white moths with brown spots, lay eggs in masses on the undersides of leaves. The hatching larvae spin a web and feed together inside it for 4 to 6 weeks. Larvae are about 1 inch long, hairy, and pale green or yellow. When fully grown, they leave the web and pupate on the bark or in plant debris. Garden webworms have a similar life cycle. Larvae are ¾ inch long, hairy, and green to black, often with a stripe. Adults are ¾-inch brown moths with gold and gray wing markings.

Damage and detection: As larvae chew on the leaves, they spin a conspicuous web around that part of the host, sometimes entirely covering the plant. Webworms can completely defoliate hosts.

Control: PHYSICAL—Handpick larvae; prune and destroy branches with webs; rake up and dispose of plant debris in fall. BIOLOGICAL—Bt; trichogramma wasps. CHEMICAL—Pyrethrins; rotenone.

Weevils

Range: *widespread throughout North America*

Generations per year: *1 to 2*

Host(s): *many ornamentals and vegetables*

The weevils that attack plants in the garden include such harmful species as the Asiatic and black vine weevils. These two are particularly damaging to azalea, bramble fruit, camellia, mountain laurel, rhododendron, strawberry, and yew.

Description and life cycle: Most adult weevils have a long, jaw-tipped snout. They are nocturnal and winged but flightless; most are black or brown and are less than ½ inch long. Most weevils overwinter in the soil or in plant debris as pale, legless larvae that feed on roots. In spring they pupate and emerge as adults to feed on a wide range of hosts. Females lay eggs in soil or debris near hosts.

Damage and detection: Larvae feeding on roots cause stunting and wilting, and may kill heavily infested plants. Adults cut large holes or notches along leaf margins or eat leaves to the midrib.

Control: PHYSICAL—Use row covers; handpick adults; CULTURAL—Cultivate soil to expose overwintering larvae; destroy infested plants; remove and dispose of plant debris in fall; rotate garden crops; use sticky traps. BIOLOGICAL—Beneficial nematodes; birds. CHEMICAL—Pyrethrins; rotenone; sabadilla.

Whiteflies

Range: *southern United States and West Coast*

Generations per year: *many*

Host(s): *many ornamentals and vegetables*

The 200 or so species of whiteflies are primarily tropical pests. In warm climates they reproduce year round. In cooler regions, they infest greenhouses and feed on houseplants. They may be transported to temperate gardens in the spring on greenhouse-grown stock, but most species will not survive a cold winter. Indoors or out, whiteflies spread fast to nearby plants, and a short life cycle lets them build up destructive populations in weeks. Whiteflies attack many different plants. Preferred hosts include citrus, gerbera, lantana, poinsettia, and salvia. The ash whitefly is a serious pest in California, where it attacks many ornamental trees and shrubs.

Description and life cycle: Most whiteflies complete their life cycle in about a month; generations overlap and reproduction is continuous. Females lay a circle of black cone-shaped eggs on the undersides of older leaves. Eggs usually hatch in less than a week, and the active, young nymphs move about and begin to feed. Once established in a feeding spot, they undergo their first molt and lose their legs to become immobile. Translucent or light green, tiny and flat, the nymphs are hard to see without a hand lens. They molt into white, mothlike adults, 1/20 to 1/10 inch long. The adults'

wings are covered with a fine, powdery wax.

Damage and detection: Because of their small size, individual whiteflies are easily overlooked, but in the aggregate they are usually easy to detect because they occur in large numbers and feed in groups. When an infested plant is disturbed, they rise in a cloud, then quickly resettle. Both nymphs and adults suck plant sap, usually feeding on the youngest leaves. Nymphs feed from the undersides of leaves, which yellow and drop prematurely. Feeding whiteflies secrete honeydew, a sweet liquid that sticks to plants. Honeydew nurtures sooty mold, a fungus that blocks light, reduces photosynthesis, and further weakens plants. The

Garden Whitefly

ash whitefly's generous secretions of honeydew drip from host trees onto cars, outdoor furniture, and walkways, creating a sticky mess and attracting ants and wasps. Whiteflies transmit several viral diseases.

Control: PHYSICAL—Rinse plants to remove larvae and adults; wipe off larvae from the undersides of tender leaves with a gloved hand; destroy eggs on the undersides of older leaves; set sticky yellow traps. BIOLOGICAL—Lacewings; parasitic wasps. CHEMICAL—Horticultural oil; insecticidal soap.

White-Fringed Beetles

Range: *eastern United States from New Jersey to Florida, west to Arkansas*

Generations per year: *1 to 4*

Host(s): *most herbaceous plants*

A South American native first seen in Florida in 1936, the white-fringed beetle has spread throughout the southern states and as far north as New Jersey. It feeds on many herbaceous ornamentals including aster and goldenrod and on vegetables such as beans, okra, peas, and potatoes.

Description and life cycle: White-fringed beetles overwinter as 1/2-inch, legless white larvae, often 9 to 12 inches deep in the soil. Pupating in late spring and early summer, they emerge as adults that are 1/2 inch long, brownish gray, and hairy, with broad snouts. They have white-banded wings but do not fly. They feed in large numbers and lay eggs for up to 2 months, depositing them low down on host plants, near the soil. The larvae hatch in about 17 days and enter the soil to feed.

Damage and detection: Adult white-fringed beetles feed on lower stems, often severing them from the roots. The larvae feed on roots and tubers. Infested plants wilt and die.

Control: PHYSICAL—Dig ditches 1 foot deep around the vegetable garden to trap and destroy the flightless beetles. CULTURAL—Spade deeply in early spring to expose larvae.

White-Marked Tussock Moths

Range: *eastern United States and Canada, west to Colorado and British Columbia*

Generations per year: *1 to 3*

Host(s): *deciduous trees and shrubs*

Tussock moths are feeders of ornamental deciduous trees and shrubs and may seriously weaken them.

Description and life cycle: Tussock moths overwinter as eggs, which hatch in spring. The larvae are caterpillars, 1¼ inches long, with distinctive tufts of long black and shorter white hairs. Caterpillars feed for several weeks, then pupate. In 2 to 4 weeks, adults emerge; males are gray with dark wing markings, females are lighter and nearly wingless. Females lay eggs in masses covered with a white, frothy material that hardens as it dries. The number of generations per year varies with the climate.

Damage and detection: Tussock moths are leaf feeders. They skeletonize leaves and defoliate plants.

Control: PHYSICAL—Remove egg masses or paint them with creosote. BIOLOGICAL—Bt; trichogramma wasps. CHEMICAL—Horticultural oil.

Wireworms

Range: *widespread throughout North America*

Generations per year: *2- to 6-year life cycle*

Host(s): *many*

Wireworms are tough-skinned larvae of the various species of click beetles. These larvae live in the soil, where they feed on the underground parts of a wide range of plants, including herbaceous ornamentals and vegetables.

Description and life cycle: Some wireworm species complete their life cycle in 1 year; others take as long as 6 years. Adult click beetles overwinter in the soil, coming to the surface in spring. They are about ½ inch long, narrow, and black or brown. Females lay their eggs 1 to 6 inches below the surface. Larvae hatch within a few weeks and begin to feed, continuing for up to 6 years. Gray, creamy, or dark brown, they are ½ to 1½ inches long, jointed, and have shiny, tough skin. Pupation occurs in late summer.

Damage and detection: Wireworms feed on seeds and bore into corms, roots, and other underground plant parts, opening the plants to decay-causing bacteria and fungi.

Control: PHYSICAL—Bury pieces of potato or carrot to trap wireworms, then dig and destroy. CULTURAL—Cultivate soil often to expose larvae. BIOLOGICAL—Beneficial nematodes.

Woodborer Beetles

Range: *various species throughout the United States and southern Canada*

Generations per year: *1- to 3-year life cycle*

Host(s): *many deciduous trees*

The many species of woodboring beetles differ in their geographic ranges and preferred hosts. They are broadly classified as flatheaded or roundheaded borers, according to the shape of the larva's head. Among the many destructive species are the bronze birch borer, the lurid flatheaded borer, the flatheaded apple tree borer, and the two-lined chestnut borer.

The bronze birch borer attacks birch, cottonwood, poplar, and willow. It is found throughout the northern parts of the United States south to Virginia and in Arizona, New Mexico, and southern Canada. The lurid flatheaded borer infests hickory and alder trees throughout the eastern part of North America. The flatheaded apple tree borer attacks most deciduous shade and fruit trees and is found throughout the United States and southern Canada. The two-lined chestnut borer occurs east of the Rocky Mountains and sometimes in California; its preferred hosts include beech, chestnut, and oak.

Description and life cycle: Most borers spend the greater part of their lives as larvae, and it is during this stage that they inflict the most serious damage. Borers overwinter as larvae in their host. In spring they feed and pupate, then emerge in the summer as beetles. Females lay their eggs in bark crevices, especially near wounds. Soon the larvae hatch and bore into the tree, where they feed on the bark, the sapwood (the layer of young tissue that includes the plant's food and water conducting layer), or the older heartwood. Larvae stay in the tree for 1 or 2 years.

The adult stage of the bronze birch borer is a beetle resembling the lightning bug, ¼ to ½ inch long, with a green-black body and a bronze head. The larvae are creamy white, slender, and flattened and are ½ inch long when fully grown. Adult lurid flatheaded borers are shiny, dark brown beetles about ¾ inch long. The flatheaded apple tree borer adults are flat, dark brown, and ½ inch long; larvae are white with flat, brown heads, and reach 1¼ inches in length. The two-lined chestnut borer adult is dark green or bluish black with yellow or bronze stripes and is about ¼ inch long; the larva is cream colored and grows to about ½ inch in length. This species usually requires 2 years to complete its life cycle.

Damage and detection: The adults feed to some extent on the host's foliage, but their damage is insignificant compared to the often lethal mining done by the larvae. By the time this internal borer damage is noticed, it is usually too late to save the tree. The larvae tunnel through the young sapwood, cutting off the flow of water and nutrients up and down the tree. Leaves turn yellow and branches die back. As upper branches die, the tree sends up a great many shoots from the crown. Most trees that do survive borer infestations display swollen areas on their trunks where new tissue has grown and healed around the damage. Borers are most often attracted to trees previously damaged by other insects or mechanical injuries.

Control: PHYSICAL—Remove damaged limbs. CULTURAL—Avoid mechanical injuries to trees; feed and water trees to minimize stress and keep them healthy and vigorous; plant resistant species, such as black birch and river birch. BIOLOGICAL—Parasitic wasps; woodpeckers.

Anthracnose of Sycamore

Type of disease: *fungal*

Host(s): *sycamore*

Anthracnose of sycamore trees is a conspicuous cosmetic disease but is seldom fatal. Caused by one species of fungus, it develops in cool, damp spring weather. A number of closely related fungi cause anthracnose in other kinds of trees including ash, elm, oak, walnut, hickory, and maple.

Symptoms: There are three distinct phases of sycamore anthracnose, each affecting different portions of the plant. In the shoot-blight phase, new leaves and shoots turn brown and die rapidly; they look as if they have been killed by frost. In the leaf-blight phase, large irregular brown areas develop along the veins. Trees look tattered and may defoliate completely. Repeated defoliations weaken the tree. In the third phase, twig cankers develop and girdle and kill branches. However, when the weather warms up, the fungus recedes and a new set of leaves restores the tree's vigor.

Transmission: The fungus overwinters in twig cankers and on fallen leaves. Its growth is favored by cool, damp conditions. It is spread by wind and rain.

Control: PHYSICAL—Gather and destroy all fallen leaves and twigs in fall; fertilize trees to maintain their vigor; prune branches with cankers. CULTURAL—Replace sycamores with London plane trees, which are similar in appearance but resistant to anthracnose.

Colletotrichum Anthracnose

Type of disease: *fungal*

Host(s): *many herbaceous plants*

The term *anthracnose* is derived from the Greek word for ulcer and refers to the ulcerlike lesions that appear on leaves, stems, and fruit. There are many species of *Colletotrichum,* and each has a specific group of hosts. Herbaceous plants are more susceptible, although some woody plants are also attacked. Commonly infected ornamental plants include orchids, hollyhocks, pansies, foxgloves, and turf grasses.

Symptoms: Infected fruit, stems, or leaves develop small sunken spots with a water-soaked appearance. Spots often enlarge and may coalesce into irregular dark areas. Sometimes leaf spots turn black, the blackened tissue then falling out to leave ragged holes. In damp weather, pinkish spore masses ooze from the center of the lesions. Fruit darkens and rots.

Transmission: The fungus overwinters in seeds and in garden debris. Spores are spread by splashing water, insects, and garden tools.

Control: PHYSICAL—Prune infected stems; remove and destroy severely infected plants and fallen leaves. CULTURAL—Plant resistant varieties; use certified, disease-free seed; rotate crops; avoid handling plants when wet.

Discula Anthracnose of Dogwood

Type of disease: *fungal*

Host(s): *flowering dogwood, Pacific dogwood*

Anthracnose of dogwood, which is caused by the *Discula destructiva* fungus, was first discovered in the early 1970s. In the eastern part of the United States, the disease affects the native flowering dogwood *(Cornus florida)*; on the West Coast, it attacks another native, the Pacific dogwood.

Symptoms: In late spring, tan spots with purple margins appear on leaves. Blighted leaves remain attached to the trees. Small, uniformly spaced brown dots—spore-producing structures—appear on spotted leaves and twigs. As the infection progresses, branches die. Trees may produce numerous water sprouts. Cankers form on the trunk. When the cankers girdle the trunk, the entire tree dies.

Transmission: This fungus thrives in cool, moist conditions, and spores are spread by rain and dew. Landscape trees are less susceptible if planted in a sunny location with good air circulation.

Control: PHYSICAL—Prune water sprouts in summer. CULTURAL—Plant resistant species and varieties; plant trees in open areas with at least a half-day of sun; keep them mulched and water them deeply during dry spells but avoid wetting leaves. CHEMICAL—Spray infected trees with a fungicide containing propiconazole or chlorothalonil every 2 weeks from the time new leaves emerge until daytime temperatures are above 80°F.

Aster Yellows

Type of disease: *bacterial*

Host(s): *many herbaceous plants*

The bacteria that cause aster yellows infect more than 40 different families of plants. Ornamentals often attacked include asters, gladiolus, calendulas, cosmos, delphiniums, flax, hydrangeas, phlox, strawflowers, and zinnias.

Symptoms: Symptoms of aster yellows vary somewhat depending on the host, but infected plants generally develop spindly stems and clear veins. The internodes of stems are short and sometimes curled, giving the plant a dwarfed, bushy appearance. Flowers and leaves are frequently deformed. On asters, leaves turn yellow and flowers are green and dwarfed, if they appear at all. Gladiolus and zinnias are dramatically dwarfed.

Transmission: Aster yellows is transmitted from infected to healthy plants by leafhoppers, which pick up bacteria while feeding. The pathogens overwinter in infected perennials, including common weeds such as thistle, wild chicory, dandelion, wild carrot, and wide-leaf plantain.

Control: PHYSICAL—Eradicate potential weed hosts; remove and destroy infected plants; use row covers to protect vegetables from leafhoppers.

Black Knot of Prunus

Type of disease: *fungal*

Host(s): *many Prunus species*

Black knot is a serious disease of more than 20 species of *Prunus* including cherries, plums, flowering almond, apricot, peach, and chokecherry. It occurs throughout moist, humid regions of the United States and Canada, wherever susceptible plants are grown.

Symptoms: Rough, black, spindle-shaped swellings or knots develop on small branches over a 2-year period. The first sign of infection emerges in spring, when the bark ruptures and an olive green fungal mass appears. It can grow to 12 inches in length and may be two to four times as thick as the branch. This growth eventually hardens and turns black and knotty. As the infection progresses, branches become girdled and die. Trees are stunted and unattractive, and varieties planted for fruit are unproductive.

Transmission: Spores of this fungus are spread by wind in early spring.

Control: PHYSICAL—Prune any infected branches at least 4 inches behind any visible damage in winter or early spring, disinfecting pruners after each cut in a 10 percent bleach solution; eradicate or prune wild cherries and plums in the vicinity as a preventive measure.

Black Spot

Type of disease: *fungal*

Host(s): *roses*

While black spot of rose occurs wherever roses are grown, it is severe only in humid climates. It is especially troublesome east of the Mississippi River and on the West Coast. Rose varieties differ in their susceptibility. Those with yellow or gold flowers are generally more susceptible than varieties with red or pink flowers.

Symptoms: Round black spots with fringed margins appear on the upper surfaces of leaves and on young canes in spring. At the center of the spots are tiny blisterlike spore-producing structures that are visible with a hand lens.

Transmission: The black spot fungus survives the winter in a dormant state on infected canes and fallen leaves. In greenhouses, it is active year round. It is spread by splashing water and by the gardener's hands, tools, and clothing.

Control: PHYSICAL—Prune to increase air circulation; remove and destroy infected leaves and canes. CULTURAL—Grow resistant varieties; avoid wetting foliage when watering. CHEMICAL—Spray dormant plants with lime sulfur; during the growing season spray with a baking soda solution (*page 56*), a fungicidal soap, or a fungicide that contains triforine, mancozeb, or chlorothalonil.

Botrytis Blight

Type of disease: *fungal*

Host(s): *many*

Various *Botrytis* species cause blighting on a wide range of herbaceous and woody ornamentals, soft fruits, and vegetables. Certain species such as *B. cinerea,* which causes gray mold blight, have a broad host range. Common hosts include poinsettia, chrysanthemum, and rhododendron. Others such as *B. tulipae,* which causes a blight on tulips, and *B. paeoniae,* which causes blight on peony, are very host specific. All species produce similar symptoms and are favored by cool, moist conditions.

Symptoms: Leaves and flowers of infected plants develop irregularly shaped, water-soaked spots that dry and turn tan or brown. Similar spots on stems form cankers that girdle stems, causing dieback. Seedlings are often killed. Infected fruit turns soft and mushy. In humid conditions, a fuzzy gray mold develops on the surface of infected tissue.

Transmission: Botrytis is spread by splashing rain and wind. The fungus persists in infected tissue and in soil.

Control: PHYSICAL—Remove and destroy fading blossoms and infected plants or plant parts. CULTURAL—Space plants to promote air circulation; avoid wetting plants; use healthy plants and bulbs for propagation. CHEMICAL—Spray with a fungicide containing chlorothalonil or mancozeb.

Cercospora Leaf Blight

Type of disease: *fungal*

Host(s): *many*

There are hundreds of *Cercospora* species, which attack leaves and shoots of trees, shrubs, vegetables, and herbaceous ornamentals. Most species apparently attack one or a few closely related plants. Often infected are arborvitae, azalea, cryptomeria, cypress, dahlia, geranium, mountain laurel, and red cedar.

Symptoms: Leaves or needles of infected plants develop spots, sometimes with dark purple margins, that often enlarge and coalesce. On carrot, celery, geranium and many other hosts the spots are yellowish at first, then turn ash gray and become paper-thin as they enlarge. Entire leaves die, and in severe cases all of the foliage dies. A fine gray mold develops on infected tissue. Leaf spots may be bordered by a dark purple margin. On cypress and arborvitae, needles and branchlets turn brown or purplish and drop off, especially on the lower portion of the plant.

Transmission: Leaf-blight fungus overwinters in or on seed or on infected leaves or needles. Warm, humid weather favors its spread and development. Spores are spread by wind and rain.

Control: PHYSICAL—Prune out infected stems or branches and rake up and destroy infected leaves or needles. CULTURAL—Plant disease-free seed. CHEMICAL—Spray with Bordeaux mixture or a fungicide containing chlorothalonil.

Diplodia Tip Blight

Type of disease: *fungal*

Host(s): *2- and 3-needle pines*

Diplodia tip blight infects older pines, especially those under stress. Most often attacks Scotch, Austrian, mugho, and ponderosa pines, red, scrub, and Japanese black pines

Symptoms: The first symptom usually noted is the browning of new needles, particularly on branches near the base of the tree. The dead needles remain attached to the tree; infected branches ooze resin. Close observation reveals small black spore-producing structures embedded under the needle sheath and in dead needles, on old cones, and in bark. After several seasons of repeated infection, branches take on a clubbed appearance and eventually die.

Transmission: Spores are produced from early spring to late fall, especially during periods of wet weather. They are spread by splashing rain, insects, birds, and pruning tools. The fungus invades the tree through young needles, buds, and shoots or through wounds. It persists over winter on infected trees and on the ground nearby.

Control: PHYSICAL—Prune and destroy dead branches in fall; collect and destroy infected needles and twigs on the ground. CHEMICAL—Spray with a fixed-copper fungicide, thiophanate-methyl, or Bordeaux mixture when new needles begin to emerge from the candles and again 10 days later.

Fire Blight

Type of disease: *bacterial*

Host(s): *members of the rose family*

Fire blight occurs only in plants belonging to the rose family. Landscape plants often damaged include crab apple, cotoneaster, flowering quince, hawthorn, mountain ash, pear, and pyracantha.

Symptoms: In early spring bees and other pollinators carry bacteria into flowers, which turn brown and shrivel. The bacteria then invade twigs, producing cankers. Bacteria oozing from cankers can be blown or splashed onto young shoots and leaves. The shoots turn dark brown or black, and leaves turn black and remain on the tree, which looks as if it has been scorched by fire. In highly susceptible plants, cankers form on the trunk and large branches.

Transmission: The bacteria overwinter in branch and trunk cankers. In humid weather bacteria-laden ooze is produced along the edges of cankers. Insects feedings on the ooze carry the bacteria to flowers. Throughout the growing season bacteria may be spread from blighted shoots, and cankers may be spread by wind. Fire blight is most severe in regions of warm, humid weather.

Control: PHYSICAL—During winter or dry weather prune out all visible cankers; avoid wounding plants. CULTURAL—Plant resistant cultivars; avoid excessive nitrogen fertilizer because it produces very succulent growth that is more susceptible to fire blight.

Southern Blight

Type of disease: *fungal*

Host(s): *many*

Southern blight occurs in the eastern United States from New York south but is most serious in the Southeast because it is a disease of hot, humid weather. It infects hundreds of herbaceous and woody plants and is particularly hard on ajuga, artemisia, chrysanthemum, lamb's ears, lavender, santolina, sage, thyme, and the tomato and legume families.

Symptoms: The southern blight fungus can be recognized by the sclerotia—small tan lumps about the size of a mustard seed—that appear on the blighted plant and the surrounding soil or mulch. Infection starts from these "mustard seed" sclerotia in soil or mulch. Plants rapidly yellow, wilt, and die. Infected bulbs and fleshy roots rot. Look for a white cottony growth on stems and surrounding soil. Small, round fruiting bodies about $\frac{1}{16}$ inch in diameter may be present near the soil surface in warm, humid conditions.

Transmission: The fungus survives in the soil for many years as sclerotia. Its growth is favored by hot, wet weather and acidic soils. It is spread by running water and infested tools, soil, mulch, or compost.

Control: PHYSICAL—Remove and destroy diseased plants and the white, cottony fungal growth around them. CULTURAL—Solarize the soil of a new bed; thin perennials to improve air circulation; mulch plants with a thin layer of solarized or sterile sharp sand.

Bacterial Canker of Stone Fruit

Type of disease: *bacterial*

Host(s): *fruits, shrubs, and vegetables*

Different forms of the bacterium *Pseudomonas syringae* are responsible for canker of stone fruit, infecting many unrelated hosts and causing a variety of symptoms. Ornamentals affected include flowering stock, lilac, oleander, rose, and sweet pea.

Symptoms: All parts of peach, plum, apricot, and other stone fruit trees are subject to infection, but the most destructive symptoms are the gummy cankers on branches and trunk, which exude a foul-smelling secretion. Flower buds may be killed while they are still dormant or after they have emerged; leaves may wilt or die. On lilacs, leaves and shoots display brown, water-soaked spots, and flower buds turn black. Infected oleanders develop oozing, bacteria-laden galls on branches, leaves, and flowers.

Transmission: The bacteria responsible for these diseases are spread by water. Mild, wet weather favors their growth and development.

Control: PHYSICAL—Prune and destroy infected branches, disinfecting pruners after each cut. CULTURAL—Thin plants to encourage good air circulation and avoid the use of high-nitrogen fertilizers.

Canker and Dieback

Type of disease: *fungal*

Host(s): *many woody plants*

Botryosphaeria dothidea infects over 50 species of woody plants including apple, azalea, eucalyptus, fig, forsythia, pecan, pyracantha, quince, rhododendron, rose, sequoia, sweet gum, and willow. This fungus is also responsible for the most destructive canker disease of redbud.

Symptoms: On redbud, cankers begin as small, sunken, oval spots that enlarge and girdle branches, causing wilting and dieback above the canker. The canker turns black at the center and cracks at the margins. Similar symptoms occur on forsythia. On roses, leaves turn brown and die but remain on the plant. On rhododendron, watery spots occur on leaves and twigs, followed by twig dieback. Cankers on the trunks of willows are generally fatal in a few years. Apple trees develop watery lesions on the bark, and vigor gradually declines. When an infected branch or stem is cut crosswise, there is usually a pie-shaped section of discolored tissue.

Transmission: Canker and dieback fungi are spread by wind, rain, insects, and on pruning tools.

Control: PHYSICAL—Cut infected branches to wood that is not discolored and destroy, disinfecting pruners with a 10 percent bleach solution after each cut. CULTURAL—Maintain plants in vigorous state and keep them watered during periods of drought.

Cytospora Canker

Type of disease: *fungal*

Host(s): *many trees and shrubs*

Many species of fungi cause cankers on trees and shrubs; most have a narrow host range. Cytospora canker is especially troublesome on Norway spruce, Colorado blue spruce, and *Prunus* species. Other species attack maple, cottonwood, black cherry, willow, and poplar.

Symptoms: On spruce, the cankers most often form on branches near the ground and enlarge to girdle the branches. Needles dry up, and the branches die back. Infected areas ooze an amber-colored sap that turns white as it dries. On poplar, cankers form on the trunk and the larger branches, discoloring the bark and causing dieback. Weakened trees often die.

Transmission: These fungi survive the winter on infected plant parts. They are spread by washing and splashing rain, insects, and pruning tools. Trees that have suffered injuries or have been weakened by conditions like drought, hail, or a late-spring freeze are more likely to be infected than healthy, intact trees. Wounds and leaf scars provide entry points for fungi.

Control: PHYSICAL—Remove and destroy infected branches when the weather is dry, making pruning cuts at least 6 inches below the canker and disinfecting pruners with a 10 percent bleach solution after each cut. CULTURAL—Keep plants vigorous; avoid wounding and excessive use of nitrogen fertilizer; do only essential pruning on susceptible species.

Nectria Canker

Type of disease: *fungal*

Host(s): *many trees and shrubs*

Coral spot nectria canker, tubercularia canker, and perennial nectria canker are common in landscape plants including apple, beech, boxwood, elm, honey locust, magnolia, maple, and zelkova.

Symptoms: Coral spot and tubercularia cankers are usually noticed in late spring, when shoots or entire branches wilt and die. At the base of the diseased branch are peach-colored to orange-red fruiting bodies emerging through openings or wounds in the bark. If the plant is in good health, it can usually wall off the fungus.

Perennial nectria cankers, which persist for years, begin as small sunken areas, often surrounding a twig stub or a wound. As they grow they develop a series of concentric ridges of bark around the original spot; in time the ridges can become quite large. Bright red-orange fruiting bodies are produced on the bark ridges and on exposed wood in the canker's center from fall through spring.

Transmission: Nectria fungi produce spores that are spread by wind, rain, insects, and animals.

Control: PHYSICAL—Prune out cankered branches in late spring through summer. Do not prune in fall and winter. CULTURAL—Avoid wounding plants; select species that are well adapted to your climate to avoid damage from environmental stress; fertilize properly and water during droughts to maintain plant vigor.

Damping-Off

Type of disease: *fungal*

Host(s): *most seedlings*

Damping-off is a disease of seedlings caused by a variety of different fungi, including species of *Pythium* and *Rhizoctonia.* These fungi may attack seeds, emerging seedlings, or older plants.

Symptoms: When these fungi attack seeds, the disease is known as preemergent damping-off. Seeds rot without germinating. Called postemergent damping-off when seedlings are infected, the disease usually occurs at or just below the soil line. The stem turns soft and brown, and the seedling topples over and dies. When the fungi attack older plants, brown lesions form on the stem or roots. When abundant, these lesions cause stunting, wilting, and sometimes death.

Transmission: The fungi responsible for damping-off are found in soil and water throughout the world. They survive on dead organic matter when they have no living host.

Control: CULTURAL—Use a soilless growing medium for seedling propagation; promote rapid growth with optimum light and temperature levels and provide good drainage and air circulation; rotate crops in the vegetable garden. CHEMICAL—Buy pretreated seeds or treat seeds with captan.

Decline

Type of disease: *infectious/environmental*

Host(s): *trees and shrubs*

Decline is a general loss of health that is not attributable to a single pathogen or pest. Rather, it is the result of stress that can arise from a variety of factors, usually over a period of years. Both infectious agents and environmental conditions may be involved. They may act on the plant at the same time or in sequence.

Symptoms: Symptoms of decline vary among plant species. Generally, yellowing and wilting of leaves, dieback of branches, and stunted or distorted growth are seen. Declining trees show reduced twig growth, and in advanced decline dead branches, or stag heads, protrude from the healthy canopy. Eventually the plant may die, although this may take years. Some of the factors often associated with decline are repeated insect infestations, infectious disease, soil compaction, root damage, injury to the roots or trunk, an inappropriate site, girdling roots, a chronic water deficit, and poorly drained soil. Plants weakened by adverse cultural conditions may be especially vulnerable to pathogens and are very attractive to woodboring insects.

Control: Once decline has become obvious, it is often too late to save the plant. However, it is important to identify the source or sources of stress so you can take measures to prevent decline in new plants installed in the same area.

Blossom-End Rot

Type of disease: *environmental*

Host(s): *tomatoes and other vegetables*

Blossom-end rot is a disease caused by a deficiency of calcium at the blossom end of susceptible fruit. Plants frequently affected include tomato, pepper, watermelon, and squash. While there may be a substantial supply of calcium in the soil, it may not reach rapidly growing fruit when the weather is hot and dry and irrigation is irregular or inadequate. Another common factor is overzealous nitrogen fertilization.

Symptoms: Blossom-end rot first appears as a brown discoloration at the blossom end of a tomato or other susceptible fruit. The spot enlarges and darkens, eventually becoming sunken and leathery. This tissue may cover the bottom third to one-half of the fruit and is subject to invasion by pathogens.

Control: CULTURAL—Apply limestone or gypsum to provide adequate soil calcium. A soil test can determine how much to apply; mulch to moderate soil moisture; provide additional water during drought; avoid excessive nitrogen fertilization.

Iron Deficiency

Type of disease: *nutritional*

Host(s): *all plants*

While iron is rarely deficient in soils, it may be unavailable to plants because it exists in an insoluble form. This is a common problem for acid-loving plants growing in neutral or alkaline soils, which have a pH of 7 or higher. Iron may also become chemically bound and unavailable to plants when large amounts of phosphate fertilizers have been added to the soil. Plants growing in sandy soils in cold, wet conditions are more likely to experience iron deficiency.

Symptoms: Iron is essential for chlorophyll synthesis, and when it is deficient young leaves are yellow with green veins, a symptom called interveinal chlorosis. Leaves are smaller than normal, and their margins often turn brown. If the deficiency is severe, leaves turn reddish brown and drop prematurely. Overall growth of the plant is stunted.

Control: CULTURAL—Avoid liming turf near acid-loving trees and shrubs; apply iron sulfate to soil to both supply iron and acidify soil; replace acid-loving species and varieties with plants that tolerate a higher soil pH.

Magnesium Deficiency

Type of disease: *nutritional*

Host(s): *all plants*

Magnesium is required for healthy plant growth and development because it is a constituent part of the chlorophyll molecule. It is also essential for various processes controlled by enzymes. This element may be naturally deficient in soils, as is common on the Atlantic and Gulf Coasts, or it may have been removed by heavy cropping or constant leaching by rain. This deficiency is common in very acid soils and in gardens to which excessive amounts of potassium fertilizers have been applied.

Symptoms: Deficiency symptoms show up first on older growth. The tip and margins of an affected leaf typically turn yellow, then brown, though in some plants the discoloration is reddish. The abnormal color spreads between the veins to the center and base of the leaves, which often drop prematurely. On some plants the leaves become puckered. In the case of conifers, needles 2 years old and above turn yellow. Continued magnesium deficiency causes stunting.

Control: CULTURAL—Apply Epsom salts, which contain magnesium; till in dolomitic limestone, which contains magnesium and also raises the pH; use balanced fertilizers that contain magnesium; do not fertilize with wood ashes because of their high potassium content.

Nitrogen Deficiency

Potassium Deficiency

Dodder

Type of disease: *nutritional*

Host(s): *all plants*

Nitrogen is an essential element for healthy vegetative growth, protein synthesis, and other critical plant functions. A lack of available nitrogen in the soil, which is more common in unusually cold, wet conditions, results in poor growth and a weakened plant.

Symptoms: A plant's oldest leaves are the first to show signs of nitrogen deficiency: They turn yellow, then brown, and drop off. New leaves are smaller than normal and lighter in color because of the decreased synthesis of plant proteins. Leaf margins may turn brown. The plant grows slowly, and its stems are slender and weak. Fruit and vegetable yields are reduced.

Control: CULTURAL—Apply nitrogen-rich fertilizers such as blood meal, soybean meal, fish emulsion, or urea to the soil; incorporate well-rotted manure or compost into the soil every year; do not apply fresh organic matter such as uncomposted woodchips, leaves, or sawdust because soil microbes will tie up available nitrogen as they attack the cellulose in these materials.

Type of disease: *nutritional*

Host(s): *all plants*

Potassium is essential to such processes as nitrogen metabolism and water uptake and movement. It acts as a catalyst for numerous other reactions, especially in growing points—buds, shoot tips, and root tips.

Symptoms: Potassium moves easily within a plant. Because it tends to move to the youngest growth, older plant parts are the first to show signs of deficiency. Leaf margins turn yellow or brown, and the discoloration then moves into the leaf between the veins. Some leaves turn reddish purple rather than brown. Dead areas along leaf margins may drop out, giving leaves a ragged edge. Growth slows, and leaves may drop prematurely. Flowering and fruiting are reduced. Plants are more subject to damage by freezing and a variety of pathogens.

Control: CULTURAL—Fertilize with potassium-rich fertilizers such as kelp meal, or granite dust; apply wood ashes in small quantities; if the soil is very sandy, allowing potassium to leach out quickly, incorporate organic matter to increase the soil's water-holding capacity; incorporate vermiculite, which is high in slow-release potassium, into the soil.

Type of disease: *parasitic*

Host(s): *many plants*

Dodders are stringy, leafless plants that lack roots and chlorophyll and parasitize a wide range of plants to obtain water and nutrients. They are particularly troublesome in areas where clover and alfalfa, two favorite hosts, are grown.

Symptoms: Dodder seed germinates and produces a slender stem that curls around the nearest plant. The stem develops "feeding pegs," which invade the host and absorb juices. As it continues to grow, the tangled mass of yellow to orange spaghetti-like stems increases while the host plant loses color and vigor and may die. Other common names for dodder include devil's hair, gold thread, strangle weed, pull down, and hell-bind.

Transmission: Dodder is transmitted as seed in mulch, humus, compost, and soil, where it can survive for up to 5 years. Dodder seed may also contaminate commercial seed lots.

Control: PHYSICAL—Thoroughly clean tools and other equipment after use in a dodder-infested area; remove and burn all dodder and its host plants before the dodder produces seed. CULTURAL—Use dodder-free seed and nursery plants. CHEMICAL—Treat the infested area with a preemergent herbicide; kill germinating dodder seeds.

Downy Mildew

Type of disease: *fungal*

Host(s): *many*

There are seven genera of fungi that cause downy mildew. Most of these fungi have a narrow host range. Among the most common ornamental plants attacked are Boston ivy, grape, pansy, redbud, rose, snapdragon, sunflower, and viburnum.

Symptoms: The first visible symptom of downy mildew infection is the development of angular yellow spots on the upper leaf surface. These areas gradually turn brown while corresponding spots on the underside of the leaf develop a white, tan, gray, or purple downy growth that can be seen in early morning during humid weather. Fruit and young stems may also be covered with the downy fungal growth. Plants may be stunted, and grapes and other susceptible crops are often completely ruined. Most downy mildews are favored by cool weather, and all require moist conditions.

Transmission: The spores of downy mildew fungi are spread by wind, rain, insects, and in infected seed.

Control: PHYSICAL—Remove and destroy plant debris and infected plants; space plants widely to provide good air circulation. CULTURAL—Use resistant varieties; rotate crops. CHEMICAL—Spray with a copper fungicide, sulfur, Bordeaux mixture, mancozeb, or chlorothalonil.

Azalea Leaf Gall

Type of disease: *fungal*

Host(s): *many plants of the heath family*

Though seldom a serious threat, azalea leaf gall is unattractive. It is a fairly common problem on azaleas, especially in the South. Other susceptible plants include Japanese andromeda, blueberry, mountain laurel, and rhododendron.

Symptoms: Symptoms vary somewhat depending on the host. On azalea, bladder-shaped galls form on all or part of a leaf or flower. The galls are soft when they are young, eventually hardening and darkening with age. As a gall develops, a white velvety layer that produces spores appears on its surface.

Transmission: This fungus overwinters in infected tissue and rapidly spreads during periods of warm, wet weather, particularly in shade. Galls do not appear until the following spring.

Control: PHYSICAL—Handpick and destroy galls, preferably before the white sporulating layer appears. CULTURAL—Make sure susceptible plants have good air circulation; avoid watering with a sprinkler in spring, when mature galls produce spores; wet foliage increases the chance of spreading the infection.

Crown Gall

Type of disease: *bacterial*

Host(s): *many plants*

Crown gall is caused by a bacterium that lives in the soil. It has one of the broadest host ranges of any bacterial plant pathogen. Common ornamental hosts include aster, chrysanthemum, euonymus, flowering quince, forsythia, honeysuckle, and willow.

Symptoms: Rounded corky galls develop on roots, on stems near the soil line or, in the case of grafted plants, near the graft union. At first the gall is soft and either white or flesh colored. It darkens and its surface becomes rough as it grows, sometimes to several inches in diameter. Infected plants may be stunted and weakened and more susceptible to environmental stress.

Transmission: The bacterium responsible for crown gall can persist in the soil for several years. It spreads from one region to another in shipments of infected nursery stock. The bacterium enters plants through wounds.

Control: PHYSICAL—Remove and destroy infected plants. CULTURAL—Plant disease-free stock; avoid wounding plants, especially near the soil line.

Leaf Blister and Leaf Curl

Type of disease: *fungal*

Host(s): *fruit and ornamental trees*

Several species of *Taphrina* are responsible for leaf blister and leaf curl. Ornamental trees commonly infected include birch, elm, flowering cherry, maple, oak, ornamental plum, and poplar.

Symptoms: Symptoms of leaf blister and leaf curl vary somewhat depending on the plant. In the case of cherry leaf curl, which infects both ornamental and edible cherry, peach, and plum trees, portions of the leaves pucker, thicken, and turn yellow or reddish brown. Leaves drop prematurely. Twigs develop knobby swellings from which a cluster of new shoots, called a witch's broom, arises. These twigs often die over winter. Oak leaf blister often begins as raised, cup-shaped areas that range from a quarter inch to several inches in diameter and are silver-gray on the lower leaf surface and yellow above. As with cherries, the leaves drop prematurely. Similar symptoms occur on maple, poplar, elm, and birch.

Transmission: The fungus overwinters on the bark, twigs, and buds on infected trees. Spores are spread by rain and infect young tissues only.

Control: CULTURAL—Plant resistant varieties; prune to promote good air circulation. CHEMICAL—Apply lime sulfur to susceptible plants while they are dormant.

Bacterial Leaf Scorch

Type of disease: *bacterial*

Host(s): *black oak, elm, maple, sycamore*

The bacterium *Xylella fastidiosa* causes leaf scorch on a variety of landscape trees. It is common on American elm, species in the black oak group, mulberry, sycamore, and some maples. Unlike leaf scorch that is caused by drought, drying winds, or root damage, bacterial leaf scorch is unevenly distributed in the tree canopy and on individual leaves.

Symptoms: Bacterial leaf scorch appears in midsummer as irregular brown or reddish brown areas along the leaf margin. These areas are typically bordered by a yellow halo. As the scorch progresses toward the midrib of leaves, they curl and drop prematurely. Infections recur from year to year, slowing growth and causing dieback of branches. On sycamore, mulberry, and red maple, the leaves develop patterns of light brown and reddish brown that are bordered by a yellow halo. Plants may be infected with the leaf-scorch bacterium yet display few symptoms.

Transmission: Leafhoppers and spittlebugs carry the leaf-scorch bacterium from plant to plant.

Control: PHYSICAL—If only a few branches show leaf scorch, cut the infected branches back to a point well below leaves showing symptoms. CULTURAL—Remove diseased, failing trees and replace them with less susceptible varieties.

Alternaria Leaf Spot

Type of disease: *fungal*

Host(s): *many woody and herbaceous plants*

A number of *Alternaria* species cause leaf spot on a wide variety of plants, including fruits, vegetables, herbaceous perennials, and woody ornamentals, among them carnation, catalpa, chrysanthemum, flowering tobacco, geranium, hibiscus, magnolia, marigold, Shasta daisy, stock, and zinnia.

Symptoms: Leaves develop small dark brown to black spots. Often numerous, the spots first appear on the plant's lowest leaves and progress upward. As spots enlarge they develop concentric rings like a bulls-eye target. Stems may have sunken lesions that girdle and kill them, and fruit and tubers may be spotted. In moist weather the spots on fruit are sometimes covered with fuzzy black structures that produce spores.

Transmission: Alternaria fungi overwinter in infected plant debris or on seeds. Spores are spread by wind, rain, and on tools.

Control: PHYSICAL—Remove and destroy infected plant debris. CULTURAL—Plant resistant varieties; use disease-free or treated seed; rotate crops. CHEMICAL—Treat infected plants with chlorothalonil.

Bacterial Leaf Spot

Type of disease: *bacterial*

Host(s): *many*

Species of two different genera of bacteria, *Pseudomonas* and *Xanthomonas,* are responsible for leaf spots on an extremely wide range of plants. Ornamental plants susceptible to bacterial leaf spot include begonia, California laurel, English ivy, geranium, and gladiolus.

Symptoms: The spots are usually brown and are often surrounded by a yellow halo; they may appear on stems and fruit as well as on leaves. Some of the spots are round, while others are elongated streaks bounded by leaf veins running parallel to one another. A branching or fish bone vein pattern gives spots a triangular outline. As a spot enlarges, the damaged tissue may drop out, making "shot holes" in the leaf. Spots can also coalesce and cover the entire leaf. Leaves often drop prematurely—bacterial spot of English ivy, for instance, can temporarily defoliate a planting.

Transmission: The bacteria are transmitted by water and tools and in infested soil. They overwinter in infected plant parts, on seeds, and in the soil.

Control: PHYSICAL—Remove and destroy infected plants and debris; CULTURAL—Plant resistant varieties; use pathogen-free seed; rotate crops. CHEMICAL—Treat infected plants with a fungicide that contains copper.

Septoria Leaf Spot

Type of disease: *fungal*

Host(s): *many*

There are many species of *Septoria* responsible for leaf-spot and blight diseases on a wide range of plants. Common ornamental hosts include azalea, aster, chrysanthemum, dogwood, poplar, and tomato.

Symptoms: Like alternaria leaf spot, the symptoms of a septoria leaf spot arise first on lower leaves and progress upward on the plant. The typical spot is angular, small, and initially yellow, later turning brown, with black spore-producing bodies scattered over the surface. On some plants the spots have purple margins. Diseased leaves often turn yellow and drop prematurely. When a tomato plant loses a substantial portion of its foliage, the fruit exposed to the sun may be ruined by sunscald.

Transmission: Septoria spores are spread by rain, irrigation water, tools, and animals. The fungi overwinter in or on seeds and in plant debris.

Control: PHYSICAL—Remove and destroy debris. CULTURAL—Plant resistant varieties; use disease-free or treated seed; rotate crops. CHEMICAL—Use a fungicide such as Bordeaux mixture or chlorothalonil.

Mosaic

Type of disease: *viral*

Host(s): *many*

There are several viruses that cause mosaic disease, some with a narrow host range and others capable of infecting many different hosts. The tobacco mosaic virus is common in gardens and greenhouses, attacking such ornamental hosts as ash, episcia, flowering tobacco, gloxinia, petunia, and streptocarpus. Other mosaics occur on birch, canna, carnation, coleus, horse chestnut rose, and ranunculus.

Symptoms: A mottling of leaves is the most obvious symptom of a mosaic infection. The irregular patches or streaks of abnormal color range from light to dark green and yellow. The leaves are often distorted, and growth is almost always stunted.

Transmission: Some mosaic viruses are transmitted by insects such as aphids. Many are spread from an infected plant to healthy ones on a tool or on the gardener's hands, as is the case with the tobacco mosaic virus. It can persist for years in dried tobacco.

Control: PHYSICAL—Remove and destroy infected plants; smokers should wash hands before handling plants. CULTURAL—Plant resistant varieties. BIOLOGICAL—Use beneficial predators to control insects that carry the viruses. CHEMICAL—Use organic pesticides on insects that spread the viruses.

Needle Cast

Type of disease: *fungal*

Host(s): *conifers*

A variety of different species of fungi are responsible for needle cast, a name shared by several diseases in which a conifer sheds a large portion of its needles prematurely. Some species are common only in the Northwest, while others are largely limited to the Southeast and the Gulf Coast region. There are also a number of species that occur throughout the United States. Many of the needle-cast fungi attack a single species or just a few closely related species. Common hosts include Douglas fir *(Pseudotsuga)*, fir *(Abies)*, pine, and spruce.

Symptoms: Mottled yellow spots on needles are the earliest sign of disease, appearing from spring through fall. Separate at first, they tend to form bands around the needles as the disease progresses. The needles turn brown and are often shed by 6 months to a year after the first spots appear. Young trees are particularly susceptible and may be killed by repeated defoliation.

Transmission: Needle-cast spores are spread locally by rain and over great distances by wind. There must be an extended period of damp or wet weather for needles to become infected.

Control: PHYSICAL—Clean up and destroy fallen needles. CULTURAL—Plant resistant species; allow enough space around plants for good air circulation.

Foliar Nematodes

Type of disease: *parasitic*

Host(s): *many herbaceous ornamentals*

Foliar nematodes infect the leaves and buds of a variety of herbaceous plants including African violet, anemone, begonia, chrysanthemum, cyclamen, ferns, hosta, iris, lily, primrose, and orchids. They are most destructive in areas with humid summers; the nematodes move through the film of water on a wet plant from one leaf to another. These tiny roundworms enter leaves through their pores.

Symptoms: New shoots may be stunted, twisted, and misshapen. Abnormally colored areas of pale green, yellow, or red-purple appear on the leaves. These spots are bounded by the veins and are roughly triangular in plants with branching veins; in plants with parallel veins, such as hosta and lily, they are elongated stripes. The leaves turn brown or black and die.

Transmission: Foliar nematodes can survive for 3 or more years in soil, compost, and plant debris. They are common in woodland plants and are usually introduced into the garden by infected but healthy-looking plants. They are spread from plant to plant by these materials or by splashing water.

Control: PHYSICAL—Remove and destroy seriously infected plants; pick and destroy all leaves showing symptoms as well as the leaves immediately surrounding them. CULTURAL—Inspect plants for signs of infection before buying; do not plant susceptible plants in infested soil.

Pinewood Nematodes

Type of disease: *parasitic*

Host(s): *pines*

Pinewood nematodes are indigenous to the United States. Native pine species are resistant to infection but become vulnerable when subjected to drought, poor soil, or other environmental stresses. Exotic species such as Austrian, Japanese black, and Scotch pines are highly susceptible.

Symptoms: Needles turn yellow, then turn brown and wilt but remain on the tree. An infestation may kill individual branches or the entire tree.

Transmission: Pinewood nematodes are spread by the flying long-horned or cerambycid beetle, which feeds on growing branch tips. As the insect feeds, it releases nematodes that enter the plant through wounds. Inside, they multiply rapidly and spread through the trunk and branches. One beetle may carry as many as 20,000 nematodes.

Control: PHYSICAL—Remove and destroy infected trees promptly.

Root Knot Nematodes

Type of disease: *parasitic*

Host(s): *many woody and herbaceous plants*

Root knot nematodes are the most common plant parasitic nematode, infecting over 2,000 plant species. There are more than 50 species, which vary in their geographic ranges and attack different kinds of plants, among them banana, boxwood, geranium, gladiolus, grape hyacinth, morning glory, pachysandra, peony, privet, rose, and hibiscus.

Symptoms: Root knot nematodes are the easiest nematodes to identify because of the galls that form on the roots of infected plants. These galls are part of the root and cannot easily be rubbed off. Symptoms in aboveground portions of the plant include stunting, yellowing, wilting during hot weather, and death. Infected plants are more susceptible to fungal and bacterial wilts, root rots, and crown gall.

Transmission: The nematodes overwinter in infected roots or soil and are spread by soil, transplants, and on tools. They invade root tissue to feed and reproduce. A generation takes about 21 days. Each female nematode produces 200 to 500 eggs in a mass that protrudes from the galls. After the eggs hatch, the larvae move through the soil and invade the roots of other plants.

Control: CULTURAL—Plant resistant varieties; add organic matter to the soil; do not plant susceptible plants in infested soil; solarize soil to kill nematodes; rotate susceptible and nonsusceptible plants.

Powdery Mildew

Type of disease: *fungal*

Host(s): *many*

Powdery mildews are caused by more than 100 species of fungi. They occur worldwide, attacking over 7,000 kinds of plants. Ornamental hosts include begonia, chrysanthemum, euonymus, gardenia, hawthorn, hydrangea, lilac, phlox, rose, sycamore, turf grasses, and zinnia.

Symptoms: The white, powdery growth that appears on leaves and buds and occasionally on shoots makes powdery mildew easy to identify. Most species of powdery mildew fungi spread rapidly when the weather is dry and days are warm and nights cool. The fungi are also favored by poor air circulation. Infected leaves turn yellow and may drop, and growth is stunted and often distorted. Plants are weakened, and some annuals may be killed. In fall, fruiting bodies form on the mildew, starting out as tan-yellow specks before turning dark brown-black.

Transmission: Spores are spread by wind. They thrive in shade and survive overwinter on infected plants.

Control: PHYSICAL—Spray plants daily with water, which kills spores; remove and destroy badly infected plant parts or entire plants. CULTURAL—Plant resistant varieties; allow adequate room between plants and thin overcrowded growth. CHEMICAL—Spray plants with a solution of baking soda *(page 56)*; apply a summer oil or a fungicide containing propiconazole, triadimefon, or triforine.

Brown Rot of Stone Fruit

Type of disease: *fungal*

Host(s): *stone fruit and some ornamentals*

Brown rot occurs worldwide, wherever peaches, plums, cherries, and other stone fruit are grown, and is particularly troublesome in warm, humid regions. It also attacks a number of landscape ornamentals including flowering quince, chokeberry, western sand cherry, and flowering almond.

Symptoms: The first symptom to appear is brown spots on blossoms. The spots spread rapidly to cover the entire flower and stem. During humid weather, a brown fuzz covers infected parts. As the disease progresses, cankers develop on twigs near the flower stem and sometimes cause girdling and dieback. Ripe fruit develop water-soaked, brown spots that enlarge and expand rapidly. Rotted flowers and fruit shrivel and may remain on the plant for a long time. Fuzzy gray mold forms on the bark.

Transmission: Spores are spread by wind, rain, and insects. The fungus overwinters in the dry, shriveled fruit, called mummies, and on twig cankers.

Control: PHYSICAL—Dispose of fruit mummies and prune out twigs with cankers. CHEMICAL—Protect fruit with a fungicide spray such as propiconazole or triadimefon.

Mushroom Root Rot

Type of disease: *fungal*

Host(s): *many*

Mushroom root rot, also known as armillaria root rot, oak-root fungus, and shoestring root rot, occurs throughout the United States. It infects a wide range of trees and shrubs; herbaceous plants are occasionally infected. Particularly susceptible are azalea, boxwood, oak, pine, rhododendron, rose, spruce, and sycamore.

Symptoms: Plants may suffer a mild infection for years with no symptoms. Then, when they are subjected to stress from drought, defoliation by insects, or another disease, the symptoms of mushroom root rot begin to appear. These include yellowing; wilting; premature dropping of leaves; dark, spongy bark; dieback of branches; tough, fan-shaped growths under the bark; and, in fall and winter, clusters of honey brown mushrooms at the base of the plant.

Transmission: The fungus spreads underground from infected to healthy plants by the black or brown cordlike structures, or shoestrings, it produces. In addition, airborne spores from the mushrooms can enter plants through wounds to start new colonies.

Control: PHYSICAL—Remove and destroy infected plants, including stumps and roots; remove soil from around rotted stumps, since armillaria persists in soil. CULTURAL—Plant resistant species; wait several years before replanting an infected site with susceptible varieties.

Phytophthora Root Rot

Type of disease: *fungal*

Host(s): *many*

Several *Phytophthora* species with different geographical ranges and different hosts cause root rots in a wide range of trees, shrubs, and herbaceous plants. Ornamentals often infected include azalea, calla lily, camellia, eucalyptus, Fraser fir, oak, periwinkle, pine, rhododendron, rose, snapdragon, and yew. Wet soils and cool temperatures favor the fungus.

Symptoms: Small feeder roots die back, and brown lesions appear on larger roots. Because of this damage, roots cannot take up adequate amounts of water and nutrients. The symptoms produced vary in different hosts. Wilting is common, growth is frequently stunted, and twigs may suffer dieback. Foliage may be sparse, yellowed, abnormally small, or misshapen. Infected plants are especially vulnerable to environmental stresses and to other diseases. Established plants may survive for a number of years, while seedlings may succumb within days of infection.

Transmission: Phytophthora root rot fungi overwinter in infected roots or soil. Spores are spread by infested soil and water, and in some cases on seed.

Control: PHYSICAL—Remove and destroy seriously infected plants. CULTURAL—Plant resistant species or varieties; incorporate composted tree bark into the soil to suppress fungus growth; improve soil drainage.

Rust

Type of disease: *fungal*

Host(s): *many*

Some 4,000 species of rust fungi are known to cause diseases on plants. Many of these fungi require two different kinds of plants in order to complete their life cycle, while a smaller number infect only one kind of plant. Commonly infected ornamentals include carnation, crab apple, hollyhock, red cedar, rose, snapdragon, spruce, and white pine.

Symptoms: Crusty rust-colored, orange, dark brown, or purplish spots dot the undersides of leaves and stems. The upper surfaces of infected leaves become mottled with yellow. On a severely infected plant, leaves shrivel but remain attached. Plants are weakened, and their growth is often stunted.

Transmission: Rust fungi overwinter on infected hosts and in plant debris. Spores are spread by wind and splashing water and on infected nursery plants or cuttings.

Control: PHYSICAL—Remove and destroy infected plant parts in fall and again in spring. CULTURAL—Plant resistant varieties. CHEMICAL—Spray with sulfur, lime sulfur, Bordeaux mixture, propiconazole, triadimefon, or triforine during the growing season.

Cedar-Apple Rust

Type of disease: *fungal*

Host(s): *red cedar, apple, and crab apple*

The cedar-apple rust fungus requires both an apple and a cedar host to complete its life cycle. Spores produced on red cedars *(Juniperus virginiana)* infect apple trees and ornamental crab apples, and spores produced on apples in turn infect red cedars. Spores produced on apples infect cedars only, just as spores produced on red cedars infect apples only. This disease is common from the Mississippi Valley eastward.

Symptoms: In early spring, orange gelatinous tendrils emerge from spherical leaf galls 1 to 2 inches in diameter on red cedar; the galls reach this stage 18 months after the tree is infected. In early to midsummer, bright yellow spots with orange-red margins appear on apple and crab apple leaves. The spots are ⅛ to ½ inch in diameter. Spotted leaves may turn yellow and fall prematurely. Fruit may also be infected; it will have sunken brown spots and be lumpy and deformed.

Transmission: The cedar-apple rust fungus overwinters on the cedar host as immature galls. Spores are spread by wind to the alternate host.

Control: CULTURAL—Plant resistant apple or crab apple cultivars; do not plant red cedars within 500 yards of apples.

Apple Scab

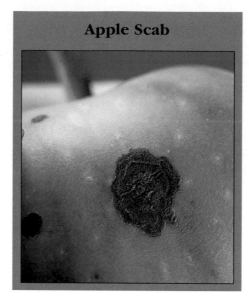

Type of disease: *fungal*

Host(s): *apple and crab apple*

Apple scab is the most important disease of apples and ornamental crab apples and can cause severe injury from defoliation. This disease is most troublesome in areas with frequent rainfall, high humidity, and mild temperatures in spring and summer.

Symptoms: Dull olive green spots ¼ inch or more in diameter with a velvety surface appear in spring on leaves, flowers, shoots, and young fruit. The spots are slightly raised on fruit and become dark, scabby, and cracked. Leaves and fruit are deformed, and if the plant is highly susceptible they fall prematurely.

Transmission: The apple-scab fungus overwinters in fallen leaves. In early spring it develops fruiting bodies that release spores that are spread by wind. During the growing season spores are washed down by rain from leaf and fruit spots to infect other leaves and fruits.

Control: PHYSICAL—Rake and destroy fallen leaves and fruit. CULTURAL—Plant resistant varieties.

Sooty Mold

Type of disease: *fungal*

Host(s): *many*

Several genera of fungi are responsible for the disorder known as sooty mold. These fungi do not attack plants directly. Instead, they feed on the sugary secretions, or honeydew, produced by sucking insects such as aphids, leafhoppers, mealybugs, psyllids, scales, and whiteflies. Besides being unsightly, a heavy growth of sooty mold can slow plant growth by shading the leaf surface and reducing photosynthesis.

Symptoms: A black growth appears on leaves and twigs that may be fine and sootlike or lumpy or crusty with spiky protuberances. The mold can be scraped off the plant surface.

Transmission: Cool, moist conditions favor the growth of sooty mold. Its spores are spread by rain and wind.

Control: PHYSICAL—If the plant is small, wipe off the mold with a damp cloth. BIOLOGICAL OR CHEMICAL—Identify the insect pest responsible for producing the honeydew and choose an appropriate control measure. If you cannot find honeydew-producing insects on a plant with sooty mold, the honeydew may be dripping down from an infested overhanging plant.

Cucumber Wilt

Type of disease: *bacterial*

Host(s): *most cucumber family members*

Bacterial wilt of cucumber is a vascular disease carried by striped and spotted cucumber beetles. It occurs throughout the United States but is most prevalent east of the Rocky Mountains, especially north of Tennessee. Hosts include cucumbers, squash, muskmelons, and pumpkins; watermelons are not susceptible.

Symptoms: At first, one or more leaves on a vine droop as if they needed watering. Soon all the leaves droop, and the vine's stem collapses. Wilted leaves shrivel and dry. When the vine is cut in two and squeezed, a viscous white liquid collects in droplets on the cut ends. When the two cut ends are put together, then pulled apart, delicate, mucuslike threads stretch between the cut ends. This symptom confirms that the plant's problem is bacterial wilt. The liquid may ooze from cracks in diseased vines.

Transmission: The cucumber-wilt bacterium survives the winter in the intestines of the striped and spotted cucumber beetle. The beetles spread the disease as they feed on susceptible plants. Other insects such as flea beetles and grasshoppers may further spread the disease during the growing season.

Control: PHYSICAL—Use row covers; remove and destroy infected plants. BIOLOGICAL—Control beetles with beneficial nematodes or tachinid flies. CHEMICAL—Control with rotenone or sabadilla.

Dutch Elm Disease

Type of disease: *fungal*

Host(s): *elms*

Dutch elm disease (DED) has caused a devastating loss of elms since its introduction to the United States around 1930. Though DED affects many species of elm, the American elm is especially susceptible and nearly always dies.

Symptoms: The fungus grows in the vascular system, producing toxins and clogging the flow of water and nutrients. Symptoms usually begin with the sudden, severe wilting of leaves on a single branch. Leaves curl, turn yellow and then brown, and may fall or stay attached to the branch. The infection can spread rapidly, causing death within a year. In some cases the disease advances slowly, and the tree dies over several years' time.

Transmission: The fungus overwinters in the bark of dead or diseased elm trees and is carried by elm bark beetles, which introduce it into healthy trees as they feed. The fungus is also transmitted through natural root grafts occurring between an infected and a healthy tree.

Control: PHYSICAL—Remove dead elms; prune wilting branches 12 inches below wood showing symptoms, disinfecting pruners between cuts. BIOLOGICAL—Control elm bark beetles with beneficial nematodes or braconid wasps. CULTURAL—Plant DED-resistant elms. This is the most effective measure against the disease. CHEMICAL—Treatment with a fungicide should be done by professionals only.

Fusarium Wilt

Type of disease: *fungal*

Host(s): *many*

Many strains and species of *Fusarium* cause wilt diseases on many herbaceous ornamentals and vegetables. Most strains are highly host specific. Common ornamental hosts include China aster, carnation, cattleya orchid, chrysanthemum, cyclamen, and gladiolus.

Symptoms: Leaves of infected plants turn yellow and droop. Brown patches appear on leaves, often spreading to cover the entire leaf. Lower leaves are usually affected first, and symptoms may initially occur on only one side of the plant. Plants may be permanently stunted or may wither and die. This is one of the most serious diseases of China asters, causing plants to wilt and die at any stage of growth; leaves turn straw yellow and curl. Leaves and flower spikes of infected gladiolus are stunted, and flowers are small and faded. The stems may split, revealing brown streaks in the conductive tissues. Cutting into a stem reveals this abnormal streaking.

Transmission: Fusarium is a soil-borne pathogen that is spread in infested soil and by infected seeds and plants. Resistant varieties may become susceptible if they are injured by insects or nematodes.

Control: CULTURAL—Plant resistant varieties; purchase disease-free plants; solarize infested soil.

Oak Wilt

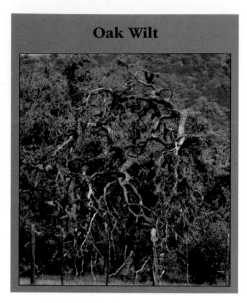

Type of disease: *fungal*

Host(s): *many oak species*

This lethal disease of oaks occurs east of the Rocky Mountains but is most troublesome in Texas and the Great Lakes area. Many species of red oaks are particularly susceptible. Also infected, though usually less severely, are species in the white oak group. One non-oak, the Chinese chestnut, is also susceptible.

Symptoms: Symptoms vary with the host. Red oaks display wilting first at the tops of trees. Leaves turn brown along their margins and yellow or brown along their veins. These symptoms progress downward and inward until all leaves are affected. Leaves fall prematurely, often before they turn brown. Total defoliation occurs within several days to several weeks. Branches die back, and trees typically die within the year. Symptoms on white oaks are similar but progress more slowly. Trees may survive for several years after infection.

Transmission: The oak-wilt fungus overwinters in infected trees. It is spread by oak bark beetles and nitidulid beetles and by natural root grafts occurring between a diseased tree and a healthy one.

Control: PHYSICAL—Remove and destroy infected trees, including stumps; prune susceptible species only when they are dormant and the carrier beetles are inactive to reduce the chance of infection.

Verticillium Wilt

Type of disease: *fungal*

Host(s): *many*

Widely occurring verticillium wilt is most troublesome in the temperate zones, attacking over 200 species of plants. Some strains are highly host specific; others attack a broad range of plants. Susceptible ornamentals include aster, azalea, barberry, catalpa, chrysanthemum, dahlia, daphne, magnolia, maple, nandina, peony, photinia, privet, and snapdragon.

Symptoms: Symptoms usually appear first on the infected plant's lower or outer leaves. Leaves develop a yellowish tinge and droop, then turn brown and die. On herbaceous plants, the leaves shrivel and remain attached to the stem for some time. Individual stems or the entire plant dies, and vascular tissue in the stems is streaked with brown. On woody plants, symptoms include elongated cankers, wilting, premature defoliation, and dieback. Symptoms may be acute, spreading over the entire plant within a few weeks, or chronic, gradually progressing over several seasons.

Transmission: Verticillium fungus is a soil-borne pathogen that enters a plant through its feeder roots or wounds. It can survive in soil for as long as 20 years.

Control: CULTURAL—Plant resistant species such as conifers and ginkgos; purchase disease-free plants; solarize infested soil; keep plants vigorous and protect them from drought stress, especially in the first 3 years after transplanting.

Acknowledgments

The editors wish to thank the following for their valuable assistance :
Beneficial Insectary, Oak Run, Calif.; Karen Bussolini, South Kent, Conn.; Ken Druse, Brook-lyn, N.Y.; Barbara H. Emerson, North Carolina Botanical Garden, University of North Carolina, Chapel Hill; Harmony Farm Supply, Graton, Calif.; Anne Heimann, Heimann-Hubbard Studios, New York, N.Y.; Lee Anne Merrill, M & R Durango, Ignacio, Colo.; Kevin Morris, National Turfgrass Evaluation Program, Beltsville Agricultural Research Center-West, Belts-ville, Md.; Necessary Trading Co., New Castle, Va.; Pest Management Supply Co., Amherst, Mass.; Susan Roth, Stony Brook, N.Y.; John Smith, New York, N.Y.

Picture Credits

The sources for the illustrations that appear in this book are listed below. Credits from left to right are separated by semicolons; credits from top to bottom are separated by dashes.

Cover: © Dwight R. Kuhn. Back cover inset: © Lefever/Grushow/ Grant Heilman Photography, Lititz, Pa.—art by Stephen R. Wagner—© Dwight R. Kuhn. End papers: © Gene Boaz. 2: Ethel Dutky. 4: Courtesy Scott Aker; courtesy Ethel Dutky. 6, 7: David and Steve Maslowski. 8, 9: Robert Walch/designed by George and Carol Miller. 11: Jerry Pavia. 13-17: Art by Sally Bensusen. 18: © Dwight R. Kuhn. 19-23: Art by Stephen R. Wagner. 24: E. R. Degginger. 25, 26: Art by Sally Bensusen. 27: Art by Stephen R. Wagner. 29: Background © Dwight R. Kuhn. 32: Art by Nicholas Fasciano. 33: Art by Stephen R. Wagner—art by Nicholas Fasciano (2). 35: Background Jerry Pavia. 36: E. R. Degginger. 37: © Dwight R. Kuhn—© Grant Heilman/Grant Heilman Photography, Lititz, Pa. 38: Marty Cordano—E. R. Degginger (2). 39: © Dwight R. Kuhn. 40: E. R. Degginger. 41: Jerry Pavia. 42, 43: © Lefever/ Grushow/Grant Heilman Photography, Lititz, Pa. 45: Virginia R. Weiler/designed by Kim Hawks, Niche Gardens, Chapel Hill, N.C. 46, 47: Art by Sally Bensusen. 48, 49: Jerry Pavia.

53, 54: Art by Stephen R. Wagner. 55: A. Murray Evans, 1977 © Time-Life Books, Inc. 57: Background E. R. Degginger. 58, 59: Jerry Pavia. 61: Background © Mark E. Gibson. 62: Leonard Phillips. 65: Jerry Pavia/courtesy Harry Jacobs, garden designed by Ron Lutsko of Lutsko Associates, San Francisco. 66: © Breck P. Kent. 67-69: Art by Stephen R. Wagner. 70: © William J. Weber/Visuals Unlimited (2); © Larry Lefever/ Grant Heilman Photography, Lititz, Pa.—© John D. Cunningham/Visuals Unlimited; Barbara H. Emerson; Science VU/Visuals Unlimited. 71: © Ted Rose/Unicorn Stock Photos; John Gerlach/Visuals Unlimited; © Walt Anderson/Visuals Unlimited— © John Colwell/Grant Heilman Photography, Lititz, Pa.; © Jane Grushow/Grant Heilman Photography, Lititz, Pa.; © Grant Heilman/Grant Heilman Photography, Lititz, Pa. 72: © Jane Grushow/Grant Heilman Photography, Lititz, Pa.; © Alan L. Detrick; John D. Cunningham/Visuals Unlimited—© Jim Strawser/Grant Heilman Photography, Lititz, Pa.; © A. Gurmankin/Unicorn Stock Photos; © Liz Ball. 73: © Alan L. Detrick; © Mark E. Gibson; © R. J. Mathews/Unicorn Stock Photos— © William J. Weber/Visuals Unlimited; © Mark E. Gibson; © Alan L. Detrick. 74, 75: © Roger Foley/designed by

Oehme, van Sweden and Associates. 77: Map by John Drummond, Time-Life Books, Inc. 78: Art by Donald Gates. 80: Ken Kay, 1971 © Time-Life Books, Inc. 82: © Betts Anderson/Unicorn Stock Photos. 83: John D. Cunningham/Visuals Unlimited—Pam Peirce; background © Dick Keen/Unicorn Stock Photos. 84: © John Colwell/ Grant Heilman Photography, Lititz, Pa.—© Jim Strawser/ Grant Heilman Photography, Lititz, Pa. 86: Paul Vincelli, except center © Stanley Schoenberger/Grant Heilman Photography, Lititz, Pa. 87: Joe Vargas; Paul Vincelli; Karen Kackley-Dutt, PhD—Paul Vincelli; Joe Vargas. 94: © Dwight R. Kuhn. 95: © J. Alcock/Visuals Unlimited; Agricultural Research Service-USDA; © Dwight R. Kuhn. 96: © Dwight R. Kuhn. 97: © Dwight R. Kuhn; © Robin Mitchell, All Rights Reserved; Animals Animals © 1995 G. A. MACLEAN/Oxford Scientific Films. 98: © Ron West; © Dwight R. Kuhn; Jan Taylor/ Bruce Coleman Ltd., Uxbridge, Middlesex. 99: © Gregory K. Scott/Nature Photos; © Ron West; © Judy Hile/Unicorn Stock Photos. 100: © Dwight R. Kuhn; © Ron West; © J. Alcock/Visuals Unlimited. 101: © Dwight R. Kuhn, except center © Grant Heilman/Grant Heilman Photography, Lititz, Pa. 102: © Science VU/Visuals Un-

limited; David J. Shetlar. 103: © Bill Beatty/Visuals Unlimited; Scott Aker; © Science VU/Visuals Unlimited. 104: Agricultural Research Service-USDA; E. R. Degginger; © Ray Kriner/Grant Heilman Photography, Lititz, Pa. 105: © Richard Thom/Visuals Unlimited; © Dwight R. Kuhn; Scott Aker. 106: © Dwight R. Kuhn (2); © Breck P. Kent. 107: © Dwight R. Kuhn; E. R. Degginger. 108: Scott Aker; E. R. Degginger; © Kenneth D. Whitney/Visuals Unlimited. 109: © K. G. Preston-Mafham/Premaphotos Wildlife, Bodmin, Cornwall; © Ron West; © Dwight R. Kuhn. 110: © Dwight R. Kuhn; Mark S. McClure; © Breck P. Kent. 111: © Runk/Schoenberger/Grant Heilman Photography, Lititz, Pa.; © Grant Heilman/ Grant Heilman Photography, Lititz, Pa.; © Dwight R. Kuhn. 112: Animals Animals © 1995 D. R. Specker; © Dwight R. Kuhn. 113: © Dwight R. Kuhn, except center David J. Shetlar. 114: Animals Animals © 1995 Richard Shiell; David J. Shetlar. 115: E. R. Degginger; © Runk/ Schoenberger/Grant Heilman Photography, Lititz, Pa.; © Ron West. 116: © Grant Heilman/ Grant Heilman Photography, Lititz, Pa.; © Glenn Oliver/Visuals Unlimited; © Bill Beatty/ Visuals Unlimited. 117: © Runk/ Schoenberger/Grant Heilman Photography, Lititz, Pa.; © Grant Heilman Photography, Lititz,

Pa.; © Ron West. 118: Scott Aker; © Dwight R. Kuhn (2). 119: © Grant Heilman/Grant Heilman Photography, Lititz, Pa.; © Dwight R. Kuhn. 120: © Douglas C. Allen; © Dwight R. Kuhn; © Runk/Schoenberger/Grant Heilman Photography, Lititz, Pa. 121: © Runk/Schoenberger/Grant Heilman Photography, Lititz, Pa.; E. R. Degginger; Animals Animals © 1995 D. R. Specker. 122: © Ron West; © Dwight R. Kuhn; Arlyn W. Evans. 123: © Jeffrey Howe/

Visuals Unlimited; © Ron West; Animals Animals © 1995 Richard Shiell. 124: E. R. Degginger; Ethel Dutky. 125: Anne Bird Sindermann; Ethel Dutky; Katharine D. Widin. 126: © Alan L. Detrick; Ethel Dutky (2). 127: Ethel Dutky; Agricultural Research Service-USDA; Anne Bird Sindermann. 128: Ethel Dutky, except center Ron Jones/Cooperative Extention Service, North Carolina State University. 129: Ethel Dutky; Ron Jones/Cooperative Exten-

tion Service, North Carolina State University; Scott Aker. 130: © John Colwell/Grant Heilman Photography, Lititz, Pa., except center Ann F. Rhoads. 131: © Runk/Schoenberger/Grant Heilman Photography, Lititz, Pa.; Potash & Phosphate Institute; E. R. Degginger. 132: G. David Lewis/E. R. Degginger; Ethel Dutky; E. R. Degginger. 133: Ethel Dutky; George W. Hudler; © Grant Heilman/Grant Heilman Photography, Lititz, Pa. 134: Ethel Dutky, except center

Arlyn W. Evans. 135: Ethel Dutky. 136: James G. Kantzes; G. David Lewis/E. R. Degginger; © Larry Lefever/Grant Heilman Photography, Lititz, Pa. 137: Ann F. Rhoads; Anne Bird Sindermann; Scott Aker. 138: © Alan L. Detrick; © Runk/Schoenberger/Grant Heilman Photography, Lititz, Pa.; Scott Aker. 139: James Dill; © Runk/Schoenberger/Grant Heilman Photography, Lititz, Pa.; E. R. Degginger. 140: © Robert & Linda Mitchell; Ethel Dutky.

Bibliography

Books:

All about Lawns. San Ramon, Calif.: Ortho Books, 1985.

An Illustrated Guide to Organic Gardening. Menlo Park, Calif.: Sunset Publishing, 1991.

Arnett, Ross H., Jr. *American Insects.* Gainesville, Fla.: Sandhill Crane Press, 1993.

Ashton, Floyd M., et al. *Weed Science: Principles and Practices.* New York: John Wiley & Sons, 1991.

Ball, Jeff, and Liz Ball: *Rodale's Landscape Problem Solver: A Plant-by-Plant Guide.* Emmaus, Pa.: Rodale Press, 1989. *Yardening.* New York: Macmillan, 1991.

Bormann, F. Herbert, Diana Balmori, and Gordon T. Geballe. *Redesigning the American Lawn.* New Haven, Conn.: Yale University Press, 1993.

Borror, Donald J., Charles A. Triplehorn, and Norman F. Johnson. *An Introduction to the Study of Insects* (6th ed.). Orlando, Fla.: Harcourt Brace, 1992.

Borror, Donald J., and Richard E. White. *A Field Guide to Insects: America North of Mexico* (Peterson Field Guide series). Boston: Houghton

Mifflin, 1970.

Bradley, Fern Marshall, and Barbara W. Ellis (Eds.). *Rodale's All-New Encyclopedia of Organic Gardening.* Emmaus, Pa.: Rodale Press, 1992.

California Center for Wildlife, with Diana Landau and Shelley Stump. *Living with Wildlife.* San Francisco: Sierra Club Books, 1994.

Carr, Anna. *Rodale's Color Handbook of Garden Insects.* Emmaus, Pa.: Rodale Press, 1979.

Carr, Anna, et al. *Rodale's Chemical-Free Yard and Garden.* Emmaus, Pa.: Rodale Press, 1991.

Cloudsley-Thompson, J. L. *Spiders, Scorpions, Centipedes, and Mites.* Oxford: Pergamon Press, 1968.

Cocannouer, Joseph A. *Weeds.* Old Greenwich, Conn.: Devin-Adair, 1950.

Controlling Weeds. San Ramon, Calif.: Ortho Books, 1989.

Cox, Jeff. *Landscaping with Nature.* Emmaus, Pa.: Rodale Press, 1991.

Dahl, Mogens, and Thyge B. Thygesen. *Garden Pests and Diseases of Flowers and Shrubs.* New York: Macmillan, 1974.

Davidson, Ralph H., and William

F. Lyon. *Insect Pests of Farm, Garden, and Orchard.* New York: John Wiley & Sons, 1987.

Denckla, Tanya. *The Organic Gardener's Home Reference* (Garden Way Publishing). Pownal, Vt.: Storey Communications, 1994.

Dirr, Michael A. *Manual of Woody Landscape Plants* (4th ed.). Champaign, Ill.: Stipes Publishing, 1990.

Ellefson, Connie Lockhart, Thomas L. Stephens, and Doug Welsh. *Xeriscape Gardening.* New York: Macmillan, 1992.

Ellis, Barbara W., and Fern Marshall Bradley (Eds.). *The Organic Gardener's Handbook of Natural Insect and Disease Control.* Emmaus, Pa.: Rodale Press, 1992.

Foley, Daniel J. *Ground Covers for Easier Gardening.* Philadelphia: Chilton, 1961.

Franklin, Stuart. *Building a Healthy Lawn* (Garden Way Publishing). Pownal, Vt.: Storey Communications, 1988.

Garden Pests and Diseases. Menlo Park, Calif.: Sunset Publishing, 1993.

Gershuny, Grace. *Start with the Soil.* Emmaus, Pa.: Rodale

Press, 1993.

Gertsch, Willis J. *American Spiders* (2d ed.). New York: Van Nostrand Reinhold, 1979.

Hamilton, Jeff (Ed.). *Organic Gardening* (RD Home Handbooks). Pleasantville, N.Y.: Reader's Digest Association, 1992.

Hansen, Michael, and the Editors of Consumer Reports Books. *Pest Control for Home and Garden.* Yonkers, N.Y.: Consumer Reports Books, 1993.

Harley, Ruth. *"Scat"* (Garden Way Publishing). Pownal, Vt.: Storey Communications, 1977.

Harper, Peter, and Jeremy Light. *The Natural Garden Book.* New York: Simon and Schuster, 1994.

Hart, Rhonda Massingham. *Bugs, Slugs, and Other Thugs* (Garden Way Publishing). Pownal, Vt.: Storey Communications, 1991.

Hudak, Joseph. *Shrubs in the Landscape.* New York: McGraw-Hill, 1984.

Improving Your Garden Soil. San Ramon, Calif.: Ortho Books, 1992.

Jenkins, Virginia Scott. *The Lawn: A History of American Obsession.* Washington, D.C.: Smithsonian Institution

Press, 1994.

Jescavage-Bernard, Karen. *Gardening in Deer Country.* Croton-on-Hudson, N.Y.: Karen Jescavage-Bernard, 1991.

Johnson, Warren T., and Howard H. Lyon. *Insects That Feed on Trees and Shrubs* (2d ed., rev.). Ithaca, N.Y.: Cornell University Press, 1994.

Kourik, Robert. *Designing and Maintaining Your Edible Landscape Naturally.* Santa Rosa, Calif.: Metamorphic Press, 1986.

Lee, Sally. *Pesticides.* New York: Franklin Watts, 1991.

Leslie, Anne R. (Ed.). *Handbook of Integrated Pest Management for Turf and Ornamentals.* Boca Raton, Fla.: Lewis Publishers, 1989.

Logsdon, Gene. *Wildlife in Your Garden.* Emmaus, Pa.: Rodale Press, 1983.

McCord, Nancy. *Please Don't Eat My Garden!* New York: Sterling Publishg, 1992.

Michalak, Patricia S., with Linda A. Gilkeson. *Controlling Pests and Diseases* (Rodale's Successful Organic Gardening series). Emmaus, Pa.: Rodale Press, 1994.

Olkowski, William, Sheila Daar, and Helga Olkowski. *Common-Sense Pest Control.* Newtown, Conn.: Taunton Press, 1991.

The Ortho Home Gardener's Problem Solver. San Ramon, Calif.: Ortho Books, 1993.

Palmer, E. Laurence. *Palmer's Fieldbook of Mammals.* New York: E. P. Dutton, 1957.

Pests of the Garden and Small Farm (Division of Agriculture and Natural Resources Publication 3332). Oakland: University of California, 1990.

Pests of Landscape Trees and Shrubs (Division of Agriculture and Natural Resources Publication 3359). Oakland, Calif.: ANR Publications, 1994.

Pfadt, Robert E. (Ed.). *Fundamentals of Applied Entomology* (3d ed.). New York: Macmillan, 1978.

Pirone, Pascal P. *Diseases and Pests of Ornamental Plants* (5th ed.). New York: John Wiley & Sons, 1978.

Pleasant, Barbara. *The Gardener's Bug Book* (Garden Way Publishing). Pownal, Vt.: Storey Communications, 1994.

Poincelot, Raymond P. *No-Dig, No-Weed Gardening.* Emmaus, Pa.: Rodale Press, 1986.

Protecting Your Garden from Animal Damage. San Ramon, Calif.: Ortho Books, 1994.

Raupp, Michael J., Roy C. Van Driesche, and John A. Davidson. *Biological Control of Insect and Mite Pests of Woody Landscape Plants.* College Park: Maryland Cooperative Extension Service, 1993.

Raymond, Dick. *Garden Way's Joy of Gardening* (Garden Way Publishing). Pownal, Vt.: Storey Communications, 1982.

Rice, Robert P., Jr. *Nursery and Landscape Weed Control Manual.* Fresno, Calif.: Thomson Publications, 1992.

Rodale Garden Books, with Jeff Cox. *Your Organic Garden.* Emmaus, Pa.: Rodale Press, 1994.

Salmon, Terrell P., and Robert E. Lickliter. *Wildlife Pest Control around Gardens and Homes.* Oakland: University of California, 1984.

Schneck, Marcus. *Butterflies: How to Identify and Attract Them to Your Garden.* Emmaus, Pa.: Rodale Press, 1990.

Schultz, Warren. *The Chemical-Free Lawn.* Emmaus, Pa.: Rodale Press, 1989.

Sinclair, Wayne A., Howard H. Lyon, and Warren T. Johnson. *Diseases of Trees and Shrubs.* Ithaca, N.Y.: Cornell University Press, 1987.

Smith, Miranda, and Anna Carr. *Rodale's Garden Insect, Disease, and Weed Identification Guide.* Emmaus, Pa.: Rodale Press, 1988.

Smith-Fiola, Deborah C. *Pest Resistant Ornamental Plants.* Toms River, N.J.: Rutgers

Cooperative Extension, 1994.

Sombke, Laurence. *Beautiful Easy Lawns and Landscapes.* Old Saybrook, Conn.: Globe Pequot Press, 1994.

Stein, Sara B. *My Weeds: A Gardener's Botany.* New York: Harper and Row, 1988.

Stokes, Donald, Lillian Stokes, and Ernest Williams. *The Butterfly Book.* Boston: Little, Brown, 1991.

Swan, Lester A., and Charles S. Papp. *The Common Insects of North America.* New York: Harper and Row, 1972.

Taylor's Guide to Gardening Techniques. Boston: Houghton Mifflin, 1991.

Tilgner, Linda. *Tips for the Lazy Gardener* (Garden Way Publishing). Pownal, Vt.: Storey Communications, 1985.

Timm, Robert M. (Ed.). *Prevention and Control of Wildlife Damage.* Lincoln: Nebraska Cooperative Extension Service, 1983.

Turnbull, Cass. *The Complete Guide to Landscape Design, Renovation, and Maintenance.* Crozet, Va.: Betterway Publications, 1991.

U.S. Department of Agriculture: *Common Weeds of the United States.* New York: Dover Publications, 1971.
Introduced Parasites and Predators of Arthropod Pests and Weeds: A World Review (Agriculture Handbook No. 480). Washington, D.C.: U.S. Government Printing Office, 1978.

U.S. Environmental Protection Agency. *Pesticide Fact Handbook* (Vol. 2). Park Ridge, N.J.: Noyes Data Corporation, 1990.

Ware, George W. *Complete Guide to Pest Control—with and without Chemicals.* Fresno, Calif.: Thomson Publications, 1988.

Waterwise Gardening. Menlo Park, Calif.: Sunset Publishing, 1991.

Webster, William David, James F. Parnell, and Walter C. Biggs, Jr. *Mammals of the Carolinas, Virginia, and Maryland.* Chapel Hill: University of North Carolina Press, 1985.

Westcott, Cynthia. *The Gardener's Bug Book* (3d ed.). New York: Doubleday, 1964.

Wyman, Donald. *Trees for American Gardens.* New York: Macmillan, 1965.

Yepsen, Roger B., Jr. (Ed.). *The Encyclopedia of Natural Insect and Disease Control.* Emmaus, Pa.: Rodale Press, 1984.

Periodicals:

Aker, Scott. "Are Natives the Solution to Pest Problems?" *Friends of the National Arboretum Newsletter,* July/August 1994.

Breene, R. G. "A New Approach for Matching Biological Control Agents to Pests." *IPM Practitioner,* August 1992.

Byczynski, Lynn:
"The Basics of Bt." *Organic Gardening,* May/June 1994.
"Listen to Your Weeds!" *Organic Gardening,* July/August 1994.

Carney, Nancy. "How to Shop for Shrubs and Trees." *Fine Gardening,* May/June 1993.

"Controlling Pests and Diseases Can Be "Earth-Kind." *Neil Sperry's Gardens,* Spring Guide 1994.

"The Environmental Gardener." *Plants & Gardens, Brooklyn Botanic Garden Record,* 1992.

Flint, Mary Louise. "Bt Controls Caterpillars." *Fine Gardening,* May/June 1994.

Gilbert, Bil. "A Groundhog's 'Day' Means More to Us Than It Does to Him." *Smithsonian,* February 1985.

Giusti, Gregory A. "Getting Rid of Gophers." *Fine Gardening,* March/April 1991.

"Gopher Strategy: Know Your Enemy. Choose Weapons. Cross Fingers." *Sunset,* April 1978.

Horn, Al. "Future Directions for Nematodes in Biological Control." *IPM Practitioner,* April 1994.

Jesiolowski, Jill. "How to Handle America's Ten Least Wanted Weeds." *Organic Gardening,* July/August 1992.

Long, Charles. "Snap Judgment." *Harrowsmith Country Life,* December 1994.

"The Natural Lawn and Alternatives." *Plants & Gardens, Brooklyn Botanic Garden Record,* 1993.

"Nematode Nomenclature and Life Cycle." *IPM Practitioner,* March 1994.

Olkowski, William, Everett Dietrick, and Helga Olkowski. "The Biological Control Industry in the United States, Part I." *IPM Practitioner,* January 1992.

Pimentel, David. "Biological Pest Control." *Fine Gardening,* July/August 1992.

Poncavage, Joanna. "A Weed-Free Garden." *Organic Gardening,* July/August 1994.

Raupp, Michael. "Who's That Insect?" *Fine Gardening,* September/October 1993.

Schmidt, Tom. "Mole Control: Trapping Does the Job." *Fine Gardening,* November/December 1989.

Wells-Gosling, Nancy. "This Little Squirrel Keeps a Big Trick Hidden in Its Sleeve." *Smithsonian,* June 1985.

Other Publications:

Hart, Rhonda Massingham. "Using Beneficial Insects." Storey Publications Bulletin A-27. Pownal, Vt.: Storey Communications, 1991.

Natural Insect Control. Handbook #139. Brooklyn, N.Y.: Brooklyn Botanic Garden, Summer 1994.

Potter-Springer, Wendy. "Grow a Butterfly Garden." Storey Publications Bulletin A-114. Pownal, Vt.: Storey Communications, 1990.

Index